Criminal Activity in the Deep South, 1700-1930

CRIMINAL ACTIVITY IN THE DEEP SOUTH, 1700-1930

An Annotated Bibliography

Compiled by
A. J. WRIGHT

Research and Bibliographical Guides in Criminal Justice, Number 1

Greenwood Press
New York • Westport, Connecticut • London

Library of Congress Cataloging-in-Publication Data

Wright, A. J.
Criminal activity in the deep South, 1700-1930 : an annotated bibliography / compiled by A. J. Wright.
p. cm.—(Research and bibliographical guides in criminal justice, ISSN 1042-4636 ; no. 1)
Bibliography: p.
Includes index.
ISBN 0-313-23798-0 (lib. bdg. : alk. paper)
1. Crime and criminals—Southern States—History—Bibliography.
I. Title. II. Series.
Z5703.5.U5W7 1989
[HV8145.A13]
016.364'975—dc19 89-1927

British Library Cataloguing in Publication Data is available.

Library of Congress Catalog Card Number: 89-1927
ISBN: 0-313-23798-0
ISSN: 1042-4636

First published in 1989

Greenwood Press, Inc.
88 Post Road West, Westport, Connecticut 06881

Printed in the United States of America

∞

The paper used in this book complies with the Permanent Paper Standard issued by the National Information Standards Organization (Z39.48-1984).

10 9 8 7 6 5 4 3 2 1

Contents

Contents

Introduction

"Every day seem like murder here"
"Every day seem like murder here."

---Charley Patton

"...we have a remarkable lack of memory where violence is concerned and have left most of our excesses a part of our buried history," Richard Hofstadter and Michael Wallace write in the introduction to their collection, American Violence: A Documentary History (Knopf, 1970). "Educated Americans...have hardly a hint of (the) striking legacy of domestic turbulence. Shirked by our historians, the subject has been repressed in the national consciousness...We do not yet know much about the patterns of American violence, and even our awareness of its past frequency is almost certain to be expanded as new areas of historical inquiry are opened."

The years since those comments were written have brought no significant change in our collective amnesia about the history of violent crime in America, indeed of crime in general, despite our media-made obsession with the subject. Americans hardly have time to examine the meaning of past criminal activity when spectacular new mass murders and other crimes are constantly competing for their attention in the midst of numerous other local, national and world events.

As Hofstadter and Wallace noted, scholars have a similar problem. "For historians violence is a difficult subject, diffuse and difficult to cope with. It is committed by isolated individuals, by small groups, and by large mobs; it is directed against individuals and crowds alike; it is undertaken for a variety of purposes (and at times for no discernable rational purpose at all), and in a variety of ways ranging from assassinations and murders to lynchings, duels, brawls, feuds and riots; it stems from criminal intent and from political idealism, from antagonisms that are entirely personal and from antagonisms of large social consequence. Hence, it has been hard to conceive of violence as a subject at all."

A statement similar to that last one could also be made about crime in general. Crime is a human activity so constant, so persuasive and so various that most writers on the subject are reduced to either indepth examination of individual crimes or criminals or wide-ranging but inevitably superficial "encyclopedias" of murders and the like.

This bibliography is a modest attempt to confront the problem. Printed material related to crime in eight southern states prior to 1930 has been examined, summarized, evaluated and organized first by georgaphy and then by type of material. Eight states were chosen in order to provide bibliographic coverage of a significant portion of the United States and yet maintain a manageable project. A termination year of 1930 was chosen because in that year Congress authorized the Department of Justice to begin collecting and compiling crime statistics. That mandate has evolved into the FBI's well-known Uniform Crime Reports, which contain statistical information about crime as reported to the FBI by police departments around the country and which is one of the major sources of our present statistical picture of crime. Before 1930 the gathering of statistics about crime in the United States was an extremely haphazard effort limited to statistics on specific types of crime in specific cities over a few years' period.

For the purposes of this bibliography "crime" has been defined as illegal activity associated with economic gain, revenge or preservation of individual or community honor. Thus, several types of criminal activity have generally been omitted completely from this work. Among the omissions are race riots and the activities of the Ku Klux Klan. These topics are deserving of individual treatment, which, in the case of the KKK, has already been completed.*

Other categories of crime or crime-related activity not covered by this work include violence associated with the labor movement, slave revolts, military crime, Indian and white relations, the evolution and enforcement of criminal laws and the evolution of penal and judicial systems. Some individual examples of these categories have undoubtedly crept into the bibliography, but as a rule I have not researched these areas for materials. These subjects also deserve individual treatment.

Despite the exclusion of such large areas, the resulting bibliography is nonetheless substantial. This appearance is somewhat illusory; much of the material published on pre-1930 southern crime is less than ideal. For instance, many books, book chapters and articles have been written about antebellum outlaw John Murrell; a great deal of it is either repititious, factually suspect or both. In fact, until 1981, when James Penick published his study of Murrell, almost nothing of scholarly worth had been published about this enigmatic figure. Material on the notorious Harpe brothers, Wiley and Micajah, who antedated Murrell by a number of years, is also plentiful and equally suspect. Serious research on those two figures--- as well as on Samuel Mason and Joseph Hare, two other major outlaws of roughly the same period---remains to be done. However, as lacking in factual value as most of the material on Murrell and the others may be, its sheer mass and content does tell us much about the continuing popularity of these men over several decades and thus a great deal about both the popular imagination in the nineteenth century South and the process by which real human lives are transformed into folklore and near-myth.

Hopefully, this bibliography, by attempting to consolidate and organize materials already published on southern crime, will reveal avenues either as yet unresearched or needing further research. Vast areas remain completely untapped, including counterfeiting, post office robbery and mass and serial murder. Other types of crime, such as lynching and dueling, urgently need new, updated or more extensive work. Numerous individual crimes and criminals await scholarly discovery. These questions are endless. How extensive was train robbery in the deep South? Bank robbery? How did technological and social developments---such as the automobile and suburban growth---affect criminal activity in the early decades of this century? What types of crime have disappeared over time as a result of societal changes, and what new crimes have appeared? This work should provide a modest foundation for efforts to answer these and innumerable other questions about crime in both the South and the United States as a whole.

Some specific points about this bibliography need to be made. Entry categories are self-explanatory with the possible exception of the "Miscellaneous" one. This category includes monograph chapters or significant portions of chapters, audio recordings and maps---in other words, items which do not fit other categories or were not completely devoted to a subject within the scope of the bibliography.

References within an entry's annotation that are accompanied by a number refer to another entry in the bibliography. For example, see entry 1, "Pitts (#20)." References without such a number refer to entries in the "Sources" listing. For example, see entry 2, "Adams (p.40)." Items in the "Sources" list have either provided entries for the bibliography or confirmed information about entries. I have tried in the entries to give some idea of any subsequent editions or reprintings of a title; however, these should not be considered exhaustive. Entries without annotation have not been examined, but are known to fall within the bibliography's criteria.

Entries for newspaper articles are a special case and attempt three goals. First, most cover specific crimes and criminals not included in the monograph and journal literature. Second, the entries include material on types of criminal activity not well-covered by that same literature: counterfeiting, moonshining, train and bank robbery, etc. Third, the inclusion of fifty newspaper articles for each state attempts to give some sense of the frequency of criminal activity; many articles over a short period of time are best for this purpose.

Finally, I would like to thank those people who have helped make this bibliography a reality. Greenwood Press Social and Behavioral Sciences Editor Mary R. Sive has been most patient and helpful. Shirley Mayfield typed most of the manuscript. Watt Espy, whose knowledge of Amercian crime and especially of capital punishment is astounding, has been most encouraging. My wife Dianne was very supportive of this project. Any errors in this bibliography are the result of my efforts, not theirs.

Comments, additions for any future update to this bibliography and corrections may be directed to the author via the publisher.

*Davis, Lenwood G. and Sims-Wood, Janet L., comp. The Ku Klux Klan: A Bibliography. Westport, Conn.: Greenwood Press, 1984.

Fisher, William Harvey. The Invisible Empire: A Bibliography of the Ku Klux Klan. Metuchen, N.J.: Scarecrow, 1980.

1

Chronology

The following chronology is designed to give an idea of the variety of criminal activity in the deep South before 1930. The listing is by no means exhaustive. For more information on these crimes, please consult the "Personal Name" or "Subject" indices.

1718 October 28

In Charleston, S.C., the trial of pirate Stede Bonnet and members of his crew begins. Bonnet will be convicted and hanged on December 10.

1718 November 22

Pirate Edward Teach, better known as Blackbeard, is killed in Ocracoke Inlet, North Carolina.

1765 March 18

At Brunswick, N.C., Alexander Simpson and Thomas Whitehurst engage in the first duel in the state.

1767

In the backcountry of South Carolina a group of vigilantes known as "Regulators" begin operation against an epidemic of thieves. The Regulators operate until 1769.

1777

On the outskirts of Savannah, Ga., Lachlan McIntosh and Button Gwinnett settle their long-running fued in a duel. Both men are only slightly wounded, but Gwinnett dies three days later due to poor medical care.

Criminal Activity in the South

1781 July 26

Molly Glass, a free quadroon, is hanged in the public square in New Orleans. Molly had been convicted of murdering fifteen year-old Emilia Davis.

1784 June 19

In New Orleans Juan San Malo and two members of his band of runaway slaves, who had been raiding plantations that spring, are hanged.

1797 or 1798

Micajah and Wiley Harpe, legendary robbers and "mad dog" killers, settle near Beaver Creek in Knox Co., Tenn.

1798 November 10

In Winston-Salem, N.C., an organization called "The Horse Society" is founded. The group, organized to pursue thieves who preyed on its members, operated until 1875--perhaps the longest-lived vigilante group in the country.

1799 summer

A posse catches legendary robber/murderer Micajah Harpe, who with his brother Wiley had operated in the Carolinas, Tennessee and the Ohio Valley, in western Kentucky. Harpe is killed, decapitated and his head displayed on a post near Dixon in Henderson County.

1804 February or March

After a trial Wiley "Little" Harpe is executed at Greenville, Mississippi Territory.

1806

John A. Murrell is born in Lunenburg County, Virginia.

1808

In Randolph Co., North Carolina, Jonathan Lewis murders his lover Naomi Wise. The crime has become the subject of considerable folklore, ballads, etc.

1809 October 11(?)

Somewhere in Tennessee the body of famed explorer Merriwether Lewis is discovered. A controversy continues to rage over whether his death was suicide or murder.

Chronology

1811 June

Future Mississippi governor George Poindexter and Federalist Abijah Hunt fight a duel in Natchez. Hunt is killed.

1811 September

Captain Edward Tinker is executed at Newbern, N.C., for the murder of sailor Edward Jones. Tinker had scuttled his vessel in an attempt to defraud the insurance company and Jones had refused to join the fraud.

1818 September 10

Joseph Hare hangs in Baltimore, Maryland, for the robbery of a mail coach. Hare and his gang had spent several previous years robbing travelers along the Natchez Trace between Nashville and Natchez. Hare's "confession" is published posthumously.

1821 December 21

Florida-based pirate Jose Gaspar supposedly commits suicide rather than submit to capture.

1822 June 2

George McDuffie, a U.S. Representative, and William Cumming, a colonel, meet in a duel at Sister's Ferry, S.C., to settle political differences. McDuffie is wounded. The two men will meet again in November, and McDuffie will again be wounded.

1826 May 25

John A. Murrell is tried for horse theft in Nashville. He is sentenced to thirty lashes, six hours in the pillory, one year in jail and the branding of the letters "HT" on his left thumb.

1827 September 18

On the Vidalia Sand Bar in the Mississippi River near Natchez, a duel between Dr. Thomas H. Maddox and Samuel L. Wells degenerates into a brawl in which two men are killed and two wounded. The legendary James Bowie is one of twelve men involved.

1827 November

Near Saluda, N.C., Sam Carson and Robert Vance engage in a duel. David Crockett is present, but does not participate.

Criminal Activity in the South

1828 January 5

At Fort Mitchell, in what is now Russell Co., Ala., George W. Crawford kills Thomas E. Burnside in a duel.

1830

Outlaw John Washburn and his gang rob the Nashville Exchange bank of $3000.

1833 July 12

In Morganton, North Carolina, Frankie Silvers is hanged for the December 22, 1831, murder of her husband Charles. According to tradition Frankie wrote a ballad about the crime on the eve of her execution.

1833 October

South Carolina College students John G. Adams and Govan Roach fight a duel to settle an argument that started over a dish of trout. Both men are wounded and Adams dies.

1834 February 9

John A. Murrell is arrested for slave stealing on the basis of charges made by Virgil Stewart. Imprisoned in Haywood Co., Tenn., to await trial in Jackson, Murrell escapes on May 7 but is recaptured in Florence, Ala., within a month. Murrell is tried, found guilty on two of ten counts and sentenced to ten years in prison.

1835 February 20

In Mobile, Ala., journeyman printer and poet Charles R.S. Boyington is hanged for the May 10, 1834, murder of his friend and fellow printer Nathaniel Frost.

1835 summer

The Walton narrative has recently been published, detailing John Murrell's vast "Mystic Clan" of outlaws and the plans for a December 1835 slave revolt across the south. At Livingston,Miss., hysteria sweeps through the populace after the narrative's contents are confirmed--under torture--by several men. A committee of thirteen men is formed in July to find local conspirators, and the lynchings begin. During the same month five gamblers are lynched at Vicksburg. Other communities in the south are also affected by the "slave revolt" fever.

Chronology

1835 October 30(?)

William H. Short, unrepentent murderer, is hanged at Point Cowpee, Miss. Short had attempted the ax murder of one employer and his family near Natchez and succeeded in killing--with an ax--his next employer.

1837

Gale H. Wages, former member of John Murrell's outlaw gang, settles in the Mobile, Ala.-Pascagoula, Miss. area and begins formation of another gang that will become known as the Copeland clan after leader James Copeland.

1839 late summer

Under cover of a fire they started, members of James Copeland's gang pillage numerous stores in Mobile for a total take of $25,000.

1843 February 10

A trio of murderers---Zebadiah Payne, Willis Green Carroll and Archibald Kirby---are hanged at Nashville, Tenn.

1844 April

John A. Murrell is released from the Nashville prison. On November 1 he dies of tuberculosis in Pikeville, Tenn.

1849 spring

Outlaw James Copeland begins serving four years for larceny at Alabama State Penitentiary in Wetumka.

1850 April

In Fayetteville, N.C., a deaf mute appears claiming to be author Herman Melville. Melville will use this incident as the basis of his novel The Confidence Man.

1851 November 11

In defense of his "honor," lawyer W.W. Avery shoots Samuel Flemming during a trial in Morganton, N.C.

1854

David T. Hines dies in a Louisiana jail. During his hey-day swindler/forger Hines operated from South Carolina to Louisiana and even wrote his autobiography in the 1840s.

1856 May 3

Joseph Flanner kills William Crawford Wilkings in the last formal duel fought in North Carolina.

Criminal Activity in the South

1857 October 30

James Copeland, leader of a gang of robbers and murderers that operated for years along the Gulf Coast, hangs in Augusta (Perry Co.), Mississippi.

1858

Henri de Riviere and Harry Maury fight several duels in Mississippi and Louisiana over a Mobile, Ala., woman named Emily Blount.

1858 November 19

William Buse is hanged at Jacinto, Miss. Buse had murdered Thomas M'Keever during an argument over a jug of whiskey.

1859

During a six-month period vigilance committees are very active in the Attakapas Country region of Louisiana.

1859 September

Nathan Maroney, manager of the Adams Express Co. office in Montgomery, Ala., is tried and convicted of embezzlement of $50,000 in company funds. Maroney, who was captured by Pinkerton agents, was sentenced to ten years in prison.

1868 March 31

Scalawag George W. Ashburn is shot to death by a group of disguised men in Columbus, Ga. Nine men are later indicted, but the charges are dropped when military rule of Georgia ends.

1871 September 27

Prominent Alabama attorney James H. Clanton is shot to death by David M. Nelson in Knoxville, Tenn.

1871 October 21

The gang of Hillary and Levi Farrington rob a train of $6000 near Union City, Tenn. In December the Farringtons will be captured by Allan and William Pinkerton. Hillary will die in an escape attempt and Levi will be lynched at Union City.

1872 September

Tom Clark, a wartime bushwhacker in Lauderdale Co., Ala., who continued to rob and murder after the fighting ended, is lynched along with two members of his gang at Florence.

Chronology

1872 October 27

In Hamilton, Ga., a man believed to be George Applewhite, a member of the notorious Lowry gang of North Carolina, is arrested. The man turns out not to be Applewhite, but too late to stop publication of a pamphlet by the captors of the "outlaw."

1873 June 14

Three black men---Noah Cherry, Robert Thompson and Harry Atkinson---hang in Wayne Co., N.C., for the ax murders earlier in the year of James Worley and his wife Appie Jane.

1875 November 29

Russell and John Allison are murdered by Joseph and George Brassell in Putnam County, Tenn. The Brassells hang for the crimes in 1878.

1877 August 23

Texas gunfighter John Wesley Hardin is arrested in Pensacola, Fla., by Texas Rangers and local officials.

1877 September 17

Texas gunfighter Brown Bowen, brother-in-law of Hardin, is arrested near Whiting, Ala. Bowen hangs in Texas in May 1878.

1878 March 27

Joseph and George Brassell are hanged in Putnam Co., Tenn., for the 1875 murders of Russell and John Allison.

1878 July

Four blacks are lynched by four to five hundred masked men at Monroe, La. Three of the victims were accused of involvement in the murder of a white constable.

1880 July 5

In one of the last formal duels fought in the deep south, E.B.C. Cash kills William M. Shannon on a bridge in Darlington Co., S.C.

1881 July

New Orleans police office David C. Hennessy captures fugitive Italian bandit Giuseppi Esposito. Esposito had fled from Italy and created an underworld group he called the Mafia in New Orleans.

Criminal Activity in the South

1882 August 19

Jack Turner is lynched in Choctaw Co., Ala., for supposedly plotting a county-wide conspiracy of blacks to murder all whites. Turner, a former slave, had been active in local politics for a number of years.

1884 August 10

In Lewis Co., Tenn., four Mormon elders are murdered by a mob.

1886 July 13

Former sheriff of Sumter Co., Ala., is taken from the jail at Livingston and lynched. Stephen S. Renfroe's fall from grace had included embezzlement, attempted murder and numerous jailbreaks.

1888 March 11

William Parker is lynched near Washington, N.C. In 1880 Civil War hero Bryan Grimes had been murdered and Parker was tried twice for the crime. The first trial ended in a mistrial, the second in acquital.

1889 June 22

The last formal duel fought in New Orleans takes place; the antagonists are E.J. LeBreton and H.S. Salvant.

1889 August 10

J.R. Williamson, president of the Rome, Chattanooga and Columbus Railroad, and Patrick Calhoun, lawyer and descendant of John Calhoun, meet in what is probably the last formal duel fought in the south. The meeting takes place somewhere along the Georgia-Alabama border; neither man is injured.

1890 March 19

In Grenada, Miss., storekeeper Mel Cheatham is hanged for the 1889 murder of James Tillman. Cheatham was the first white executed for killing a black after the Civil War.

1890 April 18

Ben Elzy, confessed murderer of 21 people in three states, hangs in Birmingham, Ala.

1890 September 1

Rube Burrow single-handedly robs an L&N train at Flomation, Ala. Burrow's take is less than $300.

Chronology

1890 October 8

Train robber Rube Burrow escapes from jail in Marengo Co., Ala., and is shot to death the next day by Dixie Carter.

1890 October 15

David C. Hennessy, New Orleans, chief of police, is assassinated, probably by organized crime elements he was investigating. In March 1891 eleven men are lynched or shot to death by an angry mob that holds them responsible for Hennessy's death.

1890 October 29

Thomas G. Woolfolk hangs in Macon, Ga., for the 1887 ax murders of his father and eight other relatives.

1891 December 3

Two masked men rob the train as it leaves Atlanta Junction.

1891 December 25

The Coctaw Co., Ala., "Sims war" climaxes in the lynching of religious cult leader Bob Sims and others.

1892

Whitecappers become active in southern Mississippi. The movement lasts only a year or so, but will reappear in 1902.

1892 August 21

Eugene F. Bunch, forger, gambler and train robber in Texas and Louisiana, is killed by members of a posse north of Franklinton, La.

1892 December 29

John Hipp and Charley Kelley are lynched in Butler Co., Ala. For the previous two years the pair had been involved in numerous robberies and viscious murders in and around the town of Georgiana in that county.

1895 April 21

In Greenville, Ala., two black men and three black women are lynched for the alleged ax murder and cremation of a white man.

1895 July 3

Escambia Co., Ala., Sheriff E.S. McMillan hears that legendary black train robber Morris "Railroad Bill" Slater is hiding out in Bluff Springs, Fla. McMillan travels to Bluff Springs and is killed by Slater. A huge manhunt for the train robber begins.

1896 March 7

Train robber Morris "Railroad Bill" Slater falls into a trap set for him at Atmore, Ala., and is killed by J.L. McGowan.

1898 January

Louis Richards hangs in St. Charles Parish, La. Before his execution Richards confesses to ten murders since 1884 in addition to the one for which he is hung.

1899 July 20

A mob in Tallulah, Madison Parish, La., lynches all five Italian residents of the town.

1900 July

In New Orleans a black named Robert Charles murders several policemen before finally being trapped and dying in a day-long seige. On one of the days that officials sought Charles, a "race riot" raged in the city for twelve hours.

1902

Whitecappers again become active in southern Mississippi; this time the movement lasts for four years.

1902 February 12

Near Lake Charles, La., Ward Earll, his wife and three children are shot to death in their home. Albert Edward Batson was tried twice for the crimes and sentenced to death.

1903 January 15

S.C. lt. governor James H. Tillman shoots his political enemy Narciso G. Gonzales, newspaper editor, in Columbia. Gonzales dies four days later; Tillman will be acquitted at his trial.

1904 July 28

Henry Hodges and four family members are murdered and their home and bodies burned near Statesboro, Ga. Will Cato and Paul Reed, two blacks, were arrested, tried and lynched for the crimes August 16.

Chronology

1905 July 8

Game Warden Guy M. Bradley is murdered at Oyster Keys, Fla., by bird poacher Walter Smith. Smith will be arrested, but later released.

1907 May 31

In Jacksonville, Fla., Hammond McNeil murders Harry Parker. The two men had fought over Cora Howorth, a madam who at one time was mistress of writer Steven Crane.

1908 October 19

Quentin Rankin, a representative of the West Tennessee Land Company, is murdered by "night riders," a vigilante organization opposed to the company's control of the Reelfoot Lake region in western Tennessee.

1908 November 10

Robin Cooper guns down former U.S. Senator Edward Carmack in Memphis, Tenn. Carmack was the political rival of Cooper's father.

1908 December 10

Notorious Memphis killer Will "Wild Bill" Latura enters a saloon and opens fire with an automatic pistol. Three blacks are killed and numerous people injured.

1911 January

A series of ritual ax murders that will eventually claim at least sixty-two victims in three states---Louisiana, Georgia and Texas---begins. The victims are all mulattoes; the murderers, also black, believed to be members of a tiny religous cult "Church of Sacrifice.

1912 September 17

Two masked men hold up the Southern railway "Memphis Special" near Stevenson, Ala.

1913 April 26

Mary Phagan, a fourteen-year-old factory worker, is murdered and her body found in the basement of the National Pencil Co. in Atlanta, Ga.

1915 August 16

Leo M. Frank is lynched near Milledgeville, Ga. Frank had been found guilty of Mary Phagan's 1913 murder and sentenced to die; Gov. John Slaton had commuted the sentence.

Criminal Activity in the South

1916 October 21

An argument over seed prices in Abbeville, S.C., escalates into the lynching of wealthy black farmer Anthony Crawford.

1920 August 5

The bank at Black Creek, N.C. is robbed of more than $100,000 in cash and bonds.

1921 January 15

In Pamplico, S.C., five members of the powerful Bigham family are murdered by one of their own, Edmund Bigham. Edmund will be sentenced to prison for the crimes and paroled in 1960.

1923 December 14

Black sharecropper and World War I veteran Joe Pullen murders his boss W.T. Sanders near Drew, Miss. Before Pullen is finally killed he also murders three and wounds four members of the thousand-man posse sent after him.

1924 November 1

John Ashley and three members of his gang of bank robbers and murderers are trapped and killed by police near Sebastian, Fla.

1924 December 24

Kinnie Wagner kills Greene Co., Miss., Deputy Sheriff Murdock McIntosh, the first of five murder victims. A folk legend is born.

1924 December 24

A branch of the Marine Bank of New Orleans is robbed of $13,000; while making his escape, the bandit kills a traffic policeman.

1926 February 25

Famed Florida bootlegger Duncan W. "Red" Shannon is killed by U.S. Coast Guardsmen.

1926 May

Labelle, Fla., is the scene of two lynchings, those of Henry Patterson and Parker Watson.

1926 October 31

Mississippi criminal Kinnie Wagner is convicted of murder at his trial in Meridian.

Chronology

1927 April 23

William Virgil Murphy, Dale Co., becomes the first person electrocuted in Alabama. Murphy dies at Kilby Prison in Montgomery for the murder of his wife.

1929 August 17

Bootlegger James Horace Alderman hangs in an abandoned hangar on a Coast Guard base near Ft. Lauderdale, Fla. Two years previously Alderman had shot and killed two U.S. Coast Guard men and a U.S. Secret Service agent.

2
Region

Monographs

1. Andrews, Johnnie, Jr., and Higgins, William David. A Digest of the Life and Confessions of James Copeland. Prichard, AL: Bienville Historical Society, Prichard Museum, 1971. 9p.

Based on Pitts (#20), although poor documentation is given. Contains numerous grammatical and punctuation errors. Gives a brief outline of the activities of Copeland and his gang of thieves and murderers in Miss., Ala. and elsewhere along the Gulf Coast between 1837 and 1857. A list of gang members is included. No index. Copeland's career deserves better treatment than this document represents.

2. Bannorris, Amanda. The Female Land Pirate; or, Awful, Mysterious, and Horrible Disclosures of Amanda Bannorris, Wife and Accomplice of Richard Bannorris, A Leader of that Terrible Band of Robbers and Murderers, Known Far and Wide as the Murrell Men...Cincinnati: E.E. Barclay, 1848. 32p. Illus.

Adams (p. 40) describes this title as "very rare" and quotes the publisher's note on the verse of the title page: "The following manuscripts were found in the cell of Amanda Bannorris, who, as all will recollect who have noticed the lists of crime in the New Orleans papers, within the past year, was found dead in her cell, from having taken poison. As she has narrated the case, it is senseless to say more; save that these manuscripts procured of the jailer, who claimed them as his property, at a heavy expense, and are now, for the first time, put before the world." Although unseen by the author, this work has the scent of fiction. Stewart (#26) does not include either Bannorris in his list of members of the Murrell clan, but that proves nothing. A check of the New Orleans newspapers for 1846-8 ought to confirm or disprove at least the existence of Amanda and her suicide. NUC Pre-1956 Imprints gives Bannorris' dates as 1817-1846.

3. Benjamin, R.C.O. Southern Outrages---A Statistical Record of Lawless Doings. Los Angeles (?): n.p., 1894. 64p.

4. Bruce, Dickson D., Jr. Violence and Culture in the Antebellum South. Austin: University of Texas Press, c1979. 322p.

Examines violence as an element of southern culture in the antebellum period. Chapters cover such topics as dueling, violence in both slaves and their masters, folklore, violence in southern fiction, etc. Numerous specific crimes are discussed. Extensive documentation. Index.

5. Clanton, Matthew. A Refutation of the Charges Made in the Western Land Pirate Against Matthew Clanton. Yalobusha Co., MS: n.p., August 1833.

In the Walton narrative (#26) Clanton was accused of being a member of John Murrell's outlaw gang. Penick (#18) says no copy of this title survives.

6. Coates, Robert Myron. The Outlaw Years: The History of the Land Pirates of the Natchez Trace. New York: Macaulay, c1930. 307p. Illus. Rep. Detroit: Gale Research, 1974.

Covers Wiley and Micajah Harpe, Joseph Hare, Samuel Mason and John A. Murrell. Responsible for perpetuating mythic aspects of these outlaws, esp. Murrell, into the twentieth century. Very conversational style. Use with extreme caution. Bibilography. No documentation or index.

7. Hall, James. The Harpe's Head: A Legend of Kentucky. Philadelphia: Key and Biddle, 1833. 256p. Rep. Philadelphia: Harrison Hall, 1835.

This title is listed in Wright, American Fiction 1774-1850 (#1907). Based on career of Wiley and Micajah Harpe. Rep. London: A.K. Newman, 1834. 2 vols., as Kentucky. A Tale.

8. Hare, Joseph. The Dying Confession of Joseph Hare, Alias Joseph Thompson Hare, One of the Mail Robbers.... Baltimore: Printed for the Publisher, 1818. 2nd ed. 23p. Rep. (microcard) Louisville, KY: Lost Cause Press, 1959.

Includes material on Hare's robberies in Louisiana, Mississippi, Tennessee and Alabama. Hare claims that he and his gang of twelve robbers made over $38,000 in gold during his time in the south. Hare and his gang hid in a cave "near the Chickasaw Bluffs" on the Mississippi River. Hare was hanged in Baltimore for mail robbery on September 10, 1818.

9. Harrison, C. Williams. Outlaw of the Natchez Trace. New York: Ballantine, 1960. 128p.

Career of John Murrell.

10. Hines, David T. The Life, Adventures and Opinions of David Theo. Hines, of South Carolina...New York: Bradley and Clark, 1840. 195p.

Hines' confessions take the form of a "Series of Letters to His Friends." Born near Pineville, S.C., around 1810, Hines grew up to a career of theft, swindling and forgery throughout the south. The book chronicles his crimes, escapes and adventures from South Carolina to Lousiana. During much of this period he practiced "medicine" in Georgia, Alabama, and Mississippi. In letter 16 Hines describes his meeting with outlaw John Murrell on the road between Montgomery and Mobile, Alabama. Murrell invited Hines to join his gang, but Hines---using his pistol for persuasion---refused. Hines claimed that Murrell "sank back with awe" when he learned Hines' identity. In the same letter Hines tells of his robbery in Mobile of $700 from an acquaintance. These letters were written---according to Hines---in the Louisville, Ky., jail. Williams (Vogues in Villainy, (# 983) says "newspaper reports of his escapades make it clear his journal is not excessively exaggerated." That view may be overly optimistic, but the journals are entertaining at the very least.

11. Howard, H.R., comp. The History of Virgil A. Stewart and His Adventure in Capturing and Exposing the Great "Western Land Pirate" and His Gang, in connection with the evidence; also of the trials, confessions, and execution of a number of Murrell's associates in the state of Mississippi during the summer of 1835, and the execution of five professional gamblers by the citizens of Vicksburg, on the 6th July 1835. New York: Harper and Brothers, 1836. Rep. 1839. 273p. Rep. Spartanburg, SC: Reprint Co., 1976. Facs. ed. intro. by Laura D.S. Sturdivant.

The book by Augustus Walton was responsible for creation of the myth surrounding John A. Murrell and his vast Mystic Clan of outlaws. This title, more than any other, has been responsible for the perpetuation of that myth. For the facts, see monograph by Penick (#18). Totally incredible and totally fascinating. No documentation, bibliography or index. Listed in Wright, American Fiction, 1744-1850, no. 235.

12. Howard, H.R. The Life and Adventures of John A. Murrel, the Great Western Land Pirate, with Twenty-One Spirited Illustrative Engravings. Philadelphia: T.B. Peterson and Brothers, 1845. 126p. Illus. Rep. New York: H. Long and Brother, 1847, 1848.

This work was reprinted under the slightly different title, Pictorial Life and Adventures of John A. Murrell ... in the 1840s, 1850s and 1860s. Listed in Wright, American Fiction, 1744-1850, no. 1237-8. Promotes the mythical Murrell.

13. Howard, H.R. The Life and Adventures of Joseph T. Hare, the Bold Robber and Highwayman, with sixteen... engravings. New York: H. Long and Brother, 1847. 107p. Illus.

Hare operated in the Alabama-Mississippi area for some time prior to his execution in Baltimore in 1818 for mail robbery. Considering what Howard did for the John Murrell legend, this title is probably more fiction than fact. Originally published in the National Police Gazette. Listed in Wright, American Fiction, 1774-1850, no. 1239, and available in the microfilm edition of that bibliography's entries, Reel H-12, issued by Research Publications.

14. Kane, Harnett T. Gentlemen, Swords and Pistols. New York: William Morrow, 1951. 306p.

A history of dueling below the Mason-Dixon line. Specific duels discussed include E.B.C. Cash vs. William Shannon (July 5, 1880) in Darlington Co., S.C.; George Crawford vs. Thomas E. Burnside (January 5, 1829) at Ft. Mitchell, Ala.; and the near-comic duel between Patrick Calhoun and J.R. Williamson (August 10, 1889) somewhere in Alabama or Georgia. Highly readable but poorly documented. Bibliography. Index.

15. Memphis, Tenn. Health Dept. A Study of Violent Deaths Registered in Atlanta, Birmingham, Memphis and New Orleans for the Years 1921 and 1922, by J.J. Durrett ...and W.G. Stromquist. Memphis, TN: Davis, 1922. 38p.

Primarily statistics.

16. Miller, Rick. The Train Robbing Bunch. College Station, TX: Creative Publishing, 1982. 175p. Illus.

Covers train robber/murderer Eugene Bunch and his gang, who robbed trains in Mississippi, Louisiana and Texas. Bunch was killed by a posse in Washington Parish, La.,

August 21, 1892. One of the few scholarly works (see Warren Rogers, Jr., for the others) completed on a southern train robber. Documentation, bibliography, index.

17. Parsons, Chuck. The Capture of John Wesley Hardin. College Station, TX: Creative Publishing, 1978. 121p. Illus. Intro. C. L. Sonnichsen.

Between the summer of 1864 and August 1877, Texas gunfighter Hardin, his wife Jane and their children lived in Florida and Alabama; the family had fled Texas due to Hardin's fear of lynching there. This title is a detailed account of those years and especially Hardin's capture in Pensacola, Fla., in August 1877. Documentation, bibliography, index. For additional material on Hardin's southern years, see (#71, #72).

18. Penick, James Lal, Jr. The Great Western Land Pirate: John A. Murrell in Legend and History. Columbia: University of Missouri Press, 1981. 197p.

A detailed investigation of the factual--as opposed to legendary--Murrell. Debunks most of the myths that have surrounded Murrell for 150 years--his leadership of a gigantic "mystic Clan" of outlaws, the formulation of a vast slave revolt from which his group would benefit, etc. Murrell turns out to have been little more than a horse thief. Fascinating, excellent work that will set a standard for future scholarship on southern criminal activity. Meticulous documentation. "Essay on Sources." Index.

19. Phares, Ross. Reverend Devil: A Biography of John A. Murrell. New Orleans: Pelican Publishing, c1941. 263p. Illus. Rep. Gretna, LA: Pelican, 1974.

Biography of the legendary Murrell. Based on Howard (#11) Coates (#6), Walton (#26), etc. For the factual Murrell see Penick (#18). No documentation. Bibliography. Index.

20. Pitts, J.R.S. Life and Confession of the noted outlaw James Copeland, executed at Augusta, Perry County, Mississippi. Leader of the Notorious Copeland and Wages Clan which Terrorized the entire Southern States, as Related by Himself in Prison after he was Condemned to Death, Giving a List of All Members of the Clan. Mystic Alphabet of the Clan for their Secret Correspondence, with an Appendix of Profound Research. Hattisburg, MS: 1858. 237pp. Illus.

21. Pitts, J.R.S. Life and Bloody Career of the Executed Criminal James Copeland, the Greater Southern Land Pirate ..... Jackson, MS: Pilot Publishing Co., 1874. 220pp. Illus.

22. Pitts, J.R.S. Life and Confession of the Noted Outlaw James Copeland. Jackson, MS: University Press of Mississippi, 1980. Rep. 1909 ed. 237p. Illus. Intro. by John D.W. Guice.

Copeland was a leader of an outlaw gang that operated primarily in Mississippi and Alabama from the late 1830s until Copeland's hanging at Augusta, Perry Co., Miss., October 30, 1857. Copeland's gang was similar in size and operation to the one supposedly led by John A. Murrell; in fact, one of Copeland's co-leaders, Gale H. Wages, had been a Murrell man. As with Murrell's gang, murder, theft, arson and counterfeiting were primary activities. One of the gang's most spectacular crimes was the 1839 burning/looting of Mobile, Ala., which netted $25,000. Fascinating. What is needed now is a scholarly examination of Copeland's life equal to that performed on Murrell's by Penick. Introduction only contains documentation. "Calendar of Events." Index.

23. Presley, Samuel C. Negro Lynching in the South. Treating of the Negro. His Past and Present Condition; of the Cause of Lynching, and of the Means to Remedy the Evil. Presenting the Northern and Southern View. Accurate Accounts of Many Notable Crimes and Lynchings, Including that of the Mafia in New Orleans. Also a Mass of Statistics About Lynching. Washington, D.C.: T.W. Cadick, 1899. 64p. Illus.

24. Quintero, J.A. The Code of Honor, Its Rationale and Uses, By the Tests of Common Sense and Good Morals, with the Effects of Its Preventive Remedies. New Orleans: E.A. Brandao and Co., 1883. 42p. 2nd. ed. rev. 1st ed. 1873.

Written by journalist Jose Quintero. Primarily regulations for dueling. Some material on specific southern duels. No documentation. No index.

25. Southern Commission on the Study of Lynching. Lynchings and What They Mean. Atlanta, GA: The Commission, 1932(?). 76p.

Primarily statistical and sociological. Some discussion of individual lynchings. Appendix gives listing of names of victims, charges, locations and dates for 1930 lynchings.

26. Walton, Augustus Q. A History of the Detection, Conviction, Life and Designs of John A. Murel, the Great Western Land Pirate; Together with his System of Villainy, and Plan of Exciting Negro Rebellion. Also a Catalogue of the Names of Four Hundred and Fifty-Five of His Mystic Clan Fellows and Followers, and a Statement of their Efforts for the Destruction of Virgil A. Stewart, the Young Man Who Detected Him. To Which is Added a Biographical Sketch of V.A. Stewart. Cincinnati: U.P. James, n.d. 84p. Illus.

Rep. Athens, TN: G. White, 1835. Rep. Lexington, KY: 1835, 185?

Walton is probably a pseudonym used by Virgil Stewart. A totally incredible, nonetheless fascinating book that created the legendary John A. Murrell and precipitated a region-wide manhunt for members of his outlaw gang who were believed to be plotting a massive slave revolt. (Several supposed members were lynched in Mississippi.) No documentation, bibliography or index.

27. Wellman, Paul I. The Devil's Disciples: The Most Dreadful of all Historic Conspiracies, brewed and finally foiled in the dark forests of America. London: W. Foulsham, c1964. 224p.

This book is as bad as its title. Yet another retelling of the various tales surrounding John A. Murrell, including the vast "Mystic Clan" he supposedly led and the "slave conspiracy" he supposedly formulated. Based on the usual dubious sources (#6,#11,#19). See Penick (#18) for the facts. Wellman claims this book is a "companion" to Spawn of Evil; it is actually a reprint of the last half of Spawn. Nothing new. Bibliography. Index.

28. Wellman, Paul I. Spawn of Evil: The Invisible Empire of Soulless Men Which for a Generation Held the Nation in a Spell of Terror. Garden City, NY: Doubleday, 1964. 350p.

Includes material on Micajah and Wiley Harpe, Samuel Mason and John Murrell. Full of the usual tall tales and will hold thinking men and women in a spell of disgust. Poor documentation. Includes annotated bibliography and index.

29. Williams, Jack K. Dueling in the Old South: Vignettes of Social History. College Station: Texas A & M University Press, 1980. 109p.

Brief survey of antebellum dueling. Covers individual duels, code of honor among combatants, opposition to dueling, etc. Reprints John Lyde Wilson's The Code of Honor (1838). Should have been more extensive. Documentation and bibliographic notes. Inexplicably, no index.

30. Wilson, John L. The Code of Honor; or, Rules for the Government of Principals and Seconds in Duelling. Charleston: T.J. Eccles, 1838. 22p. Rep. Charleston: James Phinney, 1858. (46 p.) New Orleans: Clark and Hofeline, 1873. 17p. Kennesaw, GA: Continental Book Co., 1959. 46p.

The book by which all subsequent southern duels were supposedly guided. Details the etiquette of dueling. Fascinating.

Region

Dissertations

31. Ayers, Edward Lynn. "Crime and Society in the Nineteenth Century South." Ph.D. dissertation, Yale University, 1980. 423p.

Concentrates on development of penitentiary as an institution in the antebellum south and its transformation during the first decade after the Civil War into the convict lease system.

32. Butcher, Jerry L. "A Narrative History of Selected Aspects of Violence in the New South, 1877-1920." Ph.D. dissertation, University of Missouri, Columbia, 1977. 212p.

Covers the tradition of violence, dueling, assasination, murder, Whitecapping, lynching and legal aspects. Good bibliography. Eleven former Confederate states and Kentucky are included in "South." Recommended.

33. Flanigan, Daniel J. "The Criminal Law of Slavery and Freedom, 1800-1868." Ph.D. dissertation, Rice University, 1873. 518p.

Sources include statutes, appellate court decisions and some trial court records. Covers District of Columbia and fifteen slave-holding states.

34. Rable, George Calvin. "But There Was No Peace: Violence and Reconstruction Politics." Ph.D. dissertation, Louisiana State University, 1978. 778p. 2 vols.

Covers riots, murders, etc., in the South, 1865-1876, as whites mounted a "successful and violent overthrow of these southern state governments..." (DAI, 39/11A, p. 6920).

35. Turner, Frederick William III. "Badmen, Black and White: The Continuity of American Folk Tradition." Ph.D. dissertation, University of Pennsylvania, 1965. 466p.

Chapter 4 contains material on Kinnie Wagner. Also included are discussion of Morris "Railroad Bill" Slater, Stackolee and other black outlaws. Examines legends surrounding white and black outlaws.

Theses

36. Dunlap, John M. Jr. "The Outlaw in Southern Folksong." M.A. thesis, University of North Carolina, 1949. 159p.

Dunlap examines published folksongs dealing with outlaws in fifteen "southern" states, including the eight covered by this bibliography. Numerous individual songs are discussed, as well as such broader categories as Negro songs and feud ballads. The historical background of some songs is also explored. Railroad Bill and Stagolee are two of many real criminals whose songs are discussed. The thesis is documented by footnotes and a bibliography.

37. Dunn, Margaret Carter. "Criminals Along the Natchez Trace." M.A. thesis, University of Southern Mississippi, 1970. 111p.

Separate chapters cover the development of the Natchez Trace, Micajah and Wiley Harpe, Samuel Mason, Joseph Hare and John Murrell. Dunn's sources include such questionable ones as Coates, Daniels, Wellman, Walton and Phares. Dunn notes, "...an abundance of primary source material on this topic is not readily available. This writer has depended on contemporary accounts from witnesses and victims for most of the fascinating facts concerning the unbelievable brigands" (p. 11-2). As the work of Penick on Murrell demonstrates, a little research goes a long way toward making these outlaws more believable. Considering the lack of scholarship on the careers of the Harpes, Mason and Hare, it is unfortunate that Dunn--despite her claim noted above---has merely perpetuated the fantasies of previous writers. Includes documentation and bibliography.

38. Haslinger, Ferdinand. "Crime in William Gilmore Simms's Border Romances: Violence and Frontier Justice in the Old South." M.A. thesis, University of Alabama (Tuscaloosa), 1982. 126p.

"The purpose of this paper is to examine the theme of crime and frontier justice in Simms's Border Romances and to determine what such a study can tell us about antebellum Southern society and culture" (p.2). Simms' "border romances" consist of seven novels, several of which are set in one or more of the states covered by this bibliography: _Guy Rivers_, _Richard Hurdis_, _Border Beagles_, _Helen Halsey_ and _Voltmeier_. Haslinger's claim that _Richard Hurdis_ and _Border Beagles_ follow correctly the outline of John A. Murrell's slave uprising "conspiracy" is absurd; Simms used spurious sources and the wild rumors of his day. In general, an excellent, well-documented examination of the novels.

39. Rees, Gary Lee. "The John Murrell Plot." M.A. thesis, University of Southern Mississippi, 1981.

Pretty much superceded by Penick's book (18).

40. Rogers, William Warren Jr. "Violence and Outlawry in the New South: Rube Burrow's Train Robbing Days in Alabama, Mississippi and Florida." M.A. thesis, Auburn University, 1979.

This title and Rogers' two journal articles are the only decent items yet written about Burrow. Documentation.

Journal Articles

41. Aswell, James R. "America's Worst Badman." American Mercury 1953 October; 77:68-73.

Repeats the usual nonsense about John A. Murrell's vast Mystic Clan of criminals and his 1835 slave insurrection. No documentation.

42. Ball, Larry D."Murrell in Arkansas: An Outlaw Gang in History and Tradition." Mid-South Folklore 1978 winter; 6(3):65-76.

Some material on John Murrell's activities in Tennessee and elsewhere in addition to Arkansas. This article and Penick are about the only decent pieces of scholarship ever written on Murrell. Well documented.

43. Cardwell, Guy A. "The Duel in the Old South: Crux of a Concept." South Atlantic Quarterly 1967; 66(1):50-69.

Cardwell discusses arguments for and against dueling in both fact and fiction. Brief mentions of individual duels and duelists. Some useful discussion of dueling in fiction. Article is seriously marred by very poor documentation. Cardwell committs such sins as noting "a historian reports..." without ever bothering to acknowledge the scholar by name.

44. Corbitt, D.C. "James Colbert and the Spanish Claims to the East Bank of the Mississippi." Mississippi Valley Historical Review 1938 March; 24(4):457-72.

Describes activities of Scotch pirate Colbert and his band against the Spanish along the Mississippi River, 1782-3. Corbitt describes Colbert not as a pirate--as the Spanish considered him--but "as a British officer carrying out the orders of his superiors." What a difference point of view makes. Documentation.

45. Davis, Robert Ralph, Jr., ed. "Notes and Documents: Buchanian Espionage: A Report on Illegal Slave Trading in the South in 1859." Journal of Southern History 1971 May; 37:271-8.

Reprints letter of secret agent Benjamin F. Slocumb, who investigated illegal slave trade in southern states for two months beginning in September 1859. Documentation.

46. "Disgrace of Georgia and Alabama." Current Literature 1904 October; 37:294-6.

Concerns August 16, 1904, lynching at Statesboro, Ga., of two blacks convicted of murder; and the September 7, 1904, lynching at Huntsville of another black convicted of murder. No documentation.

47. Dobie, James Frank. "James Bowie, Big Dealer." Southwestern Historical Quarterly 1957 January; 60:337-57.

Overview of Bowie's life. Includes material on slave smuggling, the sandbar "duel" near Natchez, Miss. (September 19, 1827), etc. Documentation.

48. Douglass, Frederick. "Lynch Law in the South." North American Review 1892 July; 155:17-24.

Anti-lynching; no details on specific cases. No documentation.

49. Eaton, Clement. "Mob Violence in the Old South." Mississippi Valley Historical Review 1942; 29(3):351-70.

Discusses primarily mob violence associated with efforts to stamp out abolitionist activity in the antebellum South. Some discussion of Mississippi duelist Alexander McClung, John Murrell"s supposed "slave insurrection" and the resultant massacre at Livingston, Miss., and other lynchings. Well documented.

50. "Enigmatic Folksongs of the Southern Underworld." Current Opinion 1919 September; 67"165-6.

Discusses white singer Gilda Gray's performance of blues songs in the Broadway show "Gaieties of 1919." Associates blues with the "outlaw emotions," i.e., gambling, prostitution, etc. Includes photograph of Gray. No documentation.

51. Flanigan, Daniel J. "Criminal Procedure in Slave Trials in the Antebellum South." Journal of Southern History 1974 November; 40(4):537-64.

Primarily concerned with the evolution of procedure in various southern states. Some specific crimes mentioned or cited, including rape and murder. Documentation includes numerous court cases.

52. Grantham, Dewey W., Jr. "Goebel, Gonzales, Carmack: Three Violent Scenes in Southern Politics." Mississippi Quarterly 1958 winter; 11:29-37.

Includes discussion of Columbia, S.C., shooting of Narciso G. Gonzales by James H. Tillman, lt. governor. Event took place January 15, 1903; Gonzales, Tillman's "bitter enemy" and a newspaper editor, died four days later. Tillman was acquitted at his trial. Also discusses November 9, 1908, Nashville, Tenn., murder of Edward Ward Carmack by Robin Cooper. No documentation.

53. Hair, William Ivy. "'Inquisition for Blood:' An Outbreak of Ritual Murder in Louisiana, Georgia and Texas, 1911-1912." Louisiana Studies 1972 winter; 11:274-81.

Between January 1911 and April 1912 at least sixty-two blacks were murdered "under similarly hideous circumstances," usually with an ax, in the three states. Between April and November 1911, thirteen were killed in Atlanta alone. Killers were probably also blacks, members of a tiny religious cult called "Church of Sacrifice" who were executing mulattoes. Documentation, primarily newspaper articles.

54. Hatheway, G.G. "Meet Wiley and Micajah Harpe: Unkind Men." Mankind 1968 June; 1(7):32-41.

Overview of Harpes' legendary career as viscious robbers and murderers along the Natchez Trace and elsewhere. No documentation. Suggested reading list includes such Harpe standards as Hall (Harpe's Head; and Legends of the West), Rothert and the dubious Coates. Illustrated.

55. Hughson, Shirley Carter. "The Carolina Pirates and Colonia Commerce, 1670-1740." John Hopkins University Studies in Historical and Political Science 1894; series 12:241-370.

Extensive examination of piracy along the coasts of North and South Carolina. Includes discussion of Edward Teach (spelled "Thatch" here), Stede Bonnet and others. Documentation.

56. Jordan, Philip D. "The Derringer and the Ace of Spades: Reflections on Middle Border Law and Order." Louisiana Studies 1967 winter; 6(4):315-32.

Includes material on a wide variety of crimes along the Mississippi River from New Orleans to St. Paul: robbery, prostitution, etc. Pirate James Colbert "on May 2, 1782, seized a vessel bound for St. Louis: from New Orleans "and carried off gifts intended for Indian tribes and 4,500 pesos." Extensive documentation.

57. "Lives of the Felons. no. 10. John Washburn." National Police Gazette 1846 August 29 and September 5; 1 (51-52):425-6,433-4.

Details the career of robber/murderer and gang leader Washburn, born in Rockingham Co., N.C., in 1811. Washburn operated in Florida, Mississippi, Louisiana and Tennessee as well as the midwest. Specific crimes described include an 1830 robbery of $3000 from the Nashville Exchange bank and a murder in Pensacola. Washburn was hanged in Cincinnati on January 6, 1837. Includes illustrations.

58. "Lives of the Felons. no. 11. John A. Murrell." National Police Gazette 1846 September 12-1847 April 24; 2(1)-2(33).

The Murrell legend was continued and reinforced by this lengthy series published just two years after Murrell's death. May be based on Howard and/or Walton, which were the only items about Murrell in print at the time. Told from "objective" point of view. Possibly written by the Gazette's editors, Enoch E. Camp and George Wilkes. Numerous illustrations.

59. "Lives of the Felons. no. 12. Life and Adventures of the Bold Robber and Highwayman Joseph T. Hare." National Police Gazette 1847 May 1-September 4; 2(34)-2(52).

According to this first-person account, "compiled from his own confessions, the statements of his accomplices, and information in possession of old members of the police," Joseph Thompson Hare was born in Chester Co., Penn., in 1780. In 1801 he arrived in New Orleans. His travels to Baton Rouge, Nashville, Knoxville, Pensacola and Natchez--along with robberies and murders committed during them with the help of cohorts---are described. In this version, Hare was hanged in Baltimore on Sept. 10, 1812 (instead of 1818). Numerous illustrations.

60. Locke, Raymond F. "The Natchez Trace: 'Road of Blood.'" Mankind 1975; 4(12):30-7.

Covers the usual Natchez Trace crowd: Wiley and Micajah Harpe, Samuel Mason, Joseph Hare, John Murrell (mispelled as Murrel), etc. No documentation; probably based on such standard dubious sources as Howard and Coates (#11 and #6). Illus. with photographs.

61. "Lynching and Public Sentiment." Outlook 1911 June 10; 98:289-91.

Discusses recent lynchings of blacks at Lake City, Fla., (Mark Morris and Jerry Gusto, accused of murdering white man B.B. Smith) and in Emanuel Co., Ga. Written by "A Southern Correspondent." No documentation.

62. McCulloch-Williams, Martha. "John Murrell and His Clan." Harper's New Monthly Magazine 1897 January; 94: 302-6.

Another incarnation of the legendary Murrell. Nothing new. No documentation.

63. Matthews, Albert. "Lynch Law." Nation 1902 December 4; 75:439-41.

Some accounts of individual southern lynchings, pre-1850. Discussion of the origin of the term "lynch law." Asserts that term may have begun with the South Carolina regulators, who used the practice and met at Lynch's Creek, S.C. Documentation.

64. Ogden, G.W. "Old Times Barge Pirates on the Mississippi." Everybody's 1902; 7:478-85.

Discusses such pirates as Colonel Fluger, Mike Fink and Campbell who attacked boats moving along the Mississippi River between St. Louis and New Orleans. Illustrated. No documentation.

65. Pinkerton, William A. "Highwaymen of the Railroad." North American Review 1893 November; 157:530-40.

Among others includes discussion of Pinkerton's pursuit of two southern train robbing gangs, the one led by Levi and Hillary Farrington and another led by Rube and Jim Burrow. No documentation.

66. Ramage, Burr J. "Homicide in the Southern States." Sewanee Review 1895-6; 4:212-32.

Generalized discussion of nature of and remedies for southern murder. Table includes number of 1880 and 1890 homicides for all states. No documentation.

67. Scott, Kenneth. "Some Counterfeiters of Provincial Currency." South Carolina Historical Magazine 1956 January; 57(1):14-22.

Covers specific counterfeiters in S.C. and Ga., 1735-8. Documentation.

68. Sessions, Gene A. "Myth, Mormonism, and Murder in the South." South Atlantic Quarterly 1976 spring; 75:212-25.

Describes violence against Mormons in the South, 1865-1900. Includes murder of four Mormon elders in Lewis Co., Tenn., August 10, 1884; murder of an elder at Russell Station, Miss., August 2, 1888; and severe whipping of two elders in Alabama, June 1893. Documentation.

69. "Uses and Abuses of Lynch Law." American Whig Review 1850; n.s. 5:459-76 and n.s. 6:494-501. 1851; n.s. 7:213-220.

Covers John Murrell's legendary outlaw gang and the supposed slave revolt to be led by that gang in 1835. Some documentation.

70. Wagner, Kinnie. "The Story of My Life." Vagabond Gazette 1931 May; 4(5):60-1.

Wagner was incarcerated at the Mississippi Penitentiary at Parchman when this article---followed by twelve others in subsequent issues of James Taylor Adams' journal---was published. Wagner murdered a deputy sheriff in Mississippi and two policemen in Tennessee. Fascinating. No documentation.

71. Wright, A.J. "A Gunfighter's Southern Vacation." Quarterly of the National Association and Center for Outlaw and Lawman History 1982 autumn; 7(3):12-8.

Covers John Wesley Hardin's years in Alabama and Florida, 1874-1877. Documentation.

72. Wright, A.J. "John Wesley Hardin's 'Missing' Years." Old West 1981 fall; 18(1):6-11.

Covers Hardin's years in Alabama and Florida, 1874-1877. No documentation.

Miscellaneous

73. Anthony, Irvin. Paddle Wheels and Pistols. New York: Grosset and Dunlap, c1929. 329p. Illus.

Chapter 11, "River Gods" (p. 234-54) repeats the usual bilge about John Murrell, his vast Mystic Clan of outlaws and planned slave revolt. Chapter 12, "Packet People" (p. 255-81) contains material on Mississippi River gamblers. No documentation, bibliography or index.

74. Asbury, Herbert. Sucker's Progress: An Informal History of Gambling in America from the Colonies to Canfield. New York: Dodd, Mead, 1938. 493p.

Chapter 9, "Gambling on the Western Rivers" (p.197-262) covers Mississippi River gambling between St. Louis and New Orleans. Discussion includes John Murrell, Virgil Stewart, the lynching of the Vicksburg gamblers in July 1835, James Bowie, J.J. Bryant, George DeVol and other southern figures and events. Footnotes, Bibliography. Index.

75. Baldwin, Leland D. The Keelboat Age on Western Waters. Pittsburgh: University of Pittsburgh Press, 1941. 268p. Illus.

Chapter 5, "River Pirates and the Natchez Trace" (p. 116-33), includes material on the activities of Samuel Mason and Micajah and Wiley Harpe in Tennessee and elsewhere. Much of the material comes from Rothert (#154) and Guild (#1115). The book includes an Index and Bibliography.

76. Baughman, Laurence Alan. Southern Rape Complex: Hundred Year Psychosis. Atlanta: Pendulum Books, c1966. 222p.

Contains some material on pre-1930 rapes and lynchings. Extremely poor documentation in what is more of a tract than a scholarly analysis. Selected bibliography. No index.

77. Borchard, Edwin M. Convicting the Innocent; Sixty-Five Actual Errors of Criminal Justice. Garden City, NY: Garden City Publishing, c1932. 383p. Illus.

"The Wrong Name on the Death Warrant" (p.32-8) concerns the October 1901 murder in Palatka, Fla., of H.W. Gordon by J.J. Johnson; J.B. Brown was almost hanged for the crime. "Out of the Mouths of Babes" (p.39-44) covers the prosecution in Lowndes Co., Ala., for the supposed murder of Topsey Warren by George Yelder and Louise Butler. The two were sentenced to life imprisonment on April 26, 1928; Topsey reappeared in less than a week. "Mississippi Melodrama" (p.206-13) covers the Will Purvis case; see Griffith. No documentation, bibliography or index.

78. Botkin, B.A., ed. A Treasury of Mississippi River Folklore: Stories, Ballads, Traditions and Folkways of the Mid-American River Country. New York: Crown, c1955. 620p.

Contains material on the Natchez-Under-the Hill district, etc. Part 3, "Pirates, Outlaws and Sharpers" (p.195-261) has entries on the Harpes, Samuel Mason, John A. Murrell, Jean Lafitte, gambling, etc. Sources for entries are given. Index.

79. Botkin, B.A., ed. A Treasury of Southern Folklore: Stories, Ballads, Traditions, and Folkways of the People of the South. New York: Crown, 1949. 776p.

Part 2, section 2, "Buccaneers, Bandits and Bullies" (p.189-249) includes material on Edward Teach, Jean LaFitte, Micajah and Wiley Harpe, Samuel Mason, John A. Murrell, George DeVol, Mike Fink, Morris "Railroad Bill" Slater, Rube Burrow and Kinnie Waggoner (sic). Taken from other sources, which are cited. Indexes of authors, titles, first lines of songs and subjects, names, places.

80. Breihan, Carl W. Badmen of the Frontier Days. New York: McBride, 1957. 315p. Illus.

Pages 12-28 cover career of John Murrell.

81. Breihan, Carl W. Outlaws of the Old West. New York: Signet, 1930.

Contains material on train robber Rube Burrow and his gang, p.36-113.

82. Brown, Richard Maxwell. "John A. Murrell." In Reader's Encyclopedia of the American West, ed. Howard W. Lamar. New York: Crowell, 1977. 1306p.

Pages 783-4 contain a brief overview of Murrell's legendary career. Brown is skeptical that Murrell was planning a slave rebellion in 1835. Recommended sources are Coates (#6), Howard (#11), and Miles (#763).

83. Brown, Richard Maxwell. Strain of Violence: Historical Studies of American Violence and Vigilantism. New York: Oxford University Press, 1975. 397p.

A seminal work on American vigilantism that cannot be praised too highly. Covers colonial era to modern day. Contains much material on pre-1930 southern vigilante movements and lynchings. A very useful feature is Appendix 3 (p. 305-19) which lists vigilante movements by state between 1767 and 1904. Extensive documentation. Index.

84. Browning, Frank and Gerassi, John. The American Way of Crime. New York: Putman's, c1980. 539p.

This history of U.S. crime contains material on pirate Edward Teach, the South Carolina pre-Revolution Regulators, the assasination of New Orleans police chief David Hennessy and its lynching aftermath, John A. Murrell, the lynching of Mississippi gamblers in July 1835, etc. Good overview. Documentation. Index.

85. Burrows, William E. Vigilante! New York: Harcourt Brace Jovanovich, c1976. 311p. Illus.

Chapter 3 (p.44-67), which covers the pre-Revolution South Carolina Regulators, is based primarily on Brown. Chapter 8 (p.193-223) covers the murder of New Orleans police chief David Hennessy in 1890 and the March 1891 lynchings of eleven Italians in response to that assasination. Chapter 8 based primarily on articles by Coxe (#594), and Kendall (#628). Documentation. Bibliography. Index.

86. Burt, Olive Woolley, ed. American Murder Ballads and their Stories. New York: Oxford University Press, 1958. 272p.

This book not only gives the lyrics and some melodies of numerous ballads, but a discussion of the historical crimes on which they're based as well. Pre-1930 deep south murders include those of Naomi Wise by Jonathan Lewis (1808,N.C.); Mary Phagan (April 1913; Atlanta, Ga.) for which Leo Frank was lynched; Joseph Standing and Rudger Clawson, two Mormon elders (July 1879; Whitfield Co., Ga.); Chief of Police David Hennessy (Oct. 1890, New Orleans); and murderers such as Railroad Bill, Stackalee, Kenny Wagner (Miss.), Joe and Leak Braswell (1875, Smithville, Tenn.) and the G. Raines gang of bank robbers (ca. World War I, Morrison and central Tenn.). The book has a detailed index.

87. Burton, Thomas G. and Manning, Ambrose N., eds. Collection of Folklore: Folksongs. Johnson City, TN: Institute of Regional Studies, East Tennessee State University, c1967. 114p.

Contains primarily song lyrics and music. Two songs are based on the career of Kinnie Wagner; another, "The Knoxville Girl," describes the murder of a girl from that city by her fiance. Index of song titles and first lines.

88. Byrnes, Thomas. Rogues' Gallery: 247 Professional Criminals of Nineteenth-Century America. Rep. ed. New York: Chelsea House, 1969. 433pp. Illus. Intros. by Arthur M. Schlesinger, Jr., and S.J. Perelman.

Covers primarily Northeastern criminals, especially those operating in New York City. However, the book does include figures involved in some deep South crimes such as bank robberies (pp. 92 and 115) in Charleston, SC, ca. March 1879 and Macon, GA, spring 1873; burglary (p. 174) in New Orleans, March 9, 1886; robbery (p. 147) of a U.S. paymaster in Vicksburg, MS; a hotel robbery (p.110) in Atlanta, GA, ca. 1880; and a jailbreak (p. 147) in Mobile, AL, ca. January 1871. No footnotes or bibliography. Index.

89. Capital Punishment Research Project. University of Alabama School of Law, Tuscaloosa.

For more than twelve years, director Watt Espy, has been gathering material on legal, civilian executions in the United States. As of April 1984, the number of confirmed executions in the eight deep south states were: Alabama--689; Florida--311; Georgia--991; Louisiana--586; Mississippi--336; North Carolina--665; South Carolina--620; and Tennessee--343. Espy's records are a gold mine not only for information concerning the executions, but also the murders and other crimes leading up to them.

90. Carter, Hodding. Lower Mississippi. New York: Farrar and Rinehart, c1942. 467p. Illus.

Chapter 11, "Sudden Death" (p.169-79) includes brief discussion of Richard and Amanda Bannoris (spelled here "Bamoris"), supposedly members of John Murrell"s gang of outlaws; Murrell; Joseph Hare; Samuel Mason; the Harpes; and Bras Coupe, the alias of a one-armed fugitive slave named Squier whose gang of thieves and murderers terrorized New Orleans in the 1830s. Carter's sources for much of this chapter are the dubious Coates, Howard and Walton. Carter does acknowledge that Bannoris' confession is probably fiction. Chapter 10, "Dominique You Squares Accounts" (p.159-68) discusses the pirate brothers Jean and Pierre Lafitte. Chapter 21, "Who Killa da Chief?" (p. 310-24) covers the 1890 murder of New Orleans police chief David Hennessy and its aftermath, the lynching of eleven Italians believed to have been involved in Hennessy's death. Some discussion of dueling and gambling. Bibliography. Index.

91. Chadbourn, James Harmon. Lynching and the Law. Chapel Hill: University of North Carolina Press, 1933. Rep. New York: Johnson Reprint, 1970, 221p.

Analyzes operation and failure of state anti-lynching laws. Numerous pre-1930 southern lynchings are discussed. Well-documented. Index.

92. Cochran, Hamilton. Noted American Duels and Hostile Encounters. Philadelphia: Chilton, c1963. 319p. Illus.

Chapter 10, "For the Love of a Woman" (p. 214-30) includes material on the 1858 Mississippi and Louisiana duels between Harry Maury and Henri de Riviere over a Mobile, Ala. woman, Emily Blount. Chapter 11, "Dueling in Dixie" (p. 231-52 includes the September 1827 duel near Natchez, Miss., in which James Bowie was an unofficial participant. Very poor documentation. No bibliography. Index.

93. Coffin, Tristram Potter and Cohen, Henning. The Parade of Heroes: Legendary Figures in American Lore. Garden City, NY: Anchor Press, 1978. 630p.

Includes material on pirate Jean Lafitte (p. 280-3) and James Copeland (p. 291-3), who is portrayed as a member of John Murrell's clan. Also material on Stagolee (p. 306-9) and Jesse James' supposed robbery of a bank in Huntsville, Ala. (p. 300).

94. Courlander, Harold. Negro Folk Music U.S.A. New York: Columbia University Press, c1963. 324p.

Pages 178-9 discuss "Stagolee" folksong. Author notes (p.177) that both "Stagolee" and "Railroad Bill" are ballads sung by both blacks and "white mountaineer balladeers and played by mountain jug bands." Documentation. Bibliography. Discography. Index.

95. Isaac J. The West Florida Controversy, 1798-1813. Gloucester, Mass.: Peter Smith, 1967. 699p. Rep. 1908 ed.

Contains much material on the three Kemper brothers, especially Reuben, "who long bore an unenviable reputation on the border as disturbers of the peace." Kempers operated along the American-Spanish border and made frequent marauding trips into Spanish West Florida. The July 1805 search for murderer William Flannigan in the Mississippi Territory is also described (p.165). Documentation. Index.

96. Crimes and Punishment: A Pictorial Encyclopedia of Aberrant Behavior. Symphonette Press. c1974. 20 vols.

A crime buff's delight, profusely illustrated. Unfortunately, little pre-1930 southern U.S. material is included. Leo Frank, David C. Hennessy and pirate Edward Teach are covered. No documentation. Index.

97. Cutler, James E. Lynch-Law: An Investigation into the History of Lynching in the United States. Montclair, N.J.: Patterson Smith, 1969. 287p. Rep. 1905 ed.

Unfortunately, this classic work remains the only comprehensive history of lynching. Many individual southern lynchings are covered. Well-documented. Index.

98. Daniels, Jonathan. The Devil's Backbone; The Story of the Natchez Trace. New York: McGraw-Hill, 1962. 278p.

Includes material on Wiley and Micajah Harpe, Samuel Mason, John Murrell and possible murder of Merriwether Lewis in Tennessee, October 11 (?), 1809. Sources include Coates, Howard and Rothert (#s 6, 11, 154). Primarily rehash. No documentation. Bibliography. Index.

99. Davidson, Donald. The Tennessee. New York: Rinehart, c1946. 2 vols.

Vol. 1, Chapter 15, "Boatmen and Outlaws on the Natchez Trace" (p.216-29) includes material on the Harpes, Samuel Mason (taken from Guild), Joseph Hare and John Murrell. Davidson doubts the veracity of much of the Stewart (#26) narrative. Selected bibiliography. Index.

100. Deen, Floyd H. "A Comparison of Simms's Richard Hurdis With Its Sources." Modern Language Notes 1945 June; 60:406-8.

Simms's "sources" are the wildly inflated works of Augustus Walton and H.R. Howard---as well as his supposed conversations with Virgil Stewart---concerning the John Murrell outlaw conspiracy. For a down-to-earth look at Murrell, see Penick (#18). Minimal documentation.

101. Defoe, Daniel. A General History of the Pyrates. Columbia, SC: University of South Carolina Press, c1972. 717p. Illus. Ed. Manuel Schonhorn.

Includes Edward Teach, Stede Bonnet, Charles Vane. Intro. identifies Defoe as real author of the "Johnson" work. Includes an index of names, places and subjects and one of ships.

102. Devol, George H. Forty Years a Gambler on the Mississippi. Cincinnati: Devol and Haines, 1887. 300p. Illus.

103. Devol, George H. Forty Years a Gambler on the Mississippi. New York: Devol and Haines, 1892. 300p. Illus.

104. Devol, George H. Forty Years a Gambler on the Mississippi. New York: Henry Holt, 1926. 300p. Illus.

104. Devol, George H. Forty Years a Gambler on the Mississippi. Austin, TX: Steck-Vaughn, 1967. 300p. Illus. Intro. by John O. West.

In this book Devol details his ante-bellum gambling career up and down the Mississippi River. The account contains many references to New Orleans, Baton Rouge, Natchez, etc. West describes it as "a truthful tale."

105. Dick, Everett. The Dixie Frontier: A Social History of the Southern Frontier from the First Transmontane Beginnings to the Civil War. New York: Knopf, 1948. 374p.

Excellent, thorough examination of colonial/antebellum southern frontier life. Chapter 6. "Land Greed" (p.63-79) includes material on fraud. Chapter 21, "Frontier Justice" (p. 225-35) covers vigilantism, counterfeiting, murder, etc. Some documentation. Extensive bibliography. Index.

106. Ellms, Charles. The Pirates Own Book, or Authentic Narratives of the Lives, Exploits, and Executions of the Most Celebrated Sea Robbers. Salem, MA: Marine Research Society, 1924. 469p. Illus. Rep. Boston: Samuel N. Dickinson, c1836.

Contains chapters on Jean Lafitte, Edward Teach and Charles Vane. No documentation or bibliography. Index.

107. Emrich, Duncan. American Folk Poetry: An Anthology. Boston: Little, Brown, c1974. 831p. Illus.

Includes lyrics of songs about such murderers and victims as Naomi Wise, Frankie Silvers and Tom Dula. Bibliography. Title and first line indexes.

108. Gaute, J.H.H. and Odell, Robin. The Murderers' Who's Who: Outstanding International Cases from the Literature of Murder in the Last 150 Years. New York: Methuen, c1979. 269p. Illus.

Brief but excellent coverage of hundreds of murder cases, primarily from the U.S. and Great Britain. Organized by murderer's last name. Pre-1930 southern murderers are few, but include the axe man of New Orleans (1911-1919), Etienne Deschamps (New Orleans, 1889) and Leo Frank. Includes extensive bibliography and classified index.

109. Gentry, Dorothy. Life and Legend of Lawrence County, Alabama. Tuscaloosa, AL: privately printed, 1962. 235p. Illus.

Pages 24-6 contain a quote from Nina Leftwich, Two Hundred Years at Muscle Shoals, concerning Joseph Hare, Wiley and Micajah Harpe, Samuel Mason and John A. Murrell. Usual lurid accounts. No documentation or bibliography. Index.

110. Ghent, W.J. "Samuel Mason." In Dictionary of American Biography, ed. Dumas Malone. New York: Scribner's, 1933. 12:374.

Brief overview of the Natchez Trace outlaw's career. Only source given is Rothert (#154).

111. Ginzburg, Ralph. 100 Years of Lynching. New York: Lancer Books, c1962. 270p.

Contains newspaper accounts, including many pre-1930 southern lynchings. Also includes a listing by state of blacks lynched after 1859.

112. Glaser, Lynn. Counterfeiting in America: The History of an American Way to Wealth. New York: Clarkson N. Potter, c1968. 274p. Illus.

Chapter 8, "Counterfeiting in the C.S.A." (p.149-59) covers Civil War counterfeiting in the South. No specific southern criminals mentioned. This title is a disappointing work about a neglected subject. Poor documentation. No bibliography or index.

113. Gosse, Philip. A History of Piracy. New York: Tudor, 1932. 349p. Rep. New York: Burt Franklin, 1968.

Covers piracy on a world-wide basis. Book III, "The Pirates of the West" (p.141-231) contains small amounts of material on Edward Teach, Jean Lafitte, Stede Bonnet, etc. No documentation. Bibliography. Index.

114. Gosee, Philip. The Pirate's Who's Who, Giving Particulars of the Lives and Deaths of the Pirates and Buccaneers. New York: Burt Franklin, 1968. 328p. Illus. Rep. 1924 ed.

Biographical material on numerous pirates, listed alphabetical by last name. Included are Edward Teach, Jean Lafitte, Stede Bonnet, Jose Gaspar, etc. No documentation.

115. Hall, James. Letters from the West; Containing Sketches of Scenery, Manners, and Customs; and Anecdotes Connected with the First Settlements of the Western Sections of the United States. London: Henry Colburn, 1828. 385p.

116. Hall, James. Letters from the West; Containing Sketches of Scenery, Manners and Customs; and Anecdotes Connected with the First Settlements of the Western Sections of the United States. Gainesville, FL: Scholars' Facsimilies and Reprints, 1967. Rep. 1828 ed. Intro. by John T. Flanagan. 385p.

Letter XVII (p. 265-82) covers the career of Wiley and Micajah Harpe; their crimes in Kentucky are the primary focus. Their career in Tennessee is ignored. The chapter does contain some material on Wiley's activities with Samuel Mason (spelled Meason) in Natchez and New Orleans. The account is undocumented; the book has no index. This account may be the first about the Harpes to appear in book form.

117. Hardin, John Wesley. The Life of John Wesley Hardin, from the Original Manuscript as Written by Himself. Seguin, TX: Smith and Moore, 1898. 144p. Illus.

118. Hardin, John Wesley. Life of John Wesley Hardin, Written by Himself and Published from Original Manuscript in 1896 by Smith and Moore. Bandera, TX: Frontier Times, 1925. 62p.

119. Hardin, John Wesley. The Life of John Wesley Hardin as Written by Himself. Norman: University of Oklahoma Press, 1961. 149p. Illus. Intro. by Robert G. McCubbin.

Reprint of 1898 ed. Hardin's slanted but generally accurate account of his gunfighting career. Pages 110-22 cover his years in Florida and Alabama, including his August 23, 1877, capture in Pensacola, Fla. No documentation, bibliography or index. Fascinating.

120. Hardin, John Wesley. Life of John Wesley Hardin as Written by Himself. New York: Leisure Books, 197?. 176p.

Paperback.

121. Hicks, Wanda Gatlin. "Travel on the Natchez Trace: 1790-1830." M.A. thesis, Mississippi College, 1963. 142p.

Chapter 7, "Many Dangers Faced the Travelers" (p.110-30) covers Wiley and Micajah Harpe, Joseph Hare, Samuel Mason, and John Murrell. Sources include #98, #6 and #154. Also discusses possible murder of Merriwether Lewis in 1809. Nothing new. Documentation. Bibliography.

122. Hofstadter, Richard and Wallace, Michael, eds. American Violence: A Documentary History. New York: Knopf, 1970. 478p.

Excerpts from various sources concerned with political, economic, social, personal and other types of violence. Pertinent southern incidents include the 1891 lynching of Italians at New Orleans; the 1874 "coup d'etat" by White League vigilantes in New Orleans; the 1827 sand bar duel-as-brawl near Natchez, Miss., in which James Bowie participated; the lynching of five gamblers in Vicksburg, Miss., July 1835; and the July 22, 1893, lynching of black Lee Walker in Memphis. Sources of excerpts and further readings are given. Index.

123. Holmes, Oliver Wendell. "John A. Murrell." In Dictionary of American Biography, Dumas Malone, ed. New York: Scribner's 1934. 13:369-70.

This brief, unskeptical entry gives the highlights of Murrell's life. Several sources are listed, all pertaining to the legendary---not the factual---Murrell.

124. Hoole, W. Stanley. Sam Slick in Texas. San Antonio, TX: Naylor, c1945. 78p. Illus. Intro J. Frank Dobie.

Biography of Samuel Adams Hammett (1816-1865), southwestern humorist. "No wonder he could write wisely and well about ... Jean Lafitte and the Murrell Gang..." (p.6). Documentation. Index.

125. Horan, James D. and Swiggett, Howard. The Pinkerton Story. New York: G.P. Putnam's Sons, c1951. 366p. Illus.

Chapter 2, "Gold, Guns and Gallows: (p.11-79) contains material on the Pinkertons' pursuit of several outlaws in the south. Among the criminals were Levi and Hillary Farrington, a pair of train-robbing brothers from Tennessee; the Farringtons operated in the early

1870s. Other train robbers include Captain Eugene Bunch; the Rube and Jim Burrow gang; and legendary "Old Bill" Miner. Miner, who began robbing trains in 1869, was arrested by Pinkerton agents in 1909 outside Dahlonega, GA. The book has an index, but no documentation of any kind.

126. Hough, Emerson. The Story of the Outlaw. A Study of the Western Desperado, with Historical Narratives of Famous Outlaws; the Stories of Noted Border Wars; Vigilante Movements and Armed Conflicts on the Frontier. New York: Grosset and Dunlap, 1907. 401p. Illus.

This book is described by the author as a "study of the American desperado." Chapter 4. "The Early Outlaw" (p. 35-73) contains material on Samuel Mason (spelled "Meason"), Wiley and Micajah Harpe and John Murrell. Most of the chapter is made up of a long quote from Life and Adventures of Virgil A. Stewart (New York: Harper and Brothers, 1836). This book, which offers nothing new on southern criminal activity, is poorly documented and has neither index nor bibliography.

127. Hulbert, Archer Butler. The Ohio River: A Course of Empire. New York: Putnam's 1906. 378p. Illus.

Chapter 9, "The Reign of the Rowdy and Outlaw," (p.195-225) covers outlaw activities between the Cave-in-Rock, Illinois, outlaw hideout to Natchez, Mississippi and New Orleans. The chapter includes material on Micajah and Wiley Harpe. The material is very poorly documented; the book contains an index.

128. Hummel, Ray O., Jr., ed. Southeastern Broadsides Before 1877: A Bibliography. Richmond: Virginia State Library, 1971. 501p.

Gives texts of broadsides. Some material on criminal activity. See appropriate state indexes under "Crime and criminals."

129. Hurd, Archibald. The Reign of the Pirates. London: Heath Cranton, 1925. 192p.

Chapter 4, "Captain Teach or Blackbeard" (p. 59-72) covers Edward Teach who operated, among other locations, off the coast of the Carolinas. Chapter 7, "Captain Charles Vane" (p. 103-11) covers another Carolinas pirate. No documentation. Brief bibliography. Index.

130. Jagendorf, M.A. Folk Stories of the South. New York: Vanguard Press, 1972. 355p. Illus.

Includes stories from ten southern states; "Railroad Bill" (p. 13-5) and "The Face in the Courthouse Window" (p. 16-7) are among the Alabama tales. A North Carolina story concerns pirate Edward Teach (p. 187-190). No documentation or index.

131. Johnson, Charles. A General History of the Robberies and Murders of the Most Notorious Pirates from their First Rise and Settlement in the Island of Providence to the Present Year. New York: Dodd, Mead, 1926. 603p. Illus. Ed. Arthur L. Hayward.

See Defoe. Two editions of this book were published in London in 1724, a third in 1725 and a fourth in 1726. This edition derived from the fourth. Includes Edward Teach, Stede Bonnet, Charles Vane. No documentation. Index. Shorter ed., Lives of the Most Notorious Pirates (London: Folio Society, 1962, 232p.).

132. Karraker, Cyrus H. Piracy Was a Business. Rindge, NH: Richard R. Smith, 1953. 244p.

Chapter 11, "Carolina and Blackbeard" (p. 134-64) covers Edward Teach. Chapter 12, "South Carolina Destroys the Pirates" (p.165-72) covers Stede Bonnet. Some documentation. Bibliography. Index.

133. Kelly, Bill. Bill Kelly's Encyclopedia of Gunmen. Anaheim, CA: Printer's Devil, 1976. 567p. Illus.

Includes many southern gunmen such as Rube and Jim Burrow, Levi and Hilary Farrington, Eugene Bunch, John Murrell, Wiley and Micajah Harpe, Samuel Mason, etc. Poorly documented. Index.

134. Kirkland, Edwin C. "A Check List of the Titles of Tennessee Folksongs." Journal of American Folklore 1946; 59:423-76.

Gives titles, published and recorded sources and often singer. Includes versions of ballads based on Mary Phagan (5), Naomi Wise (8), Kinnie Wagner (3), Leo Frank (1), Stagolee (2), Tom Dooley (Dula) (2) and others. Bibliography.

135. Larranaga, Robert D. Pirates and Buccaneers. Minneapolis: Lerner, 1970. 63p. Illus.

Intended for juvenile audience. Includes chapters on Edward Teach and Jean Lafitte. No documentation, bibliography or index.

136. Laws, G. Malcolm, Jr. Native American Balladry; A Descriptive Study and a Bibliographical Syllabus. Philadelphia: American Folklore Society, 1950. 276p.

Contains material on ballads based on Kennie Wagner, Frankie Silvers, Naomi Wise, Mary Phagan, Morris "Railroad Bill" Slater, "Stagolee," Albert Edward Batson, etc. Documentation, bibliography, index.

137. Lawson, John Davidson, ed. American State Trials; a Collection of the Important and Interesting Criminal Trials in the United States, from the Beginning of Our Government to the Present Day. St. Louis: Thomas Law Book Co., 1914-30. 17 vols.

Entries are divided into "The Narrative" and "The Trial" sections. Vol. 3 (p. 562-602): the trial of three blacks ---Noah Cherry, Robert Thompson and Harry Atkinson---for the spring 1873 ax murders in Wayne Co., N.C., of James Worley and his wife Appie Jane. The three were executed June 14, 1873. Vol. 4 (p. 652-722): the 1718 trials in South Carolina of Stede Bonnet and thirty-three crewmen for piracy. Vol. 5 (p. 369-527): the trial in Fayetteville, N.C., 1850, of Ann K. Simpson for the murder by poison of her husband Alexander C. Simpson. Vol 6 (p. 514-96): trial of Rev. George W. Carawan for the murder of Clement H. Lassiter, 1853, Washington N.C. Vol. 10 (p. 182-414): Leo M. Frank trial, 1913, Atlanta, Ga., for murder of Mary Phagan. Vol. 10 (p. 624-98): 1918 Atlanta trials of W.J. Cook and Mrs. Herman H. Hirsch for blackmail. Documentation. Each volume is indexed and index to entire set is available.

138. Library of Congress. Music Division. Check-List of Recorded Songs in the English Language in the Archive of American Folk Song to July 1940. Washington, DC: Library of Congress, 1942. mimeographed. 3 vols.

Includes versions of numerous relevant songs: "Batson (1), "Railroad Bill" (5), "Natchez Under the Hill" (1), "Naomi Wise" (2), "Oma Wise" (3), "Omie Wise" (6), "Frankie Silver(s)" (2) "Stagolee" (16), "Tom Dooley" (4), etc. Entries give singer; date, place and collector; and call number of recording.

139. Lomax, Alan. The Folk Songs of North America in the English Language. Garden City, New York: Double-day, c1960. 623p.

Contains background, lyrics and music to such murder-related ballads as "Omie Wise," "Tom Dula," "Stagolee" and "Railroad Bill." Notes concerning "Railroad Bill": "An American Negro Ballad---widespread in central South and found among mountain whites." Versions of these songs have been anthologized numerous times; see Patricia Pate Havlice, Popular Song Index (Metuchen, NJ: Scarecrow, 1975) for other entries.

140. McCall, Edith. Pirates and Privateers. Chicago: Childrens Press, c1963. 127p. Illus.

Intended for juvenile audience. Contains chapters on Edward Teach and Stede Bonnet. No documentation, bibliography or index.

141. McDade, Thomas M. The Annals of Murder: A Bibliography of Books and Pamphlets on American Murders from Colonial Times to 1900. Norman: University of Oklahoma Press, 1961.

This annotated bibliography contains numerous entries pertaining to the eight deep south states; see index. McDade's work cannot be praised too highly--this title is a cornucopia.

142. Nash, Jay Robert. Bloodletters and Badmen; A Narrative Encyclopedia of American Criminals from the Pilgrims to the Present. New York: M. Evans, c1973. 640p. Illus.

Entries are alphabetical by criminal. Train robbers Eugene Bunch and Rube Burrow are included. Beware of factual errors; Nash, a prolific popularizer, is no scholar. No documentation. Bibliography. Index.

143. Nash, Jay Robert. Murder, American; Homicide in the United States from the Revolution to the Present. New York: Simon and Schuster, c1980. 479p. Illus.

The bulk of Nash's book contains individual chapters on specific murders that occurred between 1778 and 1977. Only one killing--the 1852 murder of Clement Lassiter by Rev. George Washington Carawan in Goose Creek, N.C.--occurs in the deep south states prior to 1930. However, more than a hundred pages are devoted to a year-by-year chronology of murders in America; many in the deep south prior to 1930 are included. Nash omits numerous spectacular southern murder cases, but given the scope of his chronology the omissions are understandable. The book includes an excellent and lengthy bibliography and an index. Beware of factual errors.

144. National Association for the Advancement of Colored People. Burning at Stake in the United States. A Record of the Public Burning by Mobs of Six Men, During the First Months of 1919, in the States of Arkansas, Florida, Georgia, Mississippi, and Texas. New York: NAACP, 1919. 23p.

145. National Association for the Advancement of Colored People. Thirty Years of Lynching in the U.S., 1889-1918. New York: Negro Universities Press, 1969. 105p. Rep. 1919 ed.

Contains descriptions of one hundred selected U.S. lynchings during the years covered and a state-by-state listing of "all" lynchings for the same period. The master list gives date, name of lynching victim, place and charge against the victim. The entries are neither complete nor totally accurate, but would serve as a good beginning to further research. No index.

146. National Association for the Advancement of Colored People. Supplement to Thirty Years of Lynching in the United States, 1889-1918. New York: NAACP, 1919-1946.

Annual.

147. Nye, Russell B. A Baker's Dozen: Thirteen Unusual Americans. East Lansing: Michigan State University Press, c1956. 300p.

Nye devotes half of his chapter "A Brace of Villains" (p. 116-37) to John A. Murrell, Natchez Trace "land pirate. "Although in his "Note on Sources" Nye acknowledges that the Virgil Stewart narrative must be "taken with several grains of salt," he nevertheless relies on it heavily for his own account. Coates is used less extensively, as are several other suspicious sources. Nye merely repeats the myths of Murrell's huge gang, the slave insurrection conspiracy, and Stewart's incredible role in Murrell's downfall.

148. Odum, Howard W.,ed. "Folk-Song and Folk-Poetry as Found in the Secular Songs of the Southern Negroes." Journal of American Folklore 1911; 24: 255-94, 351-96.

Numbers 46 and 47 are versions of "Stagolee" (p. 288-9), a murderer widely sung about from the late nineteenth century into the rock era. Numbers 48-51 are versions of songs about Morris "Railroad Bill" Slater, legendary black Alabama train robber/murderer (p. 289-93). The "Railroad Bill" songs represent a codification of the folklore surrounding Slater just fifteen years after his death.

149. Odum, Howard W. and Johnson, Guy B. The Negro and His Songs; A Study of Typical Negro Songs in the South. Chapel Hill: University of North Carolina Press, 1925. Rep. New York: Negro Universities Press, 1968. 306p.

Divided into religious and social songs, with discussion and numerous examples of both categories. Pages 196-203 cover "Stagolee" and "Railroad Bill." No documentation. Select bibliography. Index to song titles only.

150. Pinkerton, Allan. Criminal Reminiscenses and Detective Sketches. Freeport, New York: Books for Libraries Press, 1970. 324p. Rep. 1878 ed.

Chapter 12, "Canada Bill" (p. 177-206) covers the career of William "Canada Bill" Jones, English-born gambler. Chapter is primarily devoted to Jones' midwestern career, but some material on his operations out of New Orleans with fellow gamblers George DeVol and Jerry Kendricks. Pinkerton gives description of Jones' gambling methods. Jones died in Charity Hospital, Reading, Penn., summer 1877. No documentations. Pinkerton's many books were often written by others based on outlines supplied by the detective.

151. Redfield, H.V. Homicide, North and South. Being a Comparative View of Crime Against the Person in Several Parts of the United States. Philadelphia: Lippincott, 1880. 207p.

Some material on individual murders in South Carolina, Mississippi and Louisiana. Poor documentation. No index.

152. Ripley, Thomas. They Died with Their Boots On. Garden City, NY: Doubleday, Doran, 1935. 285p.

Includes material on Texas gunfighter John Wesley Hardin's years in Florida and Alabama during the 1870s. No documentation or index.

153. Rosenbaum, H. Jon and Secerberg, Peter C., eds. Vigilante Politics. Philadelphia: University of Pennsylvania Press, 1976. 292p.

Chapter 5, "The History of Vigilantism in America" (p. 79-109) by Richard Maxwell Brown contains material on pre-revolutionary South Carolina "regulators" and other southern activity. See Brown. Documentation. Index.

154. Rothert, Otto. The Outlaws of Cave-in-Rock; Historical Accounts of the Famous Highwaymen and River Pirates who operated in Pioneer Days upon the Ohio and Mississippi rivers and over the old Natchez Trace. Cleveland: Arthur H. Clark, 1924. 364p. Illus. Rep. New York: Arno.

Includes coverage of southern activities of outlaws Wiley and Micajah Harpe and Samuel Mason, a Revolutionary War soldier. Well-researched. Documentation. Bibliography. Index.

155. Sabine, Lorenzo. Notes on Duels and Duelling, Alphabetically Arranged, with a Preliminary Historical Essay. Boston: Crosby, Nichols, and Co., 1859. 3rd. ed. 426p.

Most of Sabine's book consists of "Challenges and Duels," a listing alphabetically by participant of duels in America and Europe. Many southern duels are included, but unless the name of at least one party is known, the user must resort to scanning the list. The book has no index. Listings give some information about most duels and Sabine will sometimes acknowledge his source.

156. St. Clair, Henry. The United States Criminal Calendar: or An Awful Warning to the Youth of America; Being an Account of the Most Horrid Murders, Piracies, Highway Robberies. Boston: Charles Gaylord, 1834. 356p. Illus.

Included are chapters on murderers Edward Tinker, 1810, Newburn, Craven Co., N.C. (p. 267-70); Robert H. Sterling, who murdered Ferdinand Morgan on September 7, 1830, in Monroe, La. (p. 270-7); and Micajah and Wiley Harpe (p. 277-84). The chapter on the Harpes is based on Hall (#115). No documentation or index.

157. Samuel, Ray; Huber, Leonard V.; Ogden, Warren C. Tales of the Mississippi. New York: Hastings House, c1955. 240p. Illus.

The chapter "The Slickest Rascal on the Mississippi" (p. 195-203) is devoted to gambler George H. Devol, who operated the length of the Mississippi River during much of the nineteenth century. Bibliography. Index.

158. Schlensker, H.G. "The Pirates and Treasures of the Southeastern States." Orlando, FL: F.C. Keiser, c1952.

Map.

159. Shay, Frank. Judge Lynch: His First Hundred Years. New York: Ives Washburn, c1938. 288p.

Shay's book is a history of lynching in the United States. Much material is included on the eight states covered in this bibliography. Separate sections are devoted to the Atlanta lynching of Leo Frank (1915) and the New Orleans lynching/shooting of Italians accused of assasinating police chief David Hennessy (1890). Other specific southern lynchings are also discussed. An appendix gives statistics by year from 1882 to 1937. Bibliography. Index.

160. Sifakis, Carl. Encyclopedia of American Crime. New York: Facts on File, c1982. 802p. Illus.

Alphabetic entries include Rube Burrow, John Murrell, James Copeland, Wiley and Micajah Harpe, John Ashley, Will Purvis, Frankie Silver, Edward Tinker, etc. Fascinating for the crime buff; lack of documentation of any sort makes it virtually useless for the scholar. Index.

161. Smith, Gene and Barry, Jayne, eds. The Police Gazette. New York: Simon and Schuster, c1972. 208p. Illus. Intro. Tom Wolfe.

Articles and illustrations from the National Police Gazette, 1878-1897. Included are the lynching of three black women and two black men for the murder of a white man, Greenville, Ala., April 21, 1895 (complete with gruesome woodcut of the lynching, p. 193); prostitution in Atlanta, Ga. (p.177); 1893 lynching of Joe Payne, black, at Jellico, Tenn., for assaulting Fanny L. Cecil (p. 170); and the January 4, 1884, hanging at Baton Rouge, La., of Edward Rector, black, for the December 1883 murder of Duncan Williams (p.50). Fascinating.

162. Smith, T. Marshall. Legends of the War of Independence, and of the Earlier Settlements in the West. Louisville, KY: J.F. Brennan, 1855. 397p.

Includes descriptions of the murderous activities in Ky., N.C. and Tenn. of the Harpes, here described as cousins and called William ("Big") and Joshua ("Little"). According to this account, the Harpes fought on the Bristish side during the Revolution, participating in the battle at King's Mountain and others. Also describes "Big" Harpe's death and "Little" Harpe's escape to Natchez, where he appeared in the company of Peter Alston, son of well-known North Carolina counterfeiter Phillip Alston. No documentation. No index.

163. Stampp, Kenneth M. The Peculiar Institution: Slavery in the Ante-Bellum South. New York: Vintage, c1956. 430p.

Pages 124-32, among others, include discussion of such crimes by slaves as theft, arson and murder. Documentation, index.

164. Sternbeck, Alfred. Filibusters and Buccaneers. New York: Robert M. McBride, n.d. 272p. Illus.

Contains material on Charles Vane, Edward Teach and Stede Bonnet. No documentation or bibliography. Index.

165. Stevens, William Oliver. Pistols at Ten Paces: The Story of the Code of Honor in America. Boston: Houghton Mifflin, c1940. 293p.

Some material on southern duels. Lacks specificity of dates, names and locations. Disappointing. No documentation or bibliography. Index.

166. Stockton, Frank R. Buccaneers and Pirates of Our Coasts. New York: Grosset and Dunlap, 1898. 325p.

Includes chapter on Jean Lafitte entitled "The Pirate of the Gulf"; also material on Stede Bonnet and Edward Teach. Fifteen other editions published between 1898 and 1947.

167. Teeters, Negley K. Hang By the Neck: The Legal Use of Scaffold and Noose, Gibbet, Stake, and Firing Squad from Colonial Times to the Present. Springfield, IL: Charles C. Thomas, c1967. 483p. Written in collaboration with Jack H. Hedblom.

A cornucopia for the connoisseur of murder and execution. Teeters covers a number of Southern cases, including Charles Boyington (Mobile, Ala., 1835), Will Purvis (Miss., 1893), Tom Dula (N.C., 1868), etc., etc. Heavily documented. Indices of selected names and subjects.

168. Triplett, Frank. History, Romance and Philosophy of Great American Crimes and Criminals; Including the Great Typical Crimes that Have Marked the Various Periods of American History from the Foundation of the Republic to the Present Day. St. Louis: N.D. Thompson, 1884. 659p. Illus. Rep. Hartford, Conn.: Park Publishing, 1885.

"Land pirate" John Murrell is covered on pages 39-129. This section is probably based on Walton (#26). The career of the Harpe brothers is explored on pages 223-50. Pages 276-324 cover Joseph Hare (pp. 323-4 include a sample of his poetry!). The Lowery (sic) Band, "The Swamp Angels of North Carolina," is covered on pages 464-92. The book has no documentation of any sort and no index.

169. Truman, Ben C. The Field of Honor: Being a Complete and Comprehensive History of Duelling in All Countries: Including...Descriptions of All the Noted Hostile Meetings in Europe and America. New York: Fords, Howard and Hulbert, 1884. 599p.

Truman devotes several chapters to "Noted American Duels," many of which occurred in the eight relevant states. Truman gives many details about the duels, including names of principals, locations, dates, causes and outcomes. No documentation. Index.

170. Twain, Mark. Life on the Mississippi. New York: New American Library, c1961. 382p. Afterword by Leonard Kriegel.

Chapter 29, "A Few Specimen Bricks" (p. 177-85) discusses "Murel's (sic) Gang." Most of the material is a quote from Walton (#26).

171. Wells-Barnett, Ida B. On Lynching: Southern Horrors; A Red Record; Mob Rule in New Orleans. New York: Arno Press and The New York Times, 1969. Illus. Rep. 1892, 1895, 1900 eds.

The lynching phenomenon was perhaps the most complex and grisly of all southern criminal activity during the period covered by this bibliography. Numerous motives---including the race of the alleged criminal and the perceived inability of legal authorities to stem the tide of crime---contributed to the orgy of lynching that continued even past 1930. In the late nineteenth and early twentieth centuries Wells-Barnett conducted a one-woman anti-lynching campaign; these three pamphlets were part of her tireless efforts. The relevance of one of these works to this bibliography lies in Wells-Barnett's meticulous listing of lynchings of blacks, by type of crime, for the years 1893 and 1894 (Red Record, p. 16-9, 91-5). These listings include the date and location of the lynching and the name of the victim. Crimes covered include murder, rape, robbery, attempted murder and robbery, arson, horse theft and kidnapping. By comparing these lists with relevant local newspapers, material about specific crimes can be found. Further research will determine whether or not the lynchings themselves were motivated solely by racial animosity. Mob Rule in New Orleans concerns the "race" riot that occurred as a result of police efforts to capture black fugitive Robert Charles.

172. Wilkie, John Elbert. "Ways of the Counterfeiters." Cosmopolitan 1905 March; 38:585-92.

General discussion of U.S. counterfeiters. Photograph of unidentified North Carolina counterfeiter included. Article notes "...in the South and the middle West, imitation standard silver dollars and halves are specialties, and individual offenders practice their arts in the 'raising' of genuine bills---that is, altering a one-dollar note, say, by skilful use of scratchwork, colored inks, pen and brush to resemble generally a ten or twenty; and incidentally it may be said that some re-markably deceptive productions have found their way into circulation." (P.587). Author was Chief of U.S. Secret Service. No documentation.

173. Williams, Daniel T., comp. Eight Negro Bibliographies. New York: Kraus Reprint, 1970.

Number 7 is "The Lynching Records at Tuskegee Institute; with Lynching in America: A Bibliography. 1969." Contains general introduction; statistics by state and year, 1882-1968; causes of lynchings, 1882-1968. Unannotated bibliography of more than 400 items contains some pre-1930 deep south materials.

174. Wyatt-Brown, Bertram. Southern Honor: Ethics and Behavior in the Old South. New York: Oxford University Press, 1982. 597p.

Covers honor as "the animating force in the antebellum South, the very keystone of the slave-holding South's morality" (dust jacket). Includes material on dueling, gambling, lynching, murder, etc. Chapter 16, "Charivari and Lynch Law" (p. 435-61) covers antebellum lynching. Chapter 17, "The Anatomy of a Wife-Killing" (p. 462-95) examines the murder of Susan Foster near Natchez, Miss., in March 1834. Heavily documented.

175. Zangrando, Robert L. The NAACP Crusade Against Lynching, 1909-1950. Philadelphia: Temple University Press, c1980. 309p.

Some mention of specific pre-1930 southern lynchings, including Leo Frank's. Also that of black sharecropper Jim McIlherron, who "was chained to a tree and tortured to death with heated irons and a bonfire at Estill Springs, Tennessee, in February 1918..." (p. 41). Based on the author's dissertation. Extensive documentation and bibliography. Index.

3

Alabama

Monographs

176. Acee, Joe. You Are There With the True Adventures of Rube Burrows, Alabama's Most Famous Train Robber. Vernon, AL: Lamar Democrat, 1973 (?). 112p. Illus.

One of many nearly worthless titles on Burrow. Written like fiction, with much dialogue placed in the mouths of the "characters." No documentation, bibliography or index.

177. Boyington, Charles R.S. A Statement of the Trial of Charles R.S. Boyington, who was Indicted and Executed for the Murder of Nathaniel Frost. Written by Himself. To which is added a Number of Fugitive Pieces, in Verse, also Written and Composed by Himself. Mobile, AL: Mercantile Advertiser Office, 1835. 40p.

Boyington had supposedly killed Frost on May 10, 1834. The motive was assumed to be robbery, although Frost and Boyington were friends. This title is Boyington's version of events and his justification of his plea of innocence. Several of Boyington's poems are also included. Boyington was hanged on February 20, 1835.

178. Breihan, Carl W. Rube Burrow: King of the Train Robbers. West Allis, WI: Pine Mountain Press, c1981. 152p. Illus.

Yet another popular biography of Burrow. Use with extreme caution. No documentation, bibliography or index.

179. Diard, Francois Ludgers. The Tree: Being the Strange Case of Charles R.S. Boyington. Mobile, AL: n.p., 1949. 104p.

On May 10, 1834, New England printer Nathaniel Frost was

murdered in Mobile. Another printer and a poet, Boyington, was arrested and tried for the murder. Boyington was hanged on February 20, 1835. Diard accepts Boyington's guilt in the crime. Reprints some of Boyington's love letters to Rose de Fleur. No documentation, bibliography or index.

180. Doggette, Edith O. The Sims War. Huntsville, AL: Strode, c1982. 82p.

During 1890 and 1891 Bob Sims, a fanatically anti-government Chocataw Co. farmer, moonshiner and leader of a religious cult consisting of many relatives and about a hundred total followers, engaged in an escalating "war" with residents and law enforcement officials of the county and state. The violence eventually climaxed in the Christmas Day 1891 lynching of Sims and two others, Tom Savage and his son. Other Simites had been and would be lynched as well. This fascinating, too-little-known chain of events---which has numerous modern counterparts, including the Gordon Kahl/Posse Comitatus incidents---receives poor treatment here. Book is poorly written, its documentation is an insult to scholarship, and there is no index. The Sims "war" deserves much better than this effort.

181. Hamilton, William Thomas. The Last Hours of Charles R. S. Boyington Who Was Executed at Mobile, Alabama, for the murder of Nathaniel Frost Perpetrated May 10, 1834. Mobile, AL: Commercial Register Office, 1835. 44p.

182. Hawley, Walter L. The Life of Detective A.J. Sullivan, and a Report of his Trial for the Killing of Tom W. Ellis, "the Hornet Man About Town." Birmingham, AL: Roberts and Son, 1888. 46pp.

183. Hicks, Nora Louis. Uncle Aron, Alabama Desperado. Great Neck, NY: Todd and Honeywell, 1982. 56p. Illus.

In the early 1900s the white members of a road gang in Randolph began verbally abusing black man Aron Sledge, throwing rocks at him and destroying his watermelon patch. Sledge fired into the group, killing two men and wounding twenty-eight. Sledge fled the state ahead of a posse and returned to his birthplace in the West Indies. This fascinating story is poorly served by his niece Hicks; the year of the event is not even given! No documentation, bibliography or index.

184. Hoole, William Stanley. The Birmingham Horrors. Huntsville, AL: Strode Publishers, c1980. 272 pp. Illus.

On December 3 and 4, 1888, the wife and two daughters of Richard R. Hawes were murdered and their bodies tossed in two lakes near Birmingham, Alabama. The case created a sensation in Alabama, Georgia and elsewhere. Hawes, who apparently hired another man to do the job, was arrested, tried and hung for the crimes. Hoole's account is based on the extensive contemporary coverage of the case printed in Birmingham and Atlanta newspapers. Unfortunately, Hoole's book lacks footnotes, bibliography and index; many of his quotes from newspaper articles are difficult or impossible to identify precisely. This book is a sloppy account of a spectacular Alabama crime.

185. Hoole, William Stanley. The James Boys Rode South. Tuscaloosa, AL: privately printed, 1955. 52p.

Describes the trip by Frank and Jesse James to Alabama and their robbery of $10,000 from an army paymaster near Florence in March 1881. Also covers Frank James' trial in Huntsville for the crime in April 1884; he was acquited. No documentation or index. Bibliography.

186. Hoole, William Stanley. The Saga of Rube Burrow: King of American Train Robbers and His Band of Outlaws. Tuscaloosa, AL: Confederate Publishing Co., c1981. 144p. Illus.

Level-headed, popularized account of Burrow's career. Usefulness severely limited by lack of documentation, bibliography and index. See work of Warren Rogers, Jr. for only scholarly material yet done on Burrow.

187. Hutchinson, J.J. Proceedings in the Trial of Jeremiah Darby, for the Murder of His Wife: in the Circuit Court, for Montgomery County: May 19th, 1847. Montgomery, AL: Press of the Daily Alabama Journal, 1847. 45pp.

"He stabbed his wife Nancy Darby to death, but was acquitted on the grounds of insanity." (McDade, Annals of Murder p.241).

188. Pinkerton, Allan. The Expressman and the Detectives. Chicago: W. B. Keen, Cooke and Co., 1875. 278p. Illus.

Describes the embezzlement of $50,000 from the Adams Express Co. in Montgomery, Ala., by manager Nathan Maroney and his wife. Maroney was captured and brought to trial by the Pinkertons in Montgomery in September 1859. This title was one of Pinkerton's first of many books. Listed in Wright, American Fiction, 1851-1875, no. 1908. See article by Stewart (#233).

189. Pruitt, Wade. Bugger Saga: The Civil War Story of Guerrilla and Bushwhacker Warfare in Lauderdale County, Alabama. Columbia, Tenn.: P-Vine Press, c1977. 192pp.

This "saga" details numerous murders and robberies, especially those committed by Tom Clark and his gang between the start of the Civil War and the lynching of Clark and two others at Florence, Ala., in early September in 1872. Poor documentation. Name index only.

190. Rogers, William Warren and Ward, Robert David. August Reckoning: Jack Turner and Racism in Post-Civil War Alabama. Baton Rouge: Louisiana State University Press, c1973. 195p.

Turner, a former slave, was active in Choctaw Co. politics during Reconstruction and later. In August 1882 "evidence" of a conspiracy led by Turner to wipe out the county's white population was uncovered, Turner and some of his black political associated were arrested; on August 19 Turner was lynched. A fascinating story---sort of a small-scale, post-war version of John Murrell's mythical slave uprising. Documentation and index.

191. Rogers, William Warren and Pruitt, Ruth. Stephen S. Renfroe: Alabama's Outlaw Sheriff. Tallahassee, FL: Sentry Press, 1972. 148p.

An excellent biography of Alabama's Jekyll and Hyde lawman. Renfroe earned the respect of a grateful Sumter Co. populace with his KKK activities in the late 1860s. He was elected sheriff and promptly began to embezzle money. After his arrest on an attempted murder charge, he made the first of a series of escapes. In 1880 and 1881 Renfroe was believed to be operating with a gang of outlaws led by Ben and Robert Harrison and operating in Louisiana and Mississippi. Renfroe was finally captured and jailed at Livingston; on the night of July 13, 1886, he was taken from his cell and lynched. Well documented, with bibliography and index.

192. Stiff, Edward. Murder in Cedar Bluff. Cedar Bluff, Ala.: Messenger Office, 1846. 32p.

This pamphlet describes the murder of Lansford Stallings, sheriff of Cherokee County, Ala., by Samuel S. Hinton, an attorney. The booklet also contains material on the trial of William M. Wier, who was tried as an accessory for aiding Hinton in his escape. The murder occurred on December 3, 1845. This rare pamphlet is written in an extremely florid style.

193. University of Alabama. The Killing of Edward L. Nabors, of Pickens County, Ala., by David A. Herring, of Franklin County, Miss., at the Univ. of Ala., June 4, 1858. n.p., n.d. 7p.

According to Owen (p. 1213), this item was printed in the Tuscaloosa Monitor and reprinted in the Gainesville (AL) Independent, June 19, 1858. It was "An address to the patrons of the university, by L.C. Garland, Presd't, to which is added a full report of the testimony of witnesses, and of the trial of Herring." See James B. Sellers, History of the University of Alabama (University: University of Alabama Press, 1953), pp.253-4 for a description of this murder. Sellers spells the name of the victim as "Nabers."

194. West, Goldsmith B. The Hawes Horror and Bloody Riot at Birmingham; a Truthful Story of What Happened. Birmingham, AL: Caldwell Printing, 1888. 145p. Illus.

"This rare pamphlet, of which only three copies are known to exist, tells the Hawes story from the finding of Mary's body (Dec. 4) until the finding of Irene's (Dec. 15). It was hastily and choppily written and published...some eleven weeks before Hawes's trial actually began on April 22, 1889. It never has been reprinted." (Hoole, #184, p.113) Captures contemporary hysteria and shock which the murder of his family by Richard Hawes stirred in what was then a small town. No documentation, bibliography or index.

195. Wood, M.H. The Trial of Dr. Stephen A. Bryant, William Bryant, and James Dobbins, for the Murder of Shelby Butler, Tried in the Circuit Court, March Term, 1860. Hon. Wm. S. Mudd, Judge. Stenographically Reported by M.H. Wood. Tuscaloosa, AL: Observer office, 1860. 96p.

Journal Articles

196. "The Alabama Tragedy." National Police Gazette 1845 December 27; 1(16):147.

Quotes the Alabama Independent concerning a November (?) 27, 1845, murder in Dallas Co. Bethel Holmes shot and killed Mrs. McKean, wife of Thomas McKean "of bank-robbing memory." Mrs. McKean was the daughter of J.K.C. Poole of Perry Co. After committing the murder, Holmes shot and killed himself.

197. Bigelow, Martha Mitchell. "Birmingham's Carnival of Crime, 1871-1910." Alabama Review 1950 April; 3(2): 123-33.

Very similar to chapter 4 of the author's "Birmingham: Biography of a City of the New South." (Ph.D. dissertation, University of Chicago, 1946. 294p.) Includes discussion of gambling, murder, lynching, the Richard Hawes case, etc. Hits only the high spots. Based primarily on newspaper articles. Documentation.

198. Bragg, James W. "Captain Slick, Arbiter of Early Alabama Morals." Alabama Review 1958 April; 11(2): 125-34.

Details operation of a vigilante group active around Huntsville, Ala., and the northern part of the state in the early 1830s. Documentation.

199. Brannon, Peter A. "Dueling in Alabama." Alabama Historical Quarterly 1955 fall; 17(3):97-109.

Duels discussed include the 1832 Ft. Mitchell duel between Joseph T. Camp and Sowell Woolfolk in which the former was wounded and the latter killed; and the May 7, 1859, Mobile encounter between Henry Vick and Lawrence Washington Smith, "One of the last great formal duels in Alabama..." (p.105). Poor documentation.

200. Bush, Lewis M. "Werther on the Alabama Frontier: A Reinterpretation of Simms' Confession." Mississippi Quarterly 1968 spring; 21:119-30.

Discussion of the relationship between Goethe and Simms' novel, Confession; or the Blind Heart (1841). The novel is set in Charleston, S.C., and Montgomery, Ala., and contains material on dueling. The main character, Edward Clifford, poisons his wife Julia. Documentation.

201. Carson, John. "Rube Burrow." True West 1961 August; 8(6):39+

202. Chappell, Gordon T. "'Gentleman Jim:' Montgomery's Notorious Robber." Alabama Review 1971 January; 24 (1): 3-16.

James A. Chastaine had been arrested and convicted of embezzlement in Memphis and robbery in Kansas City. After escaping from guards on the way to prison for the latter charge, Chastaine turned up in Montgomery as Jim Sutton. Early in 1881 a number of burglaries of private residences occurred. Chastaine was finally suspected and fatally shot by one of two policemen attempting to arrest him. Documentation.

203. Childers, Neil R. "Grandfather Enfinger Tells of Flomaton Train Robbery." Escambia County (AL) Historical Quarterly 1975 December; 3(4):8-12.

Covers Rube Burrow's robbery of an L&N train on September 2, 1890. Reprinted from the Pensacola (FL) News-Journal, August 15, 1954. Peter David Enfinger was almost 100 years old when this article was originally published. No documentation.

204. Cleveland, Len G. "The Crawford-Burnside Affair and the Movement to Abolish Dueling in Georgia." Research Studies 1976; 44(4):241-7.

On January 5, 1828, Georgia political rivals Thomas E. Burnside and George W. Crawford fought a duel at Fort Mitchell in what is now Russell Co., Ala. Burnside was killed.

205. Collins, William B. "The Crawford-Burnside Duel." Gulf States Historical Magazine 1903 July; 2:54-7.

Discusses the January 5, 1828, duel between Thomas E. Burnside and George W. Crawford. The two Georgia men met over political differences at Fort Mitchell, Russell Co., Ala., since dueling was then illegal in Georgia but not in the neighboring state. The parties fired three times; Burnside was killed. No documentation.

206. Crudele, Juanita W. "A Lynching Bee: Butler County Style." Alabama Historical Quarterly 1980; 42(1-2):59-71.

Covers the April 21, 1895, lynching in Greenville of two black men (John Rattler and Zeb Colley) and three black women (Martha and Alice Greene and Mary Dean) for the alleged ax murder and cremation of Watts Murphy. Perhaps the worst multiple lynching in Alabama history.

207. "Escape of a Forger." National Police Gazette 1846 September 5; 1(52):435.

Describes the escape from the Tallapoosa County, Ala., jail on June 7, 1846, of John H. Peters, a notorious forger.

208. Figh, Margaret Gillis. "Nineteenth Century Outlaws in Alabama Folklore." Southern Folklore Quarterly 1961; 25(2): 125-35.

Folk tales collected in Alabama, 1940s and 1950s, concerning John Murrell, Jesse James, Rube Burrow and Morris "Railroad Bill" Slater. No documentation except to note who told the stories to the author.

209. Figh, Margaret Gillis. "Some Alabama Folktales." Alabama Review 1963 October; 16(4):270-8.

Includes the Bill Skeeto "unquiet grave" tale and others about such outlaws as John Murrell, James Copeland, Jesse James, Rube Burrow, and Morris "Railroad Bill" Slater. Very sketchy. Some documentation.

210. Figh, Margaret Gillis and Kirkpatrick, Margaret B. "The Development of an Alabama Folktale." Southern Folklore Quarterly 1974 June; 38:109-20.

Discusses variations of a tale of a man unjustly hanged whose spirit keeps the ground clean under the tree from which he was lynched. Source of the tale may be Bill Sketoe, who died in 1864 and is buried in Newton, Dale Co. Sketoe "is said to have returned home before" the Civil War ended "and to have been killed by an angry mob." Many versions discussed say the hanged man was a murderer. Documentation primarily identifies people who were sources of the tales collected.

211. Gordon, Eric. "'Railroad Bill' Hammers Lesson." Guardian Independent Radical Newsweekly 1981 April 8.

Review of New York Labor Theater production "Railroad Bill," written by C.R. Portz. Play toured U.S. in 1981. See also "'Railroad Bill' Begins Tour for Labor Theater" in New York Times 1981 April 8; 130:19.

212. Harlan, J.B. "Railroad Bill." L&N Employes' Magazine 1927 May; 3:30-1, 69-70.

213. Harris, W. Stuart. "Rowdyism, Public Drunkenness and Bloody Encounters in Early Perry County." Alabama Review 1980 January; 33(1):15-24.

Covers various types of lawlessness including the August 1840 hanging of the slave Harry for attempted rape of a white woman, Rebecca Harris; and the activities of a "Captain Slick Company" vigilance committee. Documentation.

214. Holmes, William F. "Moonshiners and Whitecaps in Alabama, 1893." Alabama Review 1981 January; 34(1):31-49.

Describes episodes of vigilantism in Cherokee and Cleburne counties in 1893. The "whitecaps" were moonshiners and their victims informers and revenue agents. Holmes has written widely on whitecapping in the south. Documentation.

215. Hoole, William Stanley. "Alabama and W. Gilmore Simms." Alabama Review 1963 April and July; 16:83-107, 185-99.

Covers Simms' trips through Alabama in 1824-5 and 1834-5 and the "border romances" he wrote based on those travels. Richard Hurdis (1838) was based directly on what Simms heard from Virgil A. Stewart, "the captor of Murrell," (p. 95), and other "eyewitnesses" about the John Murrell "Mystic Clan" of outlaws, etc. See Penick (#18) Documentation.

216. Howington, Arthur F. "John Barley Corn Subdued: The Enforcement of Prohibition in Alabama." Alabama Review 1970 July; 23(3):212-25.

Mostly political, administrative, statistical. Some discussion of bootlegging "rings." Documentation.

217. Howington, Arthur F. "Violence in Alabama: A Study of Late Ante-Bellum Montgomery." Alabama Review 1974 July; 27 (3);213-31.

Discusses several specific duels, hangings, murders, lynchings and vigilante activities. Documentation, including numerous newspaper articles

Alabama

218. Katz, Elaine S. "Variation as Relative Perception in the Legend of Hazel Farris." Mid-South Folklore 1978 winter; 6(3):55-64.

Farris supposedly murdered five men in Kentucky, August 1905, and fled to Bessemer, Ala., becoming either a madam or a schoolteacher. She committed suicide rather than submit to arrest. Katz gives background on Farris and the continuous exhibition of her mummified body. Katz also gives stories about Farris by eight unidentified informants. Documentation.

219. Lardent, Minnie L. "Selma's Lightning Committee." Alabama Review 1956 January; 9(1):66-7.

Description, including list of members, of a vigilance committee briefly active in late 1870.

220. McDonald, William. "The Legend of Captain Slick's Company." Journal of Muscle Shoals History 1977; 5:17-8.

Members of Slick's northwest Alabama regulator band supposedly helped recapture outlaw John Murrell after his escape from jail in Tennessee in 1834. Other work of the group is also described. No documentation.

221. McDonald, William. "The Legend of Uncle Tom Brannon and the Capture of John A. Murrell." The Journal of Muscle Shoals History 1977; 5:37-8.

Role of a negro slave in recapture of outlaw John Murrell in northwest Alabama in 1834. Notes that Brannon received $100 in reward money for his efforts. No documentation.

222. Mason, Harold. "He Gets Money with a Mummy." National Enquirer 1963 March 17; p.25.

Concerns exhibition of the mummified remains of Hazel Farris, legendary Kentucky murderess and Bessemer, Ala., madam (or schoolteacher, depending on the version), who committed suicide rather than submit to arrest. Her body has been exhibited off and on since her death ca. 1906.

223. Mitcham, Mildred Barnett. "A Tale in the Making: The Face in the Window." Southern Folklore Quarterly 1948 December; 12:241-57.

In Pickens Co., Ala., a black man named Henry Wells was arrested for arson, attempted murder and burglary; he died before his trial, set for November 16, 1876. This article explores variant tales that have developed around Wells' crimes, death and the image of his face supposedly "photographed" by lightning onto a window of the Courthouse at Carrollton. Includes thirteen versions of the story collected by the author from various sources. Documentation.

224. Pettus, Thomas C. "The Legend of Aunt Jenny Brooks." Journal of Muscle Shoals History 1977; 5:86-91.

Covers activities of Jenny Brooks and her sons in Lawrence Co. and the far west. Quotes issue of Montgomery Daily Advertiser, April 20, 1884, that describes a Lawrence Co. gunbattle between a Mr. Phillips and the gang of thieves led by Gains Brooks. Documentation.

225. Rachleff, Marshall. "Big Joe, Little Joe, Bill, and Jake: An Example of Slave-Resistance in Alabama." Alabama Review 1979 April; 32(2):141-6.

Primarily correspondence concerning the murder of Peter Hamilton by two of his slaves in Greene Co. in 1850. Documentation.

226. "Railroad Bill: The Black Robin Hood." Southern Exposure 1981 summer; 9(2):35.

Folklore concerning Morris "Railroad Bill" Slater, Alabama's black nineteenth century train robber.

227. "Re: Railroad Bill, Outlaw." Escambia County (Ala.) Historical Quarterly 1978 March; 6(1):22.

Listing dated July 5, 1895, of citizens who donated reward money for capture of Morris "Railroad Bill" Slater after he murdered Escambia County Sheriff E.S. McMillan.

228. Rogers, William Warren, Jr. "Journalistic Warfare: The Atlanta Constitution, the Birmingham Age-Herald and the Rube Burrow Interview." Alabama Historical Quarterly 1981 spring; 43(1):34-41.

Describes the efforts by a reporter for the Constitution to interview Burrow. The interview finally published was a fake; the reporter had been fooled into talking with a substitute for the train robber. Documentation.

229. "Rube Burrows in Clarke!" Clarke County Historical Society Quarterly 1982 summer; 7(1):3.

Reprints an article from the Clarke Co. Democrat (Oct. 9, 1890) concerning train robber/murderer Burrow's activities in the county just prior to his capture and death.

230. Sheridan, Susan M. "Fire Eaters and Duelists of Old Tuscumbia." Journal of Muscle Shoals History 1981; 9:136-9.

Describes a July 16, 1826 or 1827 duel at Tuscumbia between Edmond Winston and Henry S. Foote, later a U.S. Senator from and governor of Mississippi. Also details the May 13, 1892, murder of John Goodwin by Tom Steele. Documentation.

231. Sisk, Glenn. "Crime and Justice in the Alabama Black Belt, 1875-1917." Mid-America 1958 April; 40:106-13.

Covers ten Alabama counties. Primarily statistics from state attorney general reports and other state agencies. Some discussion of jail/prison conditions and individual crimes. Too cursory. Documentation.

232. Stallworth, Clarke. "Desperado---Alabama, Too, Produced Rascals." EnviroSouth 1981; 5(4):10-11.

Covers John Wesley Hardin, Frank and Jesse James, Stephen Renfroe, Rube Burrow. Nothing new. No documentation.

233. Stewart, W. Cassell. "The Pinkerton-Maroney Investigation." Alabama Review 1982 July; 35(3):163-71.

Discusses case of Nathan Maroney, manager of the Adams Express Co. in Montgomery, Ala. Maroney embezzled $50,000 from the company and was captured by the Pinkertons and tried in Montgomery in September 1859. See also Allan Pinkerton, The Expressman and the Detectives. Documentation.

234. Wiggins, Sarah Woolfolk. "Press Reaction in Alabama to the Attempted Assassination of Judge Richard Busteed." Alabama Review 1968 July; 21(3):211-9.

Busteed, U.S. District Court judge, was shot in Mobile on December 28, 1867, by U.S. District Attorney Lucien Van Buren Martin. "The trouble between Busteed and Martin seems to have begun as a personal matter" (p.212). Wiggins shows how the press attitude toward Busteed, a Republican, changed from abuse to support after the shooting. Documentation.

235. Williams, Jack K. "Crime and Punishment in Alabama, 1819-1840." Alabama Review 1953 January; 6(1):14-30.

Generalized discussion of murders, dueling, arson, robberies, vigilantism, etc. Documentation, primarily newspaper articles, will lead to specific crimes.

236. Wright, A.J. "Wanted Dead or Alive: Alabama's Outlaw Heritage." Alabama Living 1981 Jan/Feb; 1(4):29-31.

Covers John Wesley Hardin, Frank and Jesse James, Stephen Renfroe and Morris "Railroad Bill" Slater. Some photographs. No documentation.

237. Young, Mary E. "The Creek Frauds: A Study in Conscience and Corruption." Mississippi Valley Historical Review 1955 December; 42(3):411-37.

Concerns land frauds connected with allotment Creeks received in Alabama under treaty of March 24, 1832. Documentation. See also Young (#279).

Miscellaneous

238. Akens, Helen Morgan and Virginia Pounds Brown. Alabama; Mounds to Missles. Huntsville, AL: Strode, c1966. Rev. ed. Illus. by Don Davis. 245pp.

This title includes a chapter on the James brothers' March 1881 robbery near Florence (pp. 152-7) and one devoted to Alabama train robber Rube Burrow (pp. 167-75). Intended as a textbook for junior high school students, the book has an index but no footnotes or bibliography. Photographs of Frank James and Burrow, with guns, in his coffin are included. These accounts of the James brothers' robbery and Burrow's career are brief but generally accurate.

239. Ballard, Lou Ellen. "Some Tales of Local Color from Southeast Alabama." Southern Folklore Quarterly 1960 June; 24:147-56.

One of these tales is "Gypsy Kidnappers" (p. 153). Documentation gives source of tales---south Alabama residents---only.

240. Barefoot Bill. "My Crime Blues." Columbia 14510-D.

Song recorded in Atlanta, November 4, 1929, by black Alabama blues artist. The song lyrics---the plea of a man condemned for a murder he did not commit--as well as information about the singer are contained in Samuel Charters, The Bluesmen (New York: Oak Publications, c1967).

241. Betts, Edward C. Early History of Huntsville. Montgomery, AL: Brown Printing, 1916. 122p.

Pages 14-9 includes discussion of "Captain Slick" band of vigilantes active in the Huntsville area in the early 1830s. Section also describes punishment for various crimes. Pages 40-4 cover general aspects of dueling, including long quote from Wilson (#30). Some documentation. No index.

242. Botkin, B.A. and Harlow, Alvin F., eds. A Treasury of Railroad Folklore; The Stories, Tall Tales, Traditions, Ballads and Songs of the American Railroad Man. New York: Crown, c1953. 530p.

Contains "Rube Burrow's Raids" (p. 199-206) taken from Richard K. Fox's work of that title. Index.

243. Brantley, Mary E. From Cabins to Mansions: Gleanings from Southwest Alabama. Huntsville, AL: Strode, c1981. 384p. Illus.

Brief mention that Turk's Cave---better known as Sanders' Cave---near Brooklyn in Conecuh Co. was used as a hiding place by Spanish pirates and in 1806 by robber Joseph T. Hare (p. 83). Also gives one version of the career of Morris "Railroad Bill" Slater (p. 111-3). Includes documentation, bibliography, index.

244. Browne, Ray B., ed. "A Night with the Hants" and Other Alabama Folk Experiences. Bowling Green, OH: Bowling Green University Popular Press, 1976. 263p.

"Getting Out of the White Caps" (p. 24-5) concerns vigilante activity. Other tales describe the restless ghosts of murder victims. Tales were collected in early 1950s. Bibliography. Index of Motifs.

245. Brunson, Marion Bailey. Pea River Reflections: Intimate Glimpses of Area Life During Two Centuries, Tuscaloosa, AL: Portals Press, c1975. 203p. Illus.

Sketches of life in Coffee Co., Ala. Chapter 9, "Plantation Violence" (p. 45-9) describes the 1862 murder of a slave. Chapter 12, "A Death Bed Confession" (p. 59-63) describes Jim Ward and his Raiders, a group of outlaws who refused to serve the Confederacy and plundered Coffee Co. during the Civil War. Ward's murder of Columbus Holley is described. Chapter 17, "Pioneer Circuit Riding" (p. 86-91) includes description of the theft of a horse from Rev. B.J. Spivey by train robber Rube Burrow. Chapter 18, "The Headless Horseman" (p. 91-4) notes the folklore surrounding a Yankee soldier who was killed by a posse to prevent his marriage to a local woman. Chapter 26, "The Last Hanging" (p. 135-9) describes the November 1898 execution of Major (Mage) Terry for the spring 1896 rape-murder of Mrs. Van Thomas. No documentation. No Index.

246. Carmer, Carl. The Hurricane's Children: Tales from Your Neck 'O' the Woods. New York: Farrar and Rinehart, 1937, 175p. Illus. by Elizabeth Black Carmer.

A chapter in this book of "American fairy stories" tells "How Railroad Bill Chased Himself to His Girl's Home" (p. 115-21). No source for the tale is given; Carmer may have heard the story himself on his travels through Alabama in the 1920s and 1930s. The book includes a bibliography.

247. Carmer, Carl. Stars Fell on Alabama. New York: Farrar and Rinehart, 1934. Rep. New York: Hill and Wang, 1961. 291p.

A chapter of this book, "The Tombigbee Outlaws" (p. 122-41) is devoted to train robbers Rube Burrow and Morris "Railroad Bill" Slater and "outlaw" sheriff Stephen Renfroe. A portion of another chapter (p. 146-55) covers a feud known as the Bob Sims War. Information on these men and events was gathered by Carmer from stories told to him during his travels through various parts of the state. No research was done. No documentation.

248. Choctaw County Bicentennial Commission. Akokoli; The Choctaw County Bicentennial Book. The Commission, 1976. 233p. Illus.

Page 119 contains a brief anecdote about the "war" in Choctaw Co. in the nineteenth century involving Bob Sims and others. No documentation, bibliography or index.

249. Coffin, Tristram Potter and Cohen, Henning, eds. Folklore from the Working Folk of America. Garden City, NY: Anchor Press/Doubleday, 1973. 504p. Illus.

Pages 396-402 contain several stories, song lyrics and music concerning Morris "Railroad Bill" Slater, Alabama's black nineteenth century train robber. Documentation.

250. Cohen, Norm. Long Steel Rail: The Railroad in American Folksong. Urbana: University of Illinois Press, c1981. 738p. Illus.

Excellent monograph on railroad folklore. Pages 122-131 contain material on Morris "Railroad Bill" Slater, Alabama's black nineteeth century train robber. In addition to music and song lyrics, biographical information and commentary, the sections also has a list of recorded versions of "Railroad Bill" songs. Beware factual errors in biographical material. Documentation.

251. Foster, C. William. A Sense of Place: The Folk Heritage of North Alabama. Troy AL: Troy State University Press, c1978. 93p.

Some discussion (p. 77-80) of Joseph Hare, John Murrell and Frank and Jesse James, in Alabama. Nothing new. Also covers the Brooks family of Lawrence Co. (p. 80-1). "Gaines Brooks was killed in a gunfight over a stolen horse in Lawrence County in 1884" (p. 81). Henry Brooks died in a 1920 gunfight while defending his still during a raid. The matriarch of the family, "Aunt" Jenny Brooks

Johnston, who died in 1924, was rumored to have been involved in several murders. Documentation. Bibliography. No index.

252. Guns and the Gunfighters. New York: Bonanza, 1982. 224p. Illus.

Articles originally published in Guns and Ammo magazine and previously published in magazine form as Guns and Ammo Guide to Guns of the Gunfighters. Much material on western gunfighters/outlaws; beware of factual errors. A portrait of Rube Burrow in his coffin, p. 205. No documentation, bibliography or index.

253. Hahn, Marilyn Davis. Butler County in the Nineteenth Century. Birmingham (?): n.p., 1978. 209p.

Pages 146-8 cover the Georgiana robberies/murders committed during 1891-2 by two men, John Hipp and Charley Kelley. Hipp and Kelley were finally caught and lynched on December 29, 1892. A photograph of their bodies hanging in front of the courthouse is reproduced. Material based on articles in Greenville Advocate, 1891-2. No documentation or bibliography. Index.

254. Katz, Elaine S. Folklore for the time of your life. Birmingham: Oxmoor House, 1978. 242 p. Illus.

"Tracking a Legend" (pp. 205-14) covers the lore surrounding Hazel Farris. On August 6, 1905, in Louisville, Ky., Farris supposedly shot and killed her husband and four policemen. She then fled to Bessemer, Ala., and the next year killed herself rather than submit to arrest. For some reason her body dehydrated, and the mummified corpse has been exhibited intermittantly ever since. This chapter describes only the legends surrounding Farris and the exhibition of her body; no attempt is made to discover the facts of her supposed crimes. A photograph of Farris is included.

255. Katz, Elaine S., ed. and comp. The Kentuck Sampler: A Book of Alabama Lore. Northport, AL: Chamber of Commerce for the Kentuck Arts and Crafts Festival, 1975. 46p. Illus.

Contains article by Tom Dugger, "Hazel the Mummy" (p. 34-6) that covers legendary murderess Hazel Farris and the travels of her "mummy" after her suicide in Bessemer, Ala., in 1906. No documentation, bibliography or index.

256. Leach, MacEdward and Beck, Horace P. "Songs from Rappahonnock Co., Virginia." Journal of American Folklore 1950; 63:257-84.

Pages 279-80 contain the words and music of a version of the folksong "Railroad Bill," based on the exploits of nineteenth century black Alabama train robber Morris Slater.

257. McClellan, R.A. Early History of Limestone County. Athens, AL: n.p., ca. 1881.

Pages 12 and 13 describe the 1832 murders of Cap Roberts and Allen Johnson, as well as Cap's father Dick, by Charles Lewis. "This trio of homicides was attributed to the same desperate feud." Published in the Athens (Ala.) Post, June 1881. Reprinted by the Limestone County (Ala.) Democrat, June-July 1927.

258. McMillan, Malcolm. Yesterday's Birmingham. Miami, FL: E.A. Seeman, c1975. 208p. Illus.

Page 48 contains photograph of train robber Rube Burrow, with guns, lying in his casket. Also contains brief note about Burrow's career. No documentation, bibliography or index.

259. Mathis, Ray. John Horry Dent, South Carolina Aristocrat on the Alabama Frontier. University: University of Alabama Press, c1979. 267p. Illus.

Pages 100-2 describe Dent's witnessing the hangings of two slaves for murder and attempted murder at Clayton, May 27, 1859. Dent's journal, from which the descriptions are quoted, was the source. Heavily documented. Bibliography. Index.

260. Nelson, Mildred M. "Alabama Trees: Chiefly Legendary." Alabama Review 1953 April: 6(2):121-34.

Includes material on trees associated with several Alabama criminals, including Stephen Renfroe, Charles Boyington and Rube Burrow. Documentation.

261. Odum, Howard W. and Johnson, Guy B. Negro Workaday Songs. Chapel Hill: University of North Carolina Press, 1926. 278p.

Page 201 contains music and lyrics of song about train robber Morris "Railroad Bill" Slater. Selected bibliography.

262. O'Neal, Bill. Encyclopedia of Western Gunfighters. Norman: University of Oklahoma Press, c1979. 386p. Illus.

Entries include birth and death dates and locations, some biographical material and separate entries for major gunfights. Entry on Rube Burrow (p. 53-4) contains factual errors including misspelling of his last name and death date as 1889 (Burrow died in 1890). Documentation, bibliography, index.

263. Parker, Price. Tales of the Hills and Hollows. Athens, Ala. (?): n.p., n.d. 84p. Illus.

Contains two chapters on activities of Tom Clark and his gang of robbers and murderers in north Alabama in the early 1860s to 1872: "Horrors of Lonely Dead Horse Hollow Still a Mystery" (p. 23-9) and "Three Men Taken from Jail, Hanged for Killings" (p. 50-4). Second chapter includes material on lynching of Clark and others at Florence, Ala., in early September 1872. No documentation or index.

264. Perrow, E.C. "Songs and Rhymes from the South." Journal of American Folklore 1912; 25:137-55.

Page 155 contains rhymes from Alabama and Mississippi about Morris "Railroad Bill" Slater, Alabama's nineteenth century black train robber.

265. Powell, E.A. "Fifty-five Years in West Alabama." Alabama Historical Quarterly 1942 winter; 4(4):501-641.

Consists of reprints of articles originally published in the Tuscaloosa Gazette in the late 1880s. Some material (p. 502-6) on commissions of murder, trials and executions. Includes the "noted case" of William Kirby, who murdered his father and brother in Pickens Co. and was executed. No documentation.

266. Puckett, Riley. "Railroad Bill." Columbia CO-15040-D

Ballad about Morris Slater recorded by white singer on September 11, 1924. Released ca. September 1925.

267. Rennert, Vincent Paul. Western Outlaws. New York: Crowell-Collier, c1968. 152p. Illus.

Intended for a junior high school audience, this book has chapters on several well-known outlaws, including train robber Rube Burrows (sic). That particular chapter (pp. 106-23) seems to be based primarily on Agee (#1176) and contains a reprint of a reward poster and a photograph of Burrow, with guns, lying in his casket. The book includes a bibliography and index.

268. Reynolds, Hughes. The Coosa River Valley From De Stoto to Hydroelectric Power. Cnythiana, KY: Hobson Book Press, 1944. 351p.

Includes the tale of man who escaped hanging at Cedar Bluff (p. 125-8). Chapter 13, "The Pirate" (p. 131-50) covers "pirate" Abner Stubbs, Chapter 25, "The Passing of the Code" (p. 266-72) describes the August 10, 1889, duel on the banks of the Coosa between J.R. Williamson and Patrick Calhoun. No Documentation. Bibliography. Index.

269. Richards, E.G. "Reminiscenses of the Early Days in Chambers County." Alabama Historical Quarterly 1942 fall; 4(3):417-45.

Includes material (p. 434-7) on operation during late 1930s of the "Slick Company," a vigilante organization. No documentation.

270. Sandburg, Carl. American Songbag. New York: Harcourt, Brace, c1927. 495p.

Pages 384-5 contain some words and the music of "Railroad Bill" song, based on the career of Alabama's black train robber of the nineteenth century, Morris Slater. "Southern negro work gangs have fixed him in a ballad of hundreds of lines" (p. 384).

271. Scarborough, Dorothy. On the Trail of Negro Folksongs. Cambridge, MA: Harvard University Press, 1925. 280p.

Material on Morris "Railroad Bill" Slater, pages 251-3.

272. Spear, Charles. Essays on the Punishment of Death. Boston: privately printed, 1844. 237p.

Pages 43-4 contain material on the Charles Boyington case, Mobile, 1834. Thirteen editions of this title were published in London and Boston between 1844 and 1851.

273. Starr, J. Barton. To Live (and Die) in Dixie. Troy, AL: Troy State University Press, c1978. 122p.

Includes brief discussion of dueling. Mention of 1870 Alabama duel in which William A. Smith challenged editor of the Tuscaloosa Independent Monitor Ryland Randolph; Randolph "lost a leg as a result." Documentation. Bibliographic essay. No index.

274. Warren, Dorothea Orr. The Practical Dreamer: A Story of John T. Milner, His Family and Forebears. Birmingham: Southern Family Press, 1959. 293p. Illus.

Page 248 describes the wagon ride given to a member of John Murrell's outlaw gang by Willis Joshua Milner. The man had intended to rob Milner, but upon learning his identity could not rob "so good a man as" Milner "was known to be." No documentation, bibliography or index.

275. Watson, Fred S. Forgotten Trails: A History of Dale County, Alabama, 1824-1966. Birmingham: Banner Press, c1968. 288p. Ed. William R. Snell.

Chapter 1, "Stories from Dale's Past" (p. 15-26) includes material on several criminals and their executions: Bill Sketo, treason (hanged December 3, 1864); Rev. Henry Duncan, murder of his wife Dolly (hanged at Ozark, February 21, 1890); Jim Summers and Mike McCrea, blacks, August 1893 murder of Angus and Mary McSween (hanged at Ozark, November 16, 1894); and William Virgil Murphy, murder of his wife (first person electrocuted in Alabama, Kilby Prison, Montgomery, April 23, 1927). Some documentation. Index.

276. White, Newman I. American Negro Folk-Songs. Hatboro, PA: Folklore Associates, 1965. Rep. Cambridge, MA: Harvard University Press, 1928. 501p.

Pages 358-9 include material on Morris "Railroad Bill" Slater.

277. Windham, Kathryn Tucker. Alabama: One Big Front Porch. Huntsville, AL: Strode, 1975. 158p. Illus.

One short entry in this title (pp. 90-91) covers the legend of Alabama's black train robber, Morris "Railroad Bill" Slater. Repeats much of the folklore and few of the facts surrounding this outlaw.

278. Windham, Kathryn Tucker. Jeffrey's Latest 13; More Alabama Ghosts. Huntsville, AL: Strode, 1982. 146 pp. Illus.

The second chapter, "The Boyington Oak" (pp. 21-32) covers the 1834 murder of Nathaniel Frost by Charles Boyington in Mobile, Ala. The chapter also describes the oak that supposedly grew from Boyington's grave as a sign of his innocence.

279. Young, Mary Elizabeth. Redskins, Ruffleshirts and Rednecks; Indian Allotments in Alabama and Mississippi 1830-1860. Norman: University of Oklahoma Press, c1961. 217p. Illus.

Chapter 4, "The Creek Frauds" (p. 73-98) covers the 1830s land frauds in Alabama arising from the allotments to Creek Indians under the treaty of March 24, 1832. Documentation. Bibliography. Index.

Criminal Activity in the South

Newspaper Articles

280. (Untitled). Mobile Register 23 December 1836, p. 2, c.1.

This brief article notes that Philander R. Broad was found guilty of leading an attack on the mail stage in the Creek nation. The trial was held in U.S. District Court, Judge Crawford presiding.

281. "Montgomery, (ALA.) Dec. 27---Murders." Charleston (SC) Courier 4 January 1840.

This brief article covers the stabbing of Peter Quigley by Isaac Merritt during an argument. Another recent murder is also discussed.

282. "Horrible Outrage." Charleston (S.C.) Courier 6 April 1840.

A shopkeeper was shot in Mobile by one of two men who came to see him. The shopkeeper, although still alive, was not expected to survive his serious head wound.

283. "The City; Fugitive Arrested." New Orleans (LA) Daily Picayune, 24 April 1856 (p. 1, c.7).

This article notes the arrest in New Orleans of Ann Jennings, wanted in Alabama for the theft of $575 from a Mr. O'Brien of Mobile. Jennings was arrested on a requisition from the governor of Alabama.

284. "Further Developments in the Edwards-Speed Murder Case." Montgomery Advertiser, 4 January 1870. Related articles January 5, 6, 7.

This long article describes the confusion surrounding the murder of a stranger named Echols in Montgomery three months previously. Susan Simmons, a black on trial for perjury in swearing that Colonel A. Edwards and Captain S.R. Honey had murdered Echols, is described. Simmons had recanted her testimony, saying that a Mr. Speed had offered her $40 for swearing that Edwards had killed Echols.

285. "Horse Thief in Limbo." Montgomery Advertiser, 8 January 1870.

"A young white man was arrested Friday night, in the suburbs of the city, having in his possession a small sorrel mare, belonging to a gentleman in Green County, from whence the young man came. He was strapped on the back of a mule, after his arrest, and carried in triumph toward the scene of his stealing glory in Greene County."

Alabama

286. "Assasination;" "The Pillow Tragedy." Montgomery Advertiser. 19 January 1870.

These two articles, the first reprinted from the North Alabamian and the second from the Huntsville Times, describes the murder of Granville and William Pillow of LaGrange, Ala., at the hands of "Disguised" men. Both the brothers were shot to death. "Our informant stated that they were killed for cruel and persistent maltreatment of the wife of one of them."

287. "Fatal and Sad Affair." Montgomery Advertiser, 19 January 1870.

This article describes the shooting of W.H. Hogan, a grocery store clerk, by Edward J. Belser, "well known in this city." Belser, who turned himself in, claimed that Hogan (who was married) had seduced his daughter.

288. "Negro Hung." Montgomery Advertiser, 19 January 1870.

This article describes the lynching in Cherokee County of a negro for attacking with an iron pipe the daughters of a Mr. Wilson. Both daughters were severely injured. Reprinted from the Gadsden Times.

289. "Murder Near Troy, Ala." Savannah (GA) Morning News, January 11, 1872. Rep. Columbus (GA) Sun.

The article describes the murder by shotgun of a Mr. Watson. Watson was killed while riding horseback from Troy to his home six miles away. Watson "possessed considerable property."

290. (Untitled), Tuscaloosa Gazette October 4, 1877 (p. 3, c.2). Related article August 16.

"Nat Pierce (white), who was charged with being implicated in the killing of Story and Kilpatrick last August, in Pickens county, was taken from the jail at Carrollton, on the night of the 26th, by 20 masked men, and hanged. A change of venu (sic) had just been granted, and he was to be tried in this county next court."

291. "Dick Diddell (sic): Not to Be Pardoned..." Montgomery Advertiser 6 January 1883. Related articles January 6, 16, 28; March 6.

This brief article notes that the president has refused to pardon Dick Liddell for the 1881 robbery of a U.S. paymaster. Liddell was in jail at Huntsville. This crime is the same robbery for which Frank James was tried and acquited, also in Huntsville.

292. "Supposed Robbers of the Birmingham Post Office Arrested." Montgomery Advertiser, 9 February 1883. Rep. Nashville Banner. Related articles March 6, 8; April 1.

This article describes the arrest of D.W. Lambert ("well-known in this city") and a man named Simpson, who were suspected in the February 5 robbery of the post office in Birmingham. In that robbery the safe was blown and almost $7000 in cash, stamps and jewelry were stolen. The article also notes that the two men were suspected of recent robberies of a saloon in Nashville and the Bank of Franklin.

293. "Sam Kason, of Carpenter's Station, Alabama; Found Dead with a Bullet in his Brain." Montgomery Advertiser, 11 February 1883. Rep. Chattanooga Times.

This article describes the discovery on Coon Creek of the body of Sam Kason. Kason, "a noted desperado," "has murdered several men in the past five years, but in each case has managed to escape the law." The article mentions that Kason had killed a man in Jackson County, Ala., about two years previously, and that he was "well known in north Alabama."

294. "Terrible Affair at Cullman: Railroad Conductor Shot and Beaten." Montgomery Advertiser 16 February 1883.

This article describes an attack by a drunken marshall of Cullman on conductor Robert Arnold. "The foregoing may be in some respects exaggerated," the paper advises. "It is the statement of one who says he was an eyewitness."

295. "Highway Robbery! Lawrence County Tax Collector Relieved of $4300." Montgomery Advertiser 17 February 1883.

Six miles outside of Courtland, Ala., the tax collector was robbed while carrying a large sum of money to the county Superintendent of Education in Moulton. A description of the robbery is given; the robber's identity is unknown.

296. "Murderer of the Gipsey Located." Montgomery Advertiser 17 February 1883.

"Wheeler, Feb. 16. John Mead, the negro accomplice of the town marshall of Courtland in the murder of the gipsey some weeks ago, has been traced to a cave near Jonesboro, where he has been hid since the murder. They propose to smoke him out with kerosene oil; he has probably been caught before this time. He was betrayed by a negro."

297. "The Whistler Counterfeiter." Montgomery Advertiser 27 February 1883. Rep. Mobile Register.

The article covers the arrest and activities of Dr. James Furlong, a resident of Whistler, Ala., since 1869. His method of making and passing counterfeit money is described.

298. "A Notorious Outlaw." Montgomery Advertiser 10 March 1883. Related articles March 17 and 28 (p. 4,c.1).

The article notes the arrest by U.S. deputy marshall T.G. Hewlett of Joe Bennefield in Winston County, Ala. Bennefield was wanted for moonshining, counterfeiting and complicity in the murder of a Lieutenant McEntyre in Georgia in 1876. The article also describes an escape by Bennefield and eight other prisoners from a jail in Huntsville.

299. "The State versus John E. Burke." Montgomery Advertiser 28 March 1883. Related articles March 29, 30, 31.

This long article describes the attack by Burke on A.R. McCurdy in Montgomery's Ruby saloon the previous December. Burke claimed that McCurdy had sent him threatening letters, and he had thus shot McCurdy to protect himself.

300. "A Bold Outrage: Four Masked Men Near Carpenter's Station, Alabama." Montgomery Advertiser 29 March 1883. Rep. Chattanooga Times. Related article 3 April.

This article details the attack by four men on the home of Henry Porter, a Jackson County man known to keep "large sums of money in his house." The thieves got no money but burned the house down before escaping. The article notes that the "neighborhood has long been infested with a band of these...desperadoes." A posse was formed to find these four.

301. "Murderer Arrested." Montgomery Advertiser 29 March 1883.

This article notes the arrest of Ben Warrick in Apalachicola, Fla., on March 24. Warrick was wanted for the murder of John R. Lee in Pike County. Warrick, who was trying to get to Cuba, was found with a large amount of money. Since his flight to Florida, he had been living among fishermen at St. Andrews Bay,Fla.

302. "Passing Counterfeit Money." Montgomery Advertiser 5 April 1883.

The article notes the arrest of Henry Morris, a black man, for passing a "poor" counterfeit silver dollar. The recent circulation of large amounts of counterfeit silver in Montgomery is also noted.

303. "The Late Excitement at Birmingham." Pensacola (FL) Semi-Weekly Advance Advocate 11 December 1883.

Notes the arrest, trial, sentencing to death and attempted lynching of Wesley Posey, a black charged with an assault on a little girl.

304. "Two Murderers Break Jail and Escape." New Orleans (LA) Times-Picayune 6 June 1885.

The article reports on the escape of two brothers, Bill and Green Tesney, from the Walker Co. jail.

305. "Life for Life." Nashville (TN) Banner 28 August 1885.

This article notes the legal execution by hanging of Charles Townsend, a black, in Huntsville. Townsend had killed Nathan Freeman, white, for a small amount of money. That crime took place on December 9, 1884, at Madison.

306. "Appalling." Birmingham Daily News 19 April 1890. Related article April 18.

This long article is the confession of Ben Elzy. Before his execution by hanging on April 18, Elzy, a black, confessed to twenty-one murders and numerous robberies in Tennessee, Georgia and Alabama. The April 18 article covers the hanging as well as Elzy's criminal career.

307. "Counterfeiters' Metal." Birmingham Daily News 24 April 1890.

This article describes the arrest of J.N. Ligsby and another man for counterfeiting in Walker Co.

308. "Sandy Jones." Birmingham Daily News 24 April 1890. Related article May 9.

This article notes that Jones will hang on May 9 unless the supreme court reverses his case. Jones was convicted for the murder in Bessemer of policeman John Manning in April 1889. The long May 9 article covers Jones' execution and also notes the execution earlier in the year of Gilbert Lowe, Richard Hawes and Ben Elzy.

309. "Sensational Case." Birmingham Daily News 26 April 1890.

This article notes the arrest of Hattie Vandiver, "a woman of ill repute, who runs a Scratch Ankle dive," for robbing John Fie, a customer in her bar. Three other parties were also arrested.

310. "Horse Thieves." Birmingham Daily News 29 April 1890. Related article April 28.

George and William Thomas, both white, were arrested near Grace's Gap for horse theft. Both men were bound over for trial.

311. "They Got Away." Birmingham Daily News 15 May 1890.

Three white convicts escaped from the Pratt mines: Jim Morrison, Bob Crawford and Bartow Thrasher. Morrison was convicted of murder in Tuscaloosa Co. and Thrasher of burglary in Blocton. In 1889 Thrasher had also escaped and nearly died in a gunbattle with law officers near West Point, Miss.

312. "Safe Robber." Birmingham Daily News 21 May 1890.

"Detective Shackleford of Atlanta passed through the city last night in charge of O.J. Simmons, a white man, who is alleged to be an expert safe robber and burglar. He was arrested in Rome, Ga., and was being taken back to Eutaw, Ala., where it is alleged he and a pal named Dickson blew a safe open.

"Simmons is said to have operated all over the South, and is known to be a bad man. He is charged with cracking a safe at Clanton, Ala., and getting $1700. It is alleged that he blew open and robbed a safe of $600 at Verbena, Ala. Several crimes are charged against him and his partners in Georgia."

313. "Counterfeiter Arrested." Birmingham Age-Herald 22 November 1891. Related article November 25.

In Birmingham Officer J.H. Whaley arrested J.C. Jenkins, a white man. Jenkins was trying to pass counterfeit silver dollars in a saloon.

314. "Lawler Caught in Texas." Birmingham Age-Herald 27 November 1891.

W.W. Lawler was arrested near Fort Worth. Lawler was wanted for the May 8, 1891, killing in Franklin Co. of U.S. Deputy Marshal Lock Ezell.

315. "Murder in Blount." Birmingham Age-Herald 5 December 1891.

This brief article describes the fatal shooting in Blount Co. of George Brazeel by Robert Gunter. "This makes three murders within one week in Blount."

316. "Bold Jail Delivery." Birmingham Age-Herald 7 December 1891.

This article describes the escape from jail in Montgomery County of three prisoners, including Emanuel Williams. Charged with burglary in Covington Co., Williams is described as "a terror in the county to all good citizens. He is connected with some of the best families in that county."

317. "Dead Near Jesse Miller's." Birmingham Age-Herald 20 December 1891.

This article notes the discovery of the body of Will Morrison seven miles from Blocton. Morrison was killed by buckshot.

318. "Rattlehoover Robbed." Birmingham Age-Herald 21 December 1891.

This article notes the robbery by two men of Romulus Rattlehoover near Talladega. The robbers claimed over $100 by pointing double-barrelled shotguns and ordering, "Throw up your hands, or you are a dead man." The article also notes this is the third such robbery around Talladega in two weeks.

319. "The Sims Gang." Birmingham Age-Herald 25 December 1891. Related articles December 26, 27 and 29(2).

This article notes the attack by the Bob Sims gang on the house of John McMillan in Womack Hill, Choctaw Co. Mcmillan and others were wounded; nine members of Sims' gang were wounded. The article also notes that three months earlier Sims was arrested for operating a still, "which he claimed he had divine authority to run." Two of his brothers rescued him; a bystander and one of the brothers were killed. Sims and his "believers" have been "hunted vigorously ever since." Later articles describe the escalation of the violence. State troops, including an artillery detachment, were called in. Sims and several other men were lynched.

320. "Assaulted by Moonshiners." Columbus (GA) Enquirer-Sun 8 January 1892.

In DeKalb Co., Ala., Rev. J.R. Hicks, from Kentucky and visiting relatives, was attacked by three moonshiners who mistook him for detective Tom Hewlett of Birmingham. "Hicks thinks his assailants were Clayton Sprouse, Top Sprouse and Will Webb, three noted desperadoes." Hicks was beaten and robbed.

321. "Under Arrest; For the Murder of the Notorious Bill Morrison." Birmingham Age-Herald 11 January 1892.

"News has been received in Birmingham that R.R. McCulley, Fayt McCulley, Monroe Calhoun and West Reich have been arrested in Bibb County and lodged in jail, charged with the murder of Bill Morrison. A warrant is said to be out for the arrest of Jesse Miller on the same charge, but he can not be found."

322. "Further Details of the Georgia Pacific Train Robbery." Birmingham Daily News 1 April 1892. Related articles April 2, 13, 14.

Continues reportage on robbery of Georgia Pacific train #53 the night of March 30 eight miles from Birmingham. Five or six men were involved in the robbery. Long article. Notes $1000 reward being offered by U.S. government. Registered mail packages were taken. April 13 article is a long one reporting arrests.

323. "Robber Killed." Birmingham Daily News 11 April 1892. Related article April 12.

A gang of four blacks, led by Tom Wright, attempted to rob a freight train that had stopped to take on water near Falkville in Morgan Co. Wright was later killed in a gunbattle with a posse and two of his gang were captured. April 12 article is a long follow-up.

324. "Train Robbery in Alabama." New York Times 2 January 1895. (p. 8).

Reports the January 1 robbery near York of a train by two masked men who had boarded at Livingston. Contents of the express car were taken; "several thousand dollars" was believed to be involved.

325. "Counterfeiters' Outfit Captured Near Oakman, Walker County, Ala." Mobile (AL) Register, January 30, 1895. Reprinted from Montgomery (AL) Advertiser.

For three months large amounts of counterfeit money had been in circulation in the vicinity of Oakman. In January 1895 Marshal Day and Deputy E.L. Williams located molds for the manufacture of five, twenty-five and fifty-cent pieces. Other counterfeiting materials were also found. Soon the officers also managed to locate and arrest James W. Blanton, a white man, for the crime. Blanton, who had been arrested in October 1894 for the same crime, was carried to Montgomery and brought before U.S. Commissioner H.A. Wilson, who charged him "with making and passing counterfeit money."

326. "One More Victim is Notched by 'Railroad Bill,' the Negro Desperado of South Alabama." Birmingham Age-Herald 8 April 1895.

This article describes the near-capture the night of April 6 of Morris "Railroad Bill" Slater. Slater was found asleep on a water tank at Hurricane bayou. A freight conductor and several of his men tried to capture Slater, who pulled two revolvers and opened fire. The men sought shelter in a nearby house. "A second freight train came up a few minutes later, and the negro captured it, rode up to where the imprisoned crew was and filled the house with lead." Later a posse was formed, and Slater was located 2½ miles from Bay Minette. "A midnight battle ensued, during which Chief James Stewart received a rifle ball through his heart." Sheriff Ed McMillan of Brewton took up the chase, but Slater escaped in a rainstorm.

327. "Railroad Bill: The Desperate Criminal was Killed at Atmore Last Night." Montgomery (AL) Advertiser, March 8, 1896. See also Mobile (AL) Register, same date.

Both of these long articles describe Morris "Railroad Bill" Slater's criminal career and violent death "at the hands of a posse." Slater was shot to death in a store in Atmore, Ala., by members of the posse pursuing the train robber/murderer. An intense manhunt for Slater had been underway all over southern Alabama since Slater's July 1895 murder of Escambia Co. sheriff Ed McMillan.

328. "Lynched by One Man." Raleigh (NC) Gazette 18 December 1897.

"Wm. Ellis, a prominent farmer, living near Evergreen, Ala., took a negro named Cook King to a swamp, tied him to a tree and shot him to death. Intimacy with Ellis' daughter is the alleged crime."

329. "Gave Up When His Eye Dimmed; Noted Moonshiner Caught." Memphis (TN) Commercial Appeal, November 29, 1908.

Datelined Anniston, Ala., November 28, this article describes the gunbattle between U.S. revenue officers and Jim Floyd and members of his "gang." The moonshining group was active in the Turkey Haven mountains for a decade. Floyd and eight "alleged" members were finally arrested; the names of the other members are given.

330. "'Railroad Bill' Begins Tour for Labor Theater." New York Times 1981 April 9; III:17.

Notes that the play, a combination of narration, blues and projected photographs and staring Horace Foster, Jr., was set to begin a 35-city tour. Tour sponsored by United Automobile Workers, Amalgamated Clothing and Textile Workers and the NAACP.

4

Florida

Monographs

331. Caudle, Hal M. The Hanging at Bahia Mar. Ft. Lauderdale, FL: Wake-Brook House, c1976. 135p. Illus.

On August 17, 1929, bootlegger James Horace Alderman was hanged in an abandoned hanger near Ft. Lauderdale. More than two years earlier Alderman had shot and killed two Coast Guard men and a U.S. Secret Service agent. This book details events leading up to the hanging. Caudle's sources included legal materials, his own diary and newspaper articles. Author was Coast Guardsman present at many of events described. No documentation or index. Brief bibliography.

332. Lambright, Edwin Dart. The Life and Exploits of Gasparilla, Last of the Buccaneers, with the History of Ye Mystic Krewe of Gasparilla. Tampa, FL: Hillsboro Printing Co., 1936. 221p. Illus.

Biographical account of Jose Gasparilla (1756-1821), Spanish pirate headquartered at Charlotte Harbor, near Tampa. Includes material on the Gasparilla carnival held in Tampa and begun in 1904.

333. Powell, J.C. The American Siberia, or Fourteen Years in Southern Convict Camp. 1891. Rep. Montclair, NJ: Patterson Smith, 1970. 359p. Illus. Rep. Gainsville, FL: University Press of Florida, 1976.

Powell was the captain in charge of Florida's convict camp during the 1880s and an official in several capacities between 1876 and 1890. Although a supporter of the convict lease system, Powell's account is detailed, well balanced and humane. Numerous individual murderers, moonshiners, thieves, etc., and their crimes are discussed, but dates and locations are vague or non-existent. Fascinating. No documentation or bibliography. Index.

334. Stuart, Hix C. The Notorious Ashley Gang: A Saga of the King and Queen of the Everglades. Stuart, FL: St. Lucie Printing Co., c1928. 80p. Illus.

Stuart was acquainted with John Ashley and members of his gang of bank robbers/murderers---including his mistress Laura Upthegrove---who operated in Florida between 1911 and 1924. Gives details of many of the gang's crimes. As far as I can determine, this title is the only work of substance yet published on the Ashley gang. No documentation, bibliography or index.

Dissertation

335. George, Paul S. "Criminal Justice in Miami, 1896-1930." Ph.D. dissertation, Florida State University, 1975. 348p.

Primarily history of development of Miami police force during the period. Chapter 8 covers unsuccessful effort of police force to stop bootlegging during Prohibition.

Journal Articles

336. Brookfield, Charles M. "The Guy Bradley Story." Audubon Magazine 1955 July August; 57:170-4.

Bradley was a game warden murdered at Oyster Keys, Fla., on July 8, 1905, by poacher Walter Smith.

337. Buchanan, Patricia. "Miami's Bootleg Boom." Tequesta 1970; 30:13-31.

Describes bootlegging and rum-running in south Florida during the 1920s. Sections cover such whiskey smugglers as Duncan W. "Red" Shannon, killed by Coast Guardsmen on February 25, 1926; and Horace Alderman, executed for murder of two Coast Guardsmen and a Secret Service agent, August 27, 1929. No documentation. Based on the author's University of Miami, M.A. thesis, 1968.

338. Carper, N. Gordon. "Martin Tabert, Martyr of an Era." Florida Historical Quarterly 1973 October; 52(2):115-31.

Discusses January 1922 murder of convict Martin Tabert by guard Walter Higginbotham. Higginbotham was sentenced to twenty years but the case was overturned on a technicality. He was found not guilty at retrial. Nevertheless, the practice of peonage in Florida received much publicity during the case. Documentation.

339. d'Ans, Andre-Marcel; Ingalls, Marie Joele, trans. "The Legend of Gasparilla: Myth and History on Florida's West Coast." Tampa Bay History 1980; 2(2):5-29.

Jose Gaspar operated a pirate's den on the island in Charlotte Harbor, 1783-1821. Discusses various versions of the legend surrounding him.

340. Doherty, Herbert J., Jr. "Code Duello in Florida." Florida Historical Quarterly 1951 April; 29(4):243-52.

Doherty's article covers ante-bellum dueling in Florida, 1824-62. Several specific duels are discused, including one in which Leigh Read killed Augustus Alston. The article includes some brief discussion of the legal and social aspects of early Florida dueling. A non-duel dispute between Joseph M. White and Richard K. Call inexplicably occupies most of the article.

341. Felson, Paul E. "The Notorious Swepson-Littlefield Fraud: Railroad Financing in Florida, 1868-71." Florida Historical Quarterly 1954 April; 32:231-61.

Overview of "financial manipulations of George W. Swepson and Milton S. Littlefield in Florida during the hectic post-Civil War period..." (p. 231). Both men also operated a fraud in North Carolina. Neither man was punished. Documentation.

342. Friedman, Peggy. "Jacksonville's Most Famous Madam." Jacksonville 1980 May/June; 12-20.

Cora Taylor, also known as Cora Howorth and Cora Crane. See Gilkes (#358).

343. George, Paul S. "Bootleggers, Prohibitionists and Police: The Temperance Movement in Miami, 1896-1920." Tequesta 1979; 39:34-41.

344. Granade, Ray. "Slave Unrest in Florida." Florida Historical Quarterly 1976; 55(1):18-36.

Describes such non-conspiratorial forms of unrest as arson, theft and murder. Documentation.

344. "How Tampa Treats Lynchers." Literary Digest 1927 June 18; 93:12-3.

Covers June 1927 attempt in Tampa by a mob to lynch B.F. Levins, a white man and "self-confessed murderer." Levins was unhurt in the riot, but five others died. Illustrated. No documentation.

345. McGovern, James R. "'Sporting Life on the Line:' Prostitution in Progressive Era Pensacola." Florida Historical Quarterly 1975 October; 54(2):131-44.

Describes conditions of prostitution, 1900-18. Specific madams, such as Mollie McCoy, and their girls are discussed. Much information based on interviews with three elderly unidentified men. Illustrated with photographs. Documentation.

346. Martin, Richard A. "Public Hangings Were Well-Attended." Jacksonville 1982 May-June; 19:91-5.

347. Rogers, William Warren, Jr. "Rube Burrow, 'King of Outlaws,' and his Florida Adventures." Florida Historical Quarterly 1980 October; 58(4):182-98.

Describes Burrow's move to Florida early in 1890 to escape pursuit; efforts of Pinkertons and railroad detectives to find him; and his single-handed train robbery at Flomaton, Ala., on September 1, 1890. Documentation.

348. Shofner, Jerrell H. "Judge Herbert Rider and the Lynching at Labelle." Florida Historical Quarterly 1981 January; 59(3):292-306.

Discusses several lynchings, including those of Parker Watson, May 8; and Henry Patterson on May 11, 1926, in Labelle, Hendry Co. Also covers role of Rider in efforts to prosecute people responsible for the Patterson lynching. Documentation.

349. Shofner, Jerrell H. "Postscript to the Martin Tabert Case: Peonage as Usual in the Florida Turpentine Camps." Florida Historical Quarterly 1981 October; 60(2):161-73.

Follow-up to (#338). Describes other murders--such as Lewis Barker's, October 19, 1924--of convicts and continuance of peonage system into the 1940s. Documentation.

350. Shofner, Jerrell H. "The White Springs Post Office Caper." Florida Historical Quarterly 1978 January; 56(3): 339-47.

Describes 1888 Hamilton Co. shooting of C.L. Morrison by Fred P. Cone and "robbery" of White Springs post office, where Morrison was postmaster, in August 1889. Documentation.

351. True, David O. "Pirate Lore and Treasure Trove of South Florida." Tequesta 1946; p.3-13.

Some discussion of pirates in south Florida, including Billy Rogers, Lewis Leland and Black Caesar. Much of the article concerns sunken treasure. No documentation.

352. Wallace, Irving, et al. "Significa. Saved from Death." Parade 1983 July 3; p. 16.

Discusses case of Jim Williams, who was sentenced to die at the Raiford, Fla., prison farm on June 1, 1927, for the murder of his wife. Because Chief Deputy Walter Minton would not pull the switch--he was not the legal executioner--Williams did not die and was later paroled. No documentation.

353. Williamson, Edward C. "The Black Belt Political Crisis: The Savage-James Lynching, 1882." Florida Historical Quarterly 1967; 45(4):402-9.

In Madison Co., Fla., February 7, 1881, black man Charles Savage shot and killed Frank Patterson during a political argument. Savage and another black, Howard James, were both arrested, tried and sentenced to hang. In late August 1882 both men were lynched while awaiting appeal of their cases. Documentation.

354. Wright, J. Leitch, Jr. "Andrew Ranson: Seventeenth Century Pirate?" Florida Historical Quarterly 1960 October; 39(2):135-44.

Ranson was an English pirate who operated against the Spanish in the St. Augustine, Fla., area during the late 1600s. Documentation.

Miscellaneous

355. Brookfield, Charles M. and Griswold, Oliver. They All Called It Tropical; True Tales of the Romantic Everglades National Park, Cape Sable and the Florida Keys. Miami: Data Press, c1949. 77p. Illus.

Chapter entitled "A Martyr to Millinery" (p. 60-68) covers July 8, 1905, murder of Audubon Society game warden Guy M. Bradley by bird poacher Walter Smith, who was arrested but later released. No documentation, bibliography or index.

356. deCoste, Frederick. True Tales of Old St. Augustine. St. Petersburg, FL: Great Outdoors Publishing Co., for the St. Augustine Historical Society, 1966. 71p. Illus.

The fourth chapter deals with pirates during the Spanish era.

357. Dinkins, J. Lester. Dunnellon, Boomtown of the 1890s; The Story of Rainbow Springs and Dunnellon. St. Petersburg, FL: Great Outdoors Publishing, c1969. 215p. Illus.

"The Murder of Turner and Barfield, November 1895" (p. 144-8) describes the Marion Co. murders of two storekeepers, Robert Turner and James Barfield. Two blacks were responsible, and a vigilante committee formed. One black, believed to have knowledge of the crime, was lynched at Juliette and another near Dunnellon. Later lynchings also occurred. Documentation. Index.

358. Gilkes, Lillian. Cora Crane: A Biography of Mrs. Stephen Crane. Bloomington: Indiana University Press, 1960. 416p. Illus.

Includes material on Cora Howorth's life as a madam in Jacksonville, Fla., before and after her relationship with writer Stephen Crane. Also describes the May 31, 1907, murder of Harry Parker by Hammond McNeil; the two men were involved with Cora. Source notes and index.

359. Hanna, Alfred Jackson and Kathryn Abbey. Florida's Golden Sands. Indianapolis: Bobbs-Merrill, c1950. 429p.

Chapter 5, "Pirates and Privateers" (p. 66-80) primarily covers the Key West-based pirate squadron set up by the U.S. government under the command of David Porter in 1823. Some mention of specific pirates, including Black Caesar. No documentation. List of "Sources." Index.

360. Hanna, Alfred Jackson and Kathryn Abbey. Lake Okeechobee, Wellspring of the Everglades. Indianapolis: Bobbs-Merrill, c1948. 379p. Illus.

Chapter 16, "The Ashley Gang" (p. 204-16), covers the group of murderers and bank robbers led by John Ashley. The Ashley gang was active in Florida between 1915 and 1924. A list of sources, primarily Florida newspaper articles, is included.

361. Hill, Norman Alan. Florida Cruise. Baltimore: George W. King Printing Co., c1945. 430p. Illus.

Chapter 7, "Gasparilla---Last of the Buccaneers" (p. 167-205) by E.D. Lambright covers the career of Barcelona-born pirate Jose Gasper (1756-1821). Supposedly the Gulf Coast pirate, based in Florida, committed suicide on December 21, 1821, rather than submit to capture. Mentions diary kept by Gaspar in late 1700s. No documentation or bibliography. Index.

362. Morris, Alton C. Folksongs of Florida. Gainesville: University of Florida Press, 1950. 464p.

"Songs of Outlawry and Prison Experience" (p. 67-99) include "Little Mary Phagan," "Naomi Wise," "Kenney Wagner's Surrender," Harvey Logan, "Birmingham Jail" and "Frank Dupree." Dupree killed an Atlanta policeman and was executed on September 1, 1922. Melodies and lyrics included. Index of titles and first lines.

363. Muir, Helen. Miami, U.S.A. New York: Holt, c1953. 308p.

A history of the city. Chapter 9, "The Last of the Frontier Sheriffs" (p. 93-8) covers Dan Hardie, elected sheriff of Dade Co. in 1908. Briefly describes Hardie's dealings with two robber gangs, those of Leland and Frank Rice and John Ashley. No documentation. Bibliography. Index.

364. Sanford, Warner. "Ye True Chart of Pirate Treasure Lost or Hidden in the Land and Waters of Florida: Being a Map to Show the Whereabouts of Much Gold and Silver and Other Loot which with Good Cause is Beleived (sic) to be Lost or Buried by Gasparilla, Black Caesar and Other Pirates of the Spanish Main, and of Other More Honest Men...which same Treasure is Now Hidden in Florida Sand and Waters." Tallahassee, FL: R.E. Odum, c1950.

Map.

365. Titler, Dale Milton. Billy Bowleg's Owne Charte: A Charte of Olde Choctawhatchee Bay and Camp Walton, Showing Those Alleged Locations of the Buried and Sunken Pyrate Booty of Captain Billy Bowlegs, a Freebooter, as Well as the Lost Treasures, Sunken Ships and Riches of Sundry Other Pyrates and Sea Rovers Who are Believed to have Frequented these Waters, Among them the Notorious Arch Smuggler and Pyrate-Patriot "Gentleman" Jean Lafitte. Marianna, Fla: n.p., c1956.

Map showing area west of Panama City, alleged frequented by pirates between 1815 and 1844, including Bowlegs (William Rogers, 1795?-1888).

366. Wells, William James. Pioneering in the Panhandle: A Look at Selected Events and Families of Santa Rosa County, Florida. Fort Walton Beach, FL: Melvin Business Services, c1976. 285p. Illus.

Pages 73-5 cover train robber Rube Burrow and contain a sketch of Burrow.

367. Wetherell, Ellen F. Facts from Florida. Lynn, MA: n.p., 1897. 91p. Illus.

Includes material on lynching in Florida.

Newspaper Articles

368. "Murder." (p. 3) Pensacola Gazette and Florida Advertiser 23 September 1828.

Notes the stabbing murder of a man named Jim Stafford by a drunken man named Sinclair. The murderer was in jail in Jacksonville. Sinclair was hanged on August 28, 1828. See Charleston (SC) Courier September 12, 1828.

369. "Attempt to Murder." Jacksonville Courier 27 August 1835.

Notes second attempt by unknown party on life of Thomas Douglass, U.S. District Attorney for East Florida. In Jacksonville.

370. "Arrest." Jacksonville Courier 3 September 1835.

Reports the arrest of an unidentified "foreigner" in St. Augustine "for attempting to excite insurrection among the blacks in that place, and on examination disclosed that several persons were engaged in the plot in Florida, with the understanding that there was to be a general rise in all the Southern States." He did not state the time, or the arrangements but doubtless it is a part of the plan revealed by Murrell, which was to be carried into effect in December next."

371. "House Breaking." Florida Union (Jacksonville) 1 October 1868.

"The house of Mr. J.C. Greeley was broken into the other night, and nearly every portable article of any value carried off." In Jacksonville.

372. "Recaptured." Florida Union (Jacksonville) 1 October 1868.

Reports recapture of Bill Morgan, "the murderer of Winner," who had escaped from jail in Jacksonville.

373. "Robber Caught." Florida Union (Jacksonville) 1 October 1868.

Notes arrest of Charles Blake, black, who burglarized the Jacksonville house of Dr. J.C. L'Engle on August 20 and got away with "quite a sum of money."

374. "Brutal Murder of a Boy in Madison Co." Tallahassee Sentinel 22 October 1868.

John Barfield kicked to death Alexander Urquhart, aged sixteen.

375. "A Murder Case Before the Supreme Court." Tallahassee Sentinel 22 October 1868.

Appeal in the case of Silas Gladden, who had been convicted for the December 31, 1867, murder in Jackson Co. of a man named Buffington.

376. "Local News." True Southerner (Tampa) 29 October 1868.

One item notes the recent arrest of John Collins "at old Tampa, charged with larceny."

377. "Arrested." Florida Union (Jacksonville) 5 November 1868.

Notes arrest of a man named Wilkinson for the August murder at Baldwin of N. Nolan.

378. "Murder in Columbia County." True Southerner (Tampa) 5 November 1868.

Reports the October 15 murder of Ned (or Ed) Spanish by Frank Higginbotham; Spanish owed him money. Murder occurred twelve miles from Lake City. Higginbotham also reported as having murdered a man in Hamilton Co. on October 16.

379. "Robbery, the Thief Captured." Florida Union (Jacksonville) 5 November 1868.

Reports the arrest of Abraham Williams, black, for the theft of $400 from a coat belonging to Andrew Canova. In Jacksonville.

380. "Terrible Tragedy at Marianna." Tallahassee Sentinel 6 March 1869.

Reports the murder of Dr. J.L. Finlayson, Clerk of the Circuit Court. Motive and perpetrator were unknown.

381. "City and State Items." Tallahassee Sentinel 15 May 1869.

One item notes the escape of five prisoners from the Tallahassee jail.

382. "City and State Items." Tallahassee Sentinel 15 May 1869.

One item notes the arrest of Thomas George Scott for the attempted murder of his brother-in-law, Thomas Knight, in Hamilton Co.

383. "Duval County Jail." Florida Union (Jacksonville) 3 June 1869.

Primarily description of bad conditions. Mentions Orin Townsend, a prisoner convicted of adultery.

384. "Trial of Henry Miller." Florida Union (Jacksonville) 3 June 1869.

This long article reports on the Jacksonville trial of Miller, black, for the March 2 murder of Gadsden Jackson. Miller was found guilty of second degree murder.

385. "Trial of Thomas Dixon." Florida Union (Jacksonville) 3 June 1969. Related article July 22.

This long article reports on the trial of Dixon for the April 1869 murder of Jacksonville policeman Ignacio Andreu. Dixon was found guilty of first degree murder, sentenced to hang and appealed his case to the Supreme Court.

386. "Gambling." Florida Union (Jacksonville) 1 July 1869.

"We are glad to announce that our city officials have at last obtained positive evidence of a 'gambling hell' in this city."

387. "Robbery." Florida Union (Jacksonville) 22 July 1869.

John P. Johnson, mail agent, was robbed of $43 while on the train between Jacksonville and Quincy on July 14. Three men were arrested and released due to insufficient evidence.

388. "Another Victim." Florida Union (Jacksonville) 5 August 1869.

Reports that James Sullivan, "a notorious gambler," met Eli Thompson (black, from Gainesville) as Thompson left the train in Jacksonville, took him to a bar and drugged and robbed him. Sullivan had thus far eluded capture.

389. "Burglaries." Florida Union (Jacksonville) 5 August 1869.

Describes two recent burglaries in Jacksonville.

390. "State Items." Florida Express (Pensacola) 9 September 1871.

One long item concerns the murder of a black named Wash Coe in Marion Co. Another item notes the robbery of Judge Bryson in Jacksonville.

391. "The Third Body." Pensacola Mail 30 January 1872.

Notes the discovery of the murdered body of William Foren. Miles Clark was arrested and then released.

392. "An Express Robber." Savannah (GA) Morning News 10 February 1872.

This long article notes the arrest and return to Florida of C.J. Hunter, an alleged thief and bigamist.

393. "Florida Affairs." Savannah (GA) Morning News 3 February 1872.

One item notes the circulation of counterfeit money in Jacksonville; a description is given.

394. (Untitled) Pensacola Gazette 29 April 1875.

Article discusses appearance of prostitutes on the streets of the city.

395. "The Riot on Saturday." Florida Express (Pensacola) 28 August 1875.

Notes the lynching in Pensacola of two blacks who had been jailed for raping a Mrs. Taylor near Pine Barren. A riot between blacks and whites over the lynching was narrowly avoided.

396. "Jail Delivery." Pensacola Commercial 22 December 1883.

Notes the escape of four men from the Pensacola city jail. The men are named, but their offenses are not.

397. "Homicide." Pensacolian 29 and December 1883. See also Pensacola Commercial 29 December 1883 (long article) and Pensacola Semi-Weekly Advance-Gazette 1 January 1884.

Boston Hargis was killed by David Foreman in Pensacola. Both men were black.

398. "Shooting Affray." Pensacolian 29 and 30 December 1883. See also Pensacola Commercial 29 December 1883.

Notes that the carpenter from a Swedish ship in Pensacola harbor was shot three times and robbed and robbed of his watch by a black man.

399. "The Schmidt Murders." Daily Florida Herald (Jacksonville) 2 July 1885.

Describes the October 3, 1884, murder of Paul Schmidt, a German, in Orlando. Schmidt was supposedly killed by two blacks, George Lancaster (who wielded the ax) and Jim McGarr, in order to rob the German.

400. "It Grows in Horror." Birmingham (AL) Age-Herald 15 December 1891. Related article December 27.

This long article discusses the brutal murders of two women and two children at New Smyrna, near Jacksonville, Florida. Mrs. L.D. Hatch and Miss Angeline Bruce were the women. A posse of two hundred armed men with bloodhounds was "scouring the country."

401. "Color in Florida." Birmingham (AL) Age-Herald 28 December 1891.

A posse of almost one thousand armed men were searching Lake Co. for Thomas E. Mike. Mike shot J.E. Parramore on a train during an argument.

402. Black Brute Runs Amuck." Birmingham (AL) Age-Herald 8 April 1895.

This article describes the crimes of Brit Glenn, "Commonly known as 'Kid Charlie,' a negro gambler and desperado." Glenn killed Napoleon Stucks in the Rabbit Foot saloon in Jacksonville, Fla., "a notorious negro dive on West Bay Street." Glenn also killed a policeman, Edward Minor, and wounded three other men.

403. "Two Men Accused of Passing Counterfeit Money." New Orleans (LA) Daily Picayune 28 June 1897. Related article June 28.

Thomas L. and John J. Salter, claiming to be carpenters from Brewton, Ala., were arrested in Pensacola for passing counterfeit silver dollars. The second article notes that both were found innocent of the 1896 murder/robbery of a mail rider near Evergreen, Ala.

404. "Told in a Paragraph." Raleigh (NC) Gazette 11 December 1897.

One item reports the arrest of John Henry, "a Florida desperado," near Valdosta, Ga.

405. "Jail Delivery." Deland News 23 April 1909.

Notes the escape of five prisoners from the Volusia Co. jail. Two were convicted murderers, Arthur Nelson (sentenced to hang) and John Johnson (life imprisonment).

406. "Two Convicted of Murder." Deland News 23 April 1909.

In Deland. One man was John Johnson. The other was Amos Nelson, alias Fred Sawyer, sentenced to hang for the December 1907 murder of Carrie Nelson, or Carrie London, at Cow Creek, Volusia Co.

407. "Express Robbery Mystery Solved." Spartanburg (SC) Journal 13 July 1920.

Reports the arrest in Jacksonville of John Holder and L. R. Dukes (or Duges) for the July 9 train robbery near Jacksonville. Most of the $7000 stolen was recovered.

408. "2 Killed, 1 Wounded as Posses Battle Everglade Bandits." New York Times 10 January 1924 (p. 1).

Reports the death of Deputy Sheriff Fred Baker, a member of the posse in pursuit of the John Ashley-Hanford Mobley gang of bank robbers. Joe W. Ashley, 65 year-old member of the gang was also killed in the day-long gunbattle. This lengthy article describes the fight.

409. "Bloodhounds Trail Everglade Bandits." New York _Times_ 11 January 1924 (p. 19). Related article Jan. 13 (p. 8).

Reports the capture of Albert Miller, twenty-year old member of the John Ashley-Hanford Mobley gang of Florida bank robbers and the "alleged slayer" of Deputy Sheriff Fred Baker. Also reports on the search by a posse of one hundred men for Ashley and Mobley.

410. "Tracking Desperadoes in Florida Everglades." New York _Times_ 27 January 1924 (sec. 8, p. 4).

This long article describes the history of the John Ashley-Hanford Mobley gang of bank robbers and the current status of search for remaining members. Includes photo of posse member.

411. "Florida Boy Bandit in Another Exploit." New York _Times_ 16 March 1924 (sec. 2, p. 1).

Describes the exploits of Hanford Mobley, last surviving member of the John Ashley bank robbing gang and wanted for murder, piracy and bank robbery. Related New York _Times_ articles appear November 2 (p. 1), 3 (p. 14) and November 16 (sec. 8, p. 8), 1924.

412. "Alderman to Hang in Broward Jail." Belle Glade _News_ 28 June 1929.

Horace Alderman, fifty year-old "alleged bootlegger" and convicted killer of two Coast Guardsmen on the ocean off Ft. Lauderdale (August 7, 1927) was sentenced to hang on August 17, 1929, in the county jail at Ft. Lauderdale.

413. "Burglars in Office." Belle Glade _News_ 28 June 1929.

Reports the burglary of "the safe of the express company in the station at Clewiston." Valuable papers and bundles of checks were taken.

414. "Eddie Durant Sentenced for Theft of J.S. Reitz Belongings." Volusia County _Times_ 26 July 1929.

Durant, black, had stolen a quantity of household goods from the home of Joseph H. Reitz, president of the Orange City Bank.

415. "Site Where Florida Gang Was Killed is Now Paved and Almost Forgotten." Birmingham (AL) _News_ 26 July 1982.

Associated Press story, datelined Roseland, Fla. Covers the activities of the John Ashley gang of bank robbers/murderers who operated in the state between 1911 and 1924. Ashley and three gang members were killed in a gunbattle near Roseland, November 1924.

5
Georgia

Monographs

416. Alexander, Henry A. Some Facts about the Murder Notes in the Phagan Case. Privately printed, 1914. 28p. Illus.

417. Arnold, Reuben R. The Trial of Leo Frank; Reuben R. Arnold's Address to the Court in His Behalf. Baxley, GA: Classic Publishing Co., 1915. 69p. Intro. Alvin V. Sellers.

Arnold was one of Frank's defense attorneys.

418. Bruffey, E.C. A Georgia Jekyl and Hyde, being ...the story of how Thomas Edgar Stripling killed his man, was sentenced to life imprisonment, escaped from prison, became chief of police in Danville, Va., and after fourteen years of freedom under an assumed name, was apprehended, brought back to his native state, and, after making a most remarkable fight for pardon, is now serving his life term in the Georgia penitentiary. Atlanta: Appeal Publishing Co., 1911. 139p. Illus.

See Burns for similar story.

419. Burns, Robert E. I Am a Fugitive from a Georgia Chain Gang! New York: Vanguard, 1932. 257p. Rep. Detroit: Gale Research, 1972.

In 1922 Burns was forced at gunpoint to help two other men rob an Atlanta grocery store. Burns was arrested and drew a sentence on the chain gang. He escaped to Chicago, made himself a pillar of society, was re-arrested and returned to Georgia, where he escaped again. This book is the story of his bizarre career. Covers both life on the chain gang and as a magazine editor in Chicago. The basis for a famous film. No documentation, bibliography or index.

420. Connolly, Christopher Powell. The Truth about the Frank Case. New York: Vail-Ballou Co., 1915. 95p.

Based in part on Connolly's articles for Collier's.

421. Davis, Robert Scott Jr. The Georgia Black Book. Easley, SC: Southern Historical Press, 1982. 450p. Illus.

Intended as a genealogical sourcebook, this title indexes material in the Georgia Department of Archives and History. Crimes covered include horse theft and murder; records covered include governors' proclamation books. This book includes material from 1755 to 1900. Indexed.

422. Dinnerstein, Leonard. The Leo Frank Case. New York: Columbia University Press, 1968. 248p. Illus.

A meticulously-researched, well-written account of the Frank case. Based on the author's dissertation on the same subject. Heavily documented. Excellent bibliography. Index.

423. Dorsey, Hugh M. Argument of Hugh M. Dorsey, Solicitor General, Atlanta Judicial Circuit, at the Trial of Leo M. Frank, charged with the Murder of Mary Phagan. Macon, GA: N. Christophulos, 1914. 146p.

Dorsey was the victorious prosecutor in Frank's trial.

424. Erwin, Marion. The Land Pirates. A Narrative of the Great Conspiracy and Murder Case Recently Terminated in the Federal Court at Macon, Georgia. Savannah, GA: Morning News Press, 1891. 96p.

425. The Frank Case: Inside Story of Georgia's Greatest Murder Mystery. Atlanta: Atlanta Publishing, 1914.

Not listed in National Union Catalog Pre-1956 Imprints.

426. Gamble, Thomas. Savannah Duels and Duellists 1733-1877. Savannah, GA: Review Publishing and Printing Co., c1923. 302p. Illus.

Gamble's book lives up to its title in thorough, detailed examination of Savannah dueling. Numerous duels are discussed, and the book is highly readable. Unfortunately, documentation is totally lacking. Index.

427. Golden, Harry. A Little Girl is Dead. Cleveland: World, 1965. 363p. Illus.

Lengthy, readable examination of the Mary Phagan/Leo M. Frank case. An epilogue brings figures in the case up to 1965. Appendices include Georgia Governor John M. Slaton's commutation order. A useful feature is a list of major and minor characters involved. Less-than-adequate documentation. Selected bibliography. No index.

428. A History of the Capture of the Notorious Outlaw George Applewhite, Alias, Ranse Lowery, of the Lowery Gang of Outlaws, of Robeson County, N.C., Together with the Manner of His Capture, His Confessions...Written by the Captors Themselves. Columbus, GA: Thomas Gilbert, 1872. 12p. Illus.

The "George Applewhite" arrested was the wrong man. Reprinted in Edwards (#456).

429. National Association for the Advancement of Colored People. The Lynchings of May, 1918 in Brooks and Lowndes Counties, Georgia. An Investigation Made and Published by the National Association for the Advancement of Colored People. New York: NAACP, 1918. 6p.

430. O'Connor, John E., ed. I Am a Fugitive from a Chain Gang. Madison: University of Wisconsin Press, 1981. 197p. Illus.

Contains the shooting script for the 1932 Warner Brothers film of this title and other material. O'Connor's introduction includes a discussion of the life of Robert E. Burns, on whose book---I Am a Fugitive from a Georgia Chain Gang!---the movie was based. A section of notes outlines differences between the script and the finished film.

431. Roberts, DeWitt. The Story of Mass Hysteria. Atlanta: n.p., 1948.

Report on the Leo Frank case to the Anti-Defamation League (NY).

432. Samuels, Charles and Louise. Night Fell on Georgia. New York: Dell, 1956. 222p.

Covers Leo M. Frank/Mary Phagan case, 1913-5. Concludes that Phagan was actually murdered by Negro Janitor James Conley, whose perjured testimony convicted Frank.

433. Southern, Kate. The Sad Case of Mrs. Kate Southern! The Beautiful, Virtuous Georgia Wife, who, Being Maddened to Insanity by the Outrageous Taunts of a Bad Woman who had Enticed her Husband Away, Killed her...She was Arrested, Tried, Convicted and Sentenced to be Hung, notwithstanding... She Was about to Become a Mother Again! Her Sentence has been Commuted by Governor Colquit. Philadelphia: Old Franklin House, 1878, 60pp. Illus. Another ed., 31pp.

"This actual case arose from the murder of Narcissa Canart in Picken, Georgia. Public sentiment was unusually high and favored the defendant. This work is a mixture of fact and fiction." Thomas McDade, Annals of Murder (p. 265).

434. Thompson, Wytt Ephraim. A Short Review of the Frank Case. Atlanta: n.p., 1914. 32p.

435. Wells-Barnett, Ida B. Lynch Law in Georgia. Chicago: n.p., 1899.

Not listed in NUC Pre-1956 Imprints.

Dissertation

436. Dinnerstein, Leonard. "The Leo Frank Case." Ph.D. dissertation, Columbia University, 1966. 350p.

Covers murder of Mary Phagan in Atlanta in 1913 and trial and lynching of Leo Frank for the crime. See Dinnerstein's monograph on the case.

Theses

437. Rogers, William Curran. "A Comparison of the Coverage of the Leo Frank Case by the Hearst- Controlled Atlanta Georgian and the Home-Owned Atlanta Journal, April 28, 1913-August 30, 1913." M.A. thesis, University of Georgia, 1950. 108p.

Dissects coverage according to "News" and "Editorials." "News" is further examined according to headlines, tone, photographs and illustrations and space devoted to the case. Editorial tone and cartoons also examined. Includes summary of Mary Phagan's murder and subsequent events in the case. Documentation, bibliography.

438. Smith, Albert C. "Violence in Georgia's Black Belt: A Study of Crime in Baldwin and Terrell Counties, 1866-1899." M.A. thesis, University of Georgia, 1974. 172p.

Primarily generalized examination of crime and violence and their relations to cultural and economic factors. Some discussion of individual murders, acts of vigilantism, etc. Numerous tables give statistical information. Based primarily on newspaper articles. Documentation and bibliography.

Journal Articles

439. Almand, Bond. "The Ashburn Murder Case and Military Trial." Georgia Bar Journal 1947 August; 10(1): 43-8.

On March 30, 1868, George W. Ashburn, a Columbus, Ga., leader of "the radical element" of the Republican party, was murdered. On April 6 nine white and three black men were arrested for the crime by military authorities. Eight men were charged with murder; after a trial all were released. One of the men tried was William D. Chipley, who would be instrumental in the August 1877 Pensacola, Fla.,capture of Texas gunfighter John Wesley Hardin. No documentation.

440. Almand, Bond. "Code Duello in Georgia 1740-1889." Georgia Bar Journal 1950 November; 13:160-70.

Discusses a number of Georgia duels, most during the antebellum period. Poor documentation.

441. Asbury, Herbert. "Hearst Comes to Georgia." American Mercury 1926 January; 7:87-95.

Influence of William Randolph Hearst on Georgia journalism via his purchase in February 1912 of the Atlanta Georgian. Some discussion of the murder of his wife by Eugene Grace (1912? 1913?) and the Mary Phagan/Leo M. Frank case. No documentation.

442. Bonner, James C. "The Georgia Penitentiary at Milledgeville, 1817-1874." Georgia Historical Quarterly 1971 fall; 55:303-28.

Brief overview of the penitentiary "from its origin in the early 1800's through its transition to the chain gang and lease systems which came to characterize the post-war period" (p. 303). Some discussion of individual crimes and criminals, including 1816 horse thief Alfred Perry and Noyal Nelms, hanged in 1816 for counterfeiting. Documentation.

443. Bradley, F.W. "Little Mary Fagan (sic)." Southern Folklore Quarterly 1960 June; 24:144-6.

Two versions of a ballad based on the Mary Phagan/Leo M. Frank case, Atlanta, 1913-15. Sources were two South Carolina women. No documentation.

444. Bricker, L.O. "A Great American Tragedy." Shane Quarterly 1943 April; 4:89-95.

Covers Leo Frank case.

445. Colby, Elbridge. "Justice in Georgia." Nation 1926 July 14; 123:32-3.

Discusses murder of black infantryman, Private Smith, by E.J. Fulbright, a night watchman at a lumberyard in Americus, Ga. No documentation.

446. Coulter, E. Merton. "Alexander H. Stephens Challenges Benjamin H. Hill to a Duel." Georgia Historical Quarterly 1972; 56(2):175-92.

Describes a series of 1856 Georgia newspaper letters in which Stephens and Hill attacked each other, Stephens challenged Hill to a duel and Hill managed to avoid it "by a masterful use of logic and reason" (p. 176). Documentation.

447. Coulter, E. Merton. "Cudjo Fye's Insurrection." Georgia Historical Quarterly 1954 September; 38:213-5.

Describes black vigilante organization led by Fye in Jefferson Co., Ga., in August 1870. A group of armed blacks freed a fellow black "club" member from jail in Louisville; in the wake of this victory, Fye threatened great destruction if white authorities interfered with his band. Fye and others were finally caught and sentenced to jail. What Coulter describes as insurrection was indeed a capital crime in Ga. at the time. However, similar activity undertaken by whites is seldom described as insurrection. Documentation.

448. Coulter, E. Merton. "A Famous Duel that was Never Fought." Georgia Historical Quarterly 1959 December; 43:365-77.

Describes the supposed Ga. duel between Charles Tait and John M. Dooly, which never actually took place but which has been treated by various writers and historians as fact. Documentation.

449. Coulter, E. Merton. "Four Slave Trials in Elbert County, Georgia." Georgia Historical Quarterly 1957 September; 41(3):237-46.

The four trials took place between 1837 and 1849. Crimes were murder, burglary, attempted rape and arson. The criminals were three men and two women. Documentation.

450. Coulter, E. Merton. "The Great Georgia Railway Disaster Hoax on the London Times." Georgia Historical Quarterly 1972 spring; 56(1):25-50.

Explores the genesis and aftermath of an article written by John Arrowsmith concerning wholesale dueling aboard a passenger train in Georgia. Based on English and American newspaper articles. Fascinating. Well documented.

451. Coulter, E. Merton. "Hanging as a Socio-Penal Institution in Georgia and Elsewhere." Georgia Historical Quarterly 1973; 57(1):17-55.

Coulter's article discusses numerous Georgia murderers and hangings, from the execution of Alice Riley and Richard White in Savannah (1735) to that of Arthur Glover in Augusta (1908). Other hangings and crimes discussed include those of West Tate (1872), Byrd Brooks (1872), Nick Boswell (1873), Anna Hunt (1874), Enoch Spann and Susan Eberhart (1873), Jesse Williams (1882), Joseph C. Jones (1883) and Thomas G. Woolfolk (1890). Based primarily on newspaper articles.

452. Coulter, E. Merton. "The Woolfolk Murder." Georgia Historical Quarterly 1965; 49(2):115-56.

In the early morning hours of Aug. 6, 1887, Richard F. Woolfolk, his second wife Mattie, six children and Mattie's aunt were slaughtered in their beds with an ax. Richard's oldest son by his first marriage, Thomas G., was soon arrested for the Macon, Ga., crime. Thomas was tried and convicted; the verdict was appealed to the state supreme court, which ordered a new trial. Woolfolk was retried, re-convicted and hanged on October 29, 1890. Based primarily on contemporary newspaper accounts. This article was reprinted in the author's The Toombs Oak, The Tree that Owned Itself, and Other Chapters of Georgia (Athens, 1966), p. 174-211.

453. Daniel, Pete. "'We Are Going to Do Away With These Boys...'" American Heritage 1972 April; 23(3):42-7, 100-1.

Describes systematic peonage and murder on the 2,000 acre plantation of John S. Williams in Jasper Co., Ga., prior to 1921. Williams was finally arrested, tried in Covington, Ga., in April 1921. At least eleven black workers were murdered. Williams was found guilty of murder and sentenced to life imprisonment. Photographs of Williams and his black overseer Clyde Manning (also tried) are included. No documentation.

454. Daniell, Elizabeth Otto. "The Ashburn Murder Case in Georgia Reconstruction, 1868." Georgia Historical Quarterly 1975 fall; 59:296-312.

George W. Ashburn, a Scalawag, was shot to death by a group of disguised men in Columbus, Ga., on the night of March 31, 1868. Nine men were accused, their trial began and then ended when military rule in the state ceased. One of the accused, William D. Chipley, would later be involved in the capture of gunfighter John Wesley Hardin in Pensacola, Fla., August 1877. Well documented.

455. Davis, Robert S. "Georgia Murderers, Murders and Murder Victims, 1823-1840, from the Governor's Proclamations." Georgia Genealogical Society Quarterly 1979; 15(3):103-14.

456. Edwards, John C. "Harris County Bounty Men and the Ubiquitious Mr. Applewhite." Atlanta Historical Journal 1980 spring; 24(1):53-62.

Describes the "capture" of George Applewhite, a member of Henry Berry Lowry's N.C. gang of outlaws, in Hamilton, Ga., October 27, 1872. The man arrested was not Applewhite, who remained at large until July 5, 1875, when he was arrested in Goldsboro, N.C. Reprints rare pamphlet about the "capture." Documentation.

457. Edwards, John C. "Slave Justice in Four Middle Georgia Counties." Georgia Historical Quarterly 1973 summer; 57(2): 265-73.

Describes November 3, 1858, hanging of Henry Jackson in DeKalb Co. for attempted rape. Other specific crimes covered are burglary and attempted murder. Based on trial records. Documentation.

458. "End of the Frank Case." Outlook 1915 September 15; 111:114-5.

Brief note on lack of action by Georgia grand jury in lynching of Leo M. Frank. No documentation.

459. "The Frank Case." Outlook 1913 December 16; 108:859-60. Commentary on trial of Leo M. Frank. No documentation.

460. Haunton, Richard H. "Law and Order in Savannah, 1850-1860." Georgia Historical Quarterly 1972 spring; 56(1):1-24.

Generalized discussion of various types of criminal activity committed by blacks and whites during the decade. Well-documented, but covers too much ground and lacks specificity.

461. Henig, Gerald S. "'He Did Not Have a Fair Trial': California Progressives React to the Leo Frank Case." California History 1979; 58(2):166-78.

Covers response of progressive newspapers and spokesmen to the Frank case, 1913-1915. Documentation.

462. Hicks, Alfred H. "Tom Watson and the Arthur Glover Case in Georgia Politics." Georgia Historical Quarterly 1969 September; 53:265-86.

In Augusta on October 19, 1906, a white man named Arthur Glover shot and killed his lover Maud Dean. Glover was quickly tried and found guilty, but sentence was overturned by the state supreme court and a new trial ordered. Despite a plea of insanity, Glover was again found guilty; Thomas E. Watson became involved in the effort to get clemency. Glover was finally hanged on January 30, 1908. Documentation.

463. Holmes, William F. "Moonshining and Collective Violence: Georgia, 1889-1895." Journal of American History 1980 December; 67(3):589-611.

Discusses moonshining and White Cap vigilantism in five northern Georgia counties: Gilmer, Gordon, Murray, Pickens and Whitfield. Statistics on night rider attacks are included. Documentation.

464. Holmes, William F. "Whitecapping in Georgia: Carroll and Houston Counties, 1893." Georgia Historical Quarterly 1980 winter; 64(4):388-404.

Describes various episodes of vigilantism. Footnotes #16 gives citations of several Atlanta Constitution articles (1890-6) with "valuable information on the lives of moonshiners." Documentation.

465. Kurtz, Wilbur G. "The Murder of Tom Terry; a Sensational Crime of the Summer of 1861, that Occurred in Atlanta During the Period of Rejoicing that Followed the First Battle of Manassas." Atlanta Historical Bulletin 1936 November; 2 (9):39-49.

Describes early August 1861 murder in Atlanta of Thomas Terry by father and son John and James Wilson. John was convicted of manslaughter and James of murder; James was sentenced to hang December 13, 1861, but apparently the sentence was not carried out. No documentation.

466. Lack, Paul D. "Law and Disorder in Confederate Atlanta." Georgia Historical Quarterly 1982; 66(2):171-95.

Covers increase in Atlanta crime during Civil War. Types and number of crimes are given. Documentation.

467. Lamplugh, George R. "Thomas Carr and the Camden County 'War' of 1793." Atlanta Historical Bulletin 1976 fall; 20 (2):37-45.

Describes political maneuvering of Carr in Camden Co. and July 10, 1792, melee at the polls between two groups of armed men during which Abner Williams was shot and died. Documentation.

468. "Last Legal Stage of the Frank Case." Outlook 1915 April 28; 109:958-9.

Commentary on U.S. Supreme Court upholding conviction of Leo M. Frank. No documentation.

469. Lefever, Harry G. "Prostitution, Politics and Religion: The Crusade Against Vice in Atlanta in 1912." Atlanta Historical Journal 1980 spring; 24(1):7-29.

Primarily concerned with anti-prostitution campaign. Documentation includes newspaper articles that describe closing of houses of prostitution in Atlanta. Illustrated.

470. Levy, Eugene. "'Is the Jew a White Man?': Press Reaction to the Leo Frank Case, 1913-1915." Phylon 1974 June; 35:212-22.

471. McPherson, Robert, ed. "Georgia Slave Trials." American Journal of Legal History 1960; 4:257-84, 364-77.

Text of records of Elbert Co. Inferior Court, 1837, 1839, 1847, 1849. Crimes include murder, burglary, arson and attempted rape. At least one slave, a man named Peter, was hanged.

472. "Matrimony and Murder." National Police Gazette 1867 July 20; 22(1142):4.

Describes the July (?) 8 murder in Brunswick, Ga., of E. G. Westmoreland by E.J. Martin. Westmoreland had recently married a woman with whom Martin was in love.

473. Moseley, Charlton and Brogdon, Frederick. "A Lynching at Statesboro: The Story of Paul Reed and Will Cato." Georgia Historical Quarterly 1981 summer; 65(2): 104-18.

On July 28, 1904, all five members of the Henry Hodges family were murdered and their bodies burned in a fire at their home near Statesboro. Two blacks, Reed and Cato, were arrested, tried and publicly lynched on August 16. Documentation, primarily newspaper articles.

474. Moseley, Clement Charlton. "The Case of Leo M. Frank, 1913-1915." Georgia Historical Quarterly 1967 March; 51:42-62.

Covers Mary Phagan murder, trial and lynching of Leo Frank and political fallout in Georgia as a result. Well documented.

475. Murphy, Elmer R. "A Visit with Leo M. Frank in the Death Cell at Atlanta." Rhodes' Colossus 1915 March; p. 3-12.

476. National States Rights Party. The Thunderbolt: The White Man's Viewpoint (Birmingham, Ala.). 1961 February.

Entire issue of this right-wing publication devoted to the Leo M. Frank/Mary Phagan case. Illustrated.

477. "Outlaw State" Lynching of Leo M. Frank." Outlook 1915 August 25; 110:945-7.

Condemnation of the Frank lynching. No documentation.

478. Oxman, Daniel K. "California Reactions to the Leo Frank Case." Western States Jewish Historical Quarterly 1978; 10(3):216-224.

Primarily newspaper reactions. Documentation.

479. Parks, Edd Winfield. "When Paul Hamilton Hayne Fought a Duel." Georgia Review 1957 spring; 11:80-4.

Brief article describes the duel fought by poet Hayne in the summer of 1855 near Marietta, Ga. Poor documentation.

480. "The Prosecution of Leo M. Frank." Frost's Magazine 1913 August; 1:1-4.

481. Roberts, Derrell. "Duel in the Georgia State Capitol." Georgia Historical Quarterly 1963 December; 47(4):420-4.

On March 11, 1879, Robert A. Alson was killed by Edward Cox in the State Treasurer's office. The dispute arose over the convict lease system, which Alston opposed and which Cox used to his financial advantage. Cox was found guilty, given a life sentence and soon pardoned. Documentation.

482. Schmitz, R.M. "Leo Frank and Mary Phagan." Journal of American Folklore 1947; 60:59-61.

Includes fourteen stanzas of "Little Mary Phagan" as sung by Joy May Creasy of Lebanon, Ky. Story in the ballad is set in Lebanon. Documentation.

483. "Serious Robberies." National Police Gazette 1846 August 8; 1(48):402.

Describes recent robberies in Harris Co. and Hancock Co., Ga. in the former $12-15,000 was taken; in the latter a William Watts was robbed of $4000.

484. Shingleton, Royce Gordon. "The Trial and Punishment of Slaves in Baldwin County, Georgia, 1812-26." Southern Humanities Review 1974 Winter; 8(1):67-73.

Describes fourteen capital cases of murder, arson, rape, assault and burglary. Six slaves were hanged as a result of their crimes. Documentation.

485. "The Stark-Minis Duel, August 10, 1832." American Jewish Archives 1955 January; 7:73-81.

Excerpts from diaries and a letter that describe the Savannah, Ga., duel in which James Jones Stark was killed by Dr. Philip Minis.

486. Swann, Lee Ann Caldwell. "An Averted Duel: Augusta, 1843." Georgia Historical Quarterly 1981 winter; 65(4):323-8.

Describes political differences between J.W. Jones and James Gardner which almost led to a duel. Documentation.

487. Train, Arthur. "Did Leo Frank Get Justice?" _Everybody's_ 1915 March; 33:314-7.

Discusses trial of Frank. Train asserts the facts in the Mary Phagan murder case pointed to black janitor James Conley, rather than Frank. Includes photo of Frank. Published prior to Frank's lynching. No documentation.

488. "Why Was Frank Lynched' Was It Race Hatred, Dirty Politics, Yellow Journalism?" _The Forum_ 1916 December; 56: 677-92.

Written "By a Public Man of Georgia," this article is an expose of the dynamics behind Leo M. Frank's conviction and lynching for Mary Phagan's murder in Atlanta. The author is especially condemnatory of the roles of the Atlanta newspapers and Thomas E. "Tom" Watson in the case. The author claims unequivacally that Frank was innocent. No documentation.

489. Wise, Stephen S. "The Case of Leo Frank: A Last Appeal." _Free Synagogue Pulpit_ 1915 May; 4:79-96.

Miscellaneous

490. Bonner, James C. _Milledgeville, Georgia's Antebellum Capital_. Athens: University of Georgia Press, c1978. 307p. Illus.

Chapter 5, "Municipal Regulation: Slaves and Citizens" (p. 103-21) covers prostitution, rape, hanging, attempted murder, etc. Some mention of specific criminals. Documentation. Bibliography. Index.

491. Busch, Francis X. _Guilty or Not Guilty?_ Indianapolis: Bobbs-Merrill, c1952. 287p.

One of four cases covered is Leo M. Frank's (p. 15-74). Not recommended. No documentation, bibliography or index.

492. Carter, Isabel Gordon. "Songs and Ballads from Tennessee and North Carolina." _Journal of American Folklore_ 1933; 46:22-50.

Lyrics only. Includes "Little Mary Phagan." Documentation.

493. Caughey, John W. _Their Majesties the Mob_. Chicago: University of Chicago Press, c1960. 214p.

Reprints various documents concerned with history of lynching in the U.S. Sources given. "Mr. Justice Holmes Dissents" (p. 110-3) contains Oliver Wendell Holmes dissenting opinion in the Leo M. Frank case. Index.

494. Churchhill, Allen. A Pictorial History of American Crime 1849-1929. New York: Holt, Rinehart and Winston, c1964. 180p. Illus.

Brief entries on numerous well-known crimes. Chapter 31, "Judge Lynch Presiding" (p. 108-11), gives a short overview of the Mary Phagan murder/Leo M. Frank lynching. No documentation or bibliography. Index.

495. Cooper, Walter G. Official History of Fulton County. Atlanta(?): History Commission, c1934. 912p. Illus.

Pages 235-9 discuss the March 30, 1868, murder of George W. Ashburn in Columbus, Ga. No documentation or bibliography. Index.

496. Hertzberg, Steven. Strangers within the Gate City; The Jews of Atlanta, 1845-1915. Philadelphia: Jewish Publication Society of America, c1978. 325p. Illus.

Chapter 9, "The Leo Frank Case" (p. 202-15), summarizes that case. Includes reaction of Atlanta Jewish community. Selected bibliography. Documentation and index.

497. Holmes, Oliver Wendell. The Dissenting Opinions of Mr. Justice Holmes. New York: Vanguard, c1929. 314p.

Pages 58-63 contain Holmes' opinion in the Leo M. Frank case.

498. Jaher, Frederick C., ed. The Age of Industrialism in America. New York: Free Press, 1968.

Chapter 5 (p. 127-57) is Leonard Dinnerstein's "Atlanta in the Progressive Era: A Dreyfus Affair in Georgia." The chapter examines the Mary Phagan murder/Leo Frank lynching, 1913 and 1915. Documentation. See Dinnerstein (#422).

499. The Jeffersonian (Thomson, Ga.), January 30, 1913-June 30, 1919.

Weekly newspaper edited by populist Georgia politician Thomas E. Watson. Numerous issues contain material on the Mary Phagan/Leo M. Frank case.

500. Jenkins, James S. Murder in Atlanta! Sensational Crimes That Rocked the Nation. Atlanta: Cherokee, 1981. 200p. Illus.

Chapter 1, "A Miscellany of Early Twentieth Century Murders" contains some material on pre-1930 cases. How a book with this title can ignore the Mary Phagan/Leo Frank case---the most famous in Atlanta and Georgia history---is beyond me. No documentation or index.

501. Jones, Mary G. and Reynolds, eds. and comps. Coweta County Chronicles for One Hundred Years. Atlanta, GA: Stein Printing Co., 1928. 869p. Rep. Easley, S.C.: Southern Historical Press, 1975.

Year-by-year chronicles include material on robberies, murder and executions, including the hangings of Harrison Sutherland for killing J. Hillsman (1834), William Harris for killing J. McCollum (1847) and the lynching of a black, Alex Brown, charged with rape (1882). No documentation or bibliography. Index.

502. Knight, Lucian Lamar. Georgia's Landmarks, Memorials and Legends. Atlanta, GA: privately printed by Byrd Printing Co., 1913-14. 2 vols. Illus.

Section 1, Vol. 2, is "Under the Code Duello" (p. 1-48). A number of duels involving Georgians are discussed. Includes reprint of Atlanta Constitution article by Gordon Noel Hurtel, an eyewitness to the South's last formal duel, that of August 10, 1889, between J.R. Williamson and Patrick Calhoun. This account says the duel was fought 2-3 miles east of Cedar Bluff, Ala., Documentation. Index.

503. Leonard, William Ellery. The Lynching Bee and Other Poems. New York: B.W. Huebsch, 1920. 84p.

Contains a poem entitled "Leo Frank" (p. 27), based on the Frank case. Title poem (p. 11-26), although given no specific setting, is probably intended to describe a southern lynching. Title poem also printed in Nation 1920 December 29; 111:778-81.

504. Pendleton, Albert S., Jr. and Thomas, Susan McKey. In Search of the Hollidays: The Story of Doc Holliday and His Holliday Families. Valdosta, GA: Little River Press, c1973. Illus.

This book explores the life in Georgia of John H. "Doc" Holliday before his move to the west and fame around 1873. Chapter 5, "Tell Us Little Rivers," describes the "Swimming hole" episode in which "Doc" either shot over the heads of some blacks using his swimming hole or shot and killed one or more of them. The book is well-documented and contains both footnotes and bibliography but no index.

505. Stokes, Thomas L. The Savannah. New York: Rinehart and Co., c1951. 401p. Rep. Athens: University of Georgia Press, 1982.

Part 4, chapter 3, "It was a Famous Feud," (p. 138-54) covers the 1777 duel on the outskirts of Savannah, Ga., between General Lachlan McIntosh and Button Gwinnett. A long-simmering feud finally erupted when McIntosh insulted Gwinnett at a public meeting. Both men were slightly wounded, but poor medical care led to Gwinnett's death three days after the encounter.

506. Warren, Mary Bondurant. Marriages and Deaths, 1763 to 1820 Abstracted from Extant Georgia Newspapers. Danielsville, GA: Heritage Papers, c1968. 2 vols.

Some notations of causes of deaths, including murder. Index by name and place only.

507. Woodward, C. Vann. Tom Watson: Agrarian Rebel. New York: Macmillan, 1938. 430p. Rep. Savannah, GA: Beehive Press, c1973.

Chapter 23, "The Lecherous Jew" (p. 373-89) is devoted to Thomas E. Watson's role in the Leo Frank case, 1913-15. Documentation. Bibliography. Index.

Newspaper Articles

508. "Daring Robbery---Arrest of the Thief." Charleston (SC) Daily Courier 9 March 1854. Rep. Savannah Morning News.

Actually describes two Savannah robberies.

509. "Homicide in Sparta, Ga." New Orleans (LA) Daily Picayune, 22 April 1856.

This brief article notes the death by gunshot of B.R. Gardner, "a well known and respected citizen of Milledgeville." Gardner was in Sparta, his former residence, on business and was shot by O.J. Powell. A quote from the Savannah News concerning the murder is given.

510. "Important Arrests." Savannah Morning News 3 January 1872.

Reports the apprehension in Savannah of "the black thieves who for some time past have been committing robberies in this city..."

511. "The Valdosta Tragedy." Savannah Morning News, January 8, 1872. Related article January 11.

This article describes an encounter in Valdosta between William Roberts and the DeLoach brothers, Hemph and Riley. The men met on the street and Hemph slapped Roberts in the face; Roberts replied by shooting both men and wounding them seriously. "(F)or several years there has existed a family feud," and the motive for the shooting was believed to lie in that direction.

512. "Another Stabbing Affray." Savannah Morning News, January 10, 1872. Related articles January 11, 12.

This brief article describes the stabbing of one black by another in Savannah. The second article notes that Mitchell Cogden had stabbed Derry Warwick, who died the next day. Cogden escaped. The third article notes that Cogden was later found by a group of armed blacks, who "would have lynched or shot him without ceremony" if Mr. Chappell, the leader of the group, had not prevented them from doing so.

513. "A Cotton Thief Jailed." Savannah Morning News 3 February 1872.

Notes the operation of a gang of cotton thieves in Savannah and the arrest of one of them, a black woman named Sarah Miller.

514. "Arrest of E.F. Blodgett." Savannah Morning News 5 February 1872. Rep. Atlanta Constitution.

Notes the arrest of Blodgett and a hearing on the charge of embezzlement of funds of the "State Road."

515. "Murder at Springfield Plantation." Savannah Morning News 7 March 1872.

Notes the murder of Reuben Ross by another black, Albert Young. Young was still at large; the crime occurred near Savannah.

516. "The Spirit of Incendiarism Aboard." Savannah Morning News 9 March 1872.

Reports on an arson attempt at the saw mill owned by T.L. Kinsey on Hutchinson's Island. The fire was discovered and put out by a night watchman.

517. "A Bold Robbery." Savannah Morning News 20 March 1872.

Reports on a gang of robbers led by C.V. Hamilton and operating in McDuffie Co. The gang's most recent robbery at Thomson is described.

518. "The Recent Homicide." Savannah Morning News 4 May 1872.

Reports on the preliminary hearing in Savannah of Richard Wickham and three others charged with the murder of Michael Burke.

519. "A Shooting Affray." Savannah Morning News 7 May 1872.

Reports the unsuccessful attempt in Savannah by Arthur Parkhill to shoot John Bohan, with whom he had been arguing.

520. "Georgia News." Columbus Daily Enquirer-Sun 3 July 1877.

London Brown, who shot and killed Sam Hayes near Barnwell, had been arrested by police in Augusta. John Gamble, 16, was in jail at Wadley for murdering his brother. Four blacks escaped from the Twiggs Co. jail, including Peyton Jones, under death sentence for the murder of Peyton Chapman.

521. "Georgia News." Columbus Daily Enquirer-Sun 11 July 1877.

One item reports on the speech of the "boy" Thomason, hung in LaGrange a few days earlier for the murder of two children.

522. "Murdered and Burned." Nashville Banner 12 September 1884.

This article describes the murder in Augusta, Ga., of the night watchman William Vales, at the street railway office. Vales' killer attacked him with a pickaxe and then attempted to burn the body and building. Thirty-eight dollars was taken from a desk in the room.

523. "Sentenced to Hang." Nashville Banner 20 September 1884.

This article covers the sentencing of Henry Cato for the January 1883 murder of Jack Dukes on the outskirts of Decatur, Ga.

524. "D.D. Doyal Murdered." Atlanta Constitution 1 January 1885.

Bill Oliver, black, murdered Loyal when the latter attempted to break up a fight between Oliver and Loyal's son Ed. The murder occurred near Fairburn, Ga., in Campbell Co.

525. "Filled with Lead." Nashville (TN) Banner 1 August 1885.

This article describes the shooting by four masked men of Jack Hopkins, a black prisoner in the Monticello jail. Hopkins was being held for the murder of his employer, wealthy planter George Gilmore.

526. "Deeds of Outlawry." Nashville (TN) Banner 29 August 1885.

This short article notes the arrest of seventeen men for the robbery and dynamiting of a store in Crane Eater, near Calhoun, Ga. The crime was blamed on "a disreputable gang who have been infesting that locality."

527. "Alabama Men Killed." Birmingham (AL) Daily News 15 May 1890.

This article describes a gunfight in Columbus, Ga., between Louis Smith and Ed Elkin, both travelling salesman. "...there had been bad blood between the two men for nearly two years, and...there is a woman in the case." Elkin was killed in the fight.

528. "Georgia Train Robbery." Birmingham (AL) Age-Herald 4 December 1891.

Two men, "wearing slouch hats and long overcoats and black masks," robbed the East Tennessee train as it left Atlanta Junction on its way to Selma, Ala. The men got very little money (around $50), but the crime was described as a "neat and skillful job."

529. "Murder and Robbery." Columbus Enquirer-Sun 5 January 1892. Related articles January 6,7,8.

Dr. J.H.M. Barrett and his wife were beaten in their home eight miles west of Griffin, Ga. A small amount of money was taken. Mrs. Barrett died, and the doctor was seriously wounded.

530. "Eight Men Killed." Columbus Enquirer-Sun 6 January 1892.

Ed Williams and John Parker argued over cheating in a card game. Parker began shooting; before the gunfight was over, he, Williams and six other men were dead. The fight took place in Homerville, Ga., in Clinch Co.

531. "For Murdering Young Kiser." Leesburg (FL) Commercial 8 April 1892.

Datelined Fairburn, April 4. "Walter Cook, a negro, was hanged here at 11 o'clock Friday forenoon for killing Andrew Kiser, a well-known planter, last October. Cook ascended the gallows proffering readiness to die and an assurance of a bright heaven. His neck was broken by the fall. The execution was public and 10,000 people are estimated to have witnessed it.

532. "Nunnally is Free." Leesburg (FL) Commercial 8 April 1892.

Reports the release of Will Nunnally and two other men at Griffin in their trial for the "horrible murder of the aged Barrett couple." The prosecution had no case against the men.

533. "Murderer Spencer Hanged." Daily Florida Citizen (Jacksonville, FL) 2 March 1894.

Reports the execution in Thomasville March 1 of Henry Spencer, black, for the April 1893 murder of his brother-in-law Mose Green.

534. "A Bold Train Robbery." New York Times 27 June 1894.

Describes the June 26 robbery near Homerville by "six masked white men." The amount taken was $1222 in cash. The robbers headed toward the Okefenokee Swamp with a posse in pursuit.

535. "Ticket Forgeries on a Large Scale." New Orleans (LA) Daily Picayune 4 October 1896.

J. Todd was arrested in Atlanta for trying to sell forged railroad tickets.

536. "James Campbell Convicted of Murdering His Brother." New Orleans (LA) Daily Picayune 5 October 1896.

In Monticello, Campbell was convicted in the death of his brother William.

537. "Mistrial in the McEachin Murder Case." New Orleans (LA) Daily Picayune 5 October 1896.

Ed McEachin was on trial in Baxley for the murder of his brother Charley.

538. "Bound for Arson." Raleigh (NC) Gazette 31 October 1896.

"J.S. Brady, who is in jail in Dublin, Ga., was arrested on a charge of conspiracy to defraud insurance companies by committing arson...Brady is a notorious character..."

539. "A Georgia Lynching." Raleigh (NC) Gazette 30 January 1897.

Reports the lynching at Jeffersonville (Twiggs Co.) of two blacks, Charles Forsythe and Willis White. A "masked mob of 100 men" lynched the pair for the murder of a Mrs. Rowland.

540. "Address from the Gallows." New York Times 17 April 1897 (p. 7).

Reports the hanging at Wadley on April 16 of Professor Lovett Brookins, black. Brookins had been convicted of murdering his mistress, Leila McCrary and another black man, Sanders Oliphant. The text of his speech to the crowd is given. Brookins had been defended at his trial by populist politician Tom Watson.

541. "Flanagan Found Guilty." Raleigh (NC) Gazette 7 August 1897.

At Decatur Edwin Flanagan was found guilty of the December 31, 1896, murders of Nancy Allen and Ruth Slack. He was sentenced to hang on August 25.

542. "White Men to Be Hanged." Raleigh (NC) Gazette 28 August 1897. Related article October 2.

Bud Brooks and Grady Reynolds were convicted at Jeffersonville (Jackson Co.) for the murder of M.C. Hunt and sentenced to hang September 24. The second article reports the hanging was delayed due to the confession of Reynolds.

543. "Father's Terrible Vengeance." Raleigh (NC) Gazette 4 September 1897.

C.E. Womble found E.E. Low compromising the former's daughter; Womble "beat his brains out with a stone." The murder occurred in Talbot Co.

544. "Murdered in the Public Road." Raleigh (NC) Gazette 16 October 1897.

W.H. Harris and his son Robert met J.H. Neismith on the road in Moultrie and shot him to death.

545. "Merchant Thieves." Raleigh (NC) Gazette 30 October 1897.

Notes the sentencing of Walter Bohannon and members of his gang at Dalton, Ga. The group had systematically looted cars of the Southern Railway over a period of five years. A number of merchants were also convicted of receiving stolen goods. Names of gang members and merchants are given.

546. "Told in a Paragraph." Raleigh (NC) Gazette 6 November 1897.

One item notes that Taylor Delke, "a Georgia outlaw," pleaded guilty to murder at McDonough.

547. "Shot and Brained in a Potato Patch." Raleigh (NC) Gazette 20 November 1897.

Henry Turner, his wife and sister were murdered in Campbell Co.

548. "Mrs. Nobles Must Hang." Raleigh (NC) Gazette 11 December 1897.

She was convicted of killing her husband and had appealed her death sentence to the U.S. Supreme Court. That court had refused to overturn the sentence.

549. "Soldiers May Not Be Able to Protect Prisoners." New Orleans (LA) Daily-Picayune 10 January 1898.

In Dawson Jack Ingram, white, and three of his black employees were on trial for the murder of Julian King, "a prominent planter." A mob of 150 men was determined to lynch the four, and the trial was delayed until soldiers could arrive.

550. "The Right Man Hanged." Raleigh (NC) Gazette 15 January 1898.

Reports the hanging of Simon Hopkins (black) for murder at Bainbridge.

551. "Negro Beats Off a Posse." Memphis (TN) Commercial Appeal, October 19, 1908.

Datelined Lithonia, Ga., October 18, this article describes the search by posses for Charlie Mitchell. Mitchell, wanted for attempted murder, shot and killed a bailiff and a young white man and badly beat a deputy sheriff. The three men had come to his home with a warrant to arrest him.

552. "Dying, He Killed Both." Memphis (TN) Commercial Appeal, October 30, 1908.

Datelined Lafayette, Ga., October 29, this article describes a gunbattle between Sheriff John Carlock and John and Charles Henderson. The sheriff was attempting to serve a warrant on the two brothers, operators of a local coal mine, when the men opened fire. Before dying, Carlock managed to shoot and kill both Hendersons.

553. "Mormons Fear the Black Hand; Montreal, Ga., in Terror; Postmaster Appeals to Governor for Protection; Recently a Morman Church was Burned and Deed is Followed by 'Black Hand' Letters to Members. Elders Forced to Flee." Memphis (TN) Commercial Appeal 26 November 1908.

This article describes the on-going battle between members of the "mob and the Mormon Church in a small town eight miles from Atlanta. The problems arose because ten Mormon families refused to join the "mob."

554. "Probe Lynching of Columbus Negro." Birmingham (AL) Age-Herald 24 August 1912.

This brief article notes that a county grand jury in Columbus, Ga., has begun an investigation of the lynching of T.S. McEkhanes, "a negro boy." McEkhanes, "who had been convicted of killing a white boy," was taken from jail by a mob and lynched.

555. "Express Robbery Still Mystery to Detectives; No Arrests Made and None of Missing Money is Located." Montgomery (AL) Advertiser 13 September 1913.

This brief article concerns a robbery of almost $72,000 from a portable safe being transported from New York to Savannah via train. No arrests had been made and none of the money located.

556. "Bad Feeling Over Killing in Georgia." Spartanburg (SC) Journal 12 July 1920.

Reports the arrest of Floyd Dedge and E. Sandford at Alma, Ga., for the Murder of Judge C.J. Medders. The Dedge and Medders families had had "bad feeling between them" for some time.

557. "Printer Charged with Bank Robbery." Spartanburg (SC) Journal 31 July 1920.

Charles L. Davenport, white, and Sonny Zant, black, were arrested in Brunswick, Ga., for the January 11 robbery of the Glynn County bank. Several Liberty bonds and a large quantity of valuables were stolen.

6

Louisiana

Monographs

558. Arthur, Stanly Clisby. Jean Laffite, Gentleman Rover. New Orleans: Harmanson, c1952. 291p. Illus.

Examines Lafitte's patriotic/piratical career. Claims that Lafitte died of pneumonia on May 5, 1854, at Alton, Ill. Most previous versions of Lafitte's death have the event occur in the Yucatan in 1826 and the cause as fever. Author claims access to much Lafitte family material "never before published." No documentation. Bibliography. Index.

559. Asbury, Herbert. The French Quarter; An Informal History of the New Orleans Underworld. New York: Knopf, c1936. Rep. Garden City, New York: Garden City Publishing, 1938. 462p.

Includes material on Jean Lafitte, John Murrell, David Hennessy, dueling, gambling, lynching, prostitution, various murders, etc. Fascinating. No documentation. Long bibliography. Index.

560. Barde, Alexandre. Histoire des Comites de Vigilance aux Attakapas... Saint-Jean Baptiste (Louisiana) Impr. du Meschacebe et de l'Avant-coureur, 1861. 428p.

French ed. Translation and edited version by Henrietta G. Rogers.

561. Barde, Alexandre. The Vigilante Committees of the Attakapas: An Eyewitness Account of Banditry and Backlash in Southwestern Louisiana. Lafayette, LA: Acadiana Press, 1981. 307pp. Ed. and annotated by David C. Edmonds and Dennis A. Gibson, trans. by Henrietta Guilbeau Rogers.

An abridged translation from the French of Barde's Histoire des Comites de Vigilance aux Attakapas (1861); Rogers' translation originally done for her M.A. thesis at Louisiana State University (1936). Barde participated in the Lafayette Parish movement; his account is thus a rare, first-hand one of southern vigilantis. Documentation, index.

562. Bellocq, E.J. Storyville Portraits: Photographs from the New Orleans Red Light District, circa 1912. New York: Museum of Modern Art, 1970. 17p. Illus.

Contains thirty-three plates. Catalog of an exhibition. Ed. by John Szarkowski. Preface by Lee Friedlander.

563. Coulter, Ellis Merton, ed. The Other Half of Old New Orleans; Sketches of Characters and Incidents From the Recorder's Court of New Orleans in the Eighteen Forties as Reported in The Picayune. University: Louisiana State University Press, 1939. 108p. Illus.

Sketches cover primarily minor crimes, such as prostitution ("Fancy Ladies," p. 29-32), drunkenness, fighting, disturbing the peace, etc. Dates of Picayune issues are given. No index.

564. The Dark and Terrible Deeds of George Lathrop, Who, after Passing Through the Various Degrees of Crime, was Finally Convicted and Hung in New Orleans June 5, 1848. For the Robbery and Murder of his Father, March 8, 1847. New Orleans: W. Stuart, 1848. 31p. Illus.

565. Dobson, Charles M. Guilty? Side Lights on the Batson Case; A Recrudescense of the Murder of the Earll Family in Louisiana, 1902. New Orleans: L. Graham Co., 1903. 112p. Illus. 2nd. ed.

On February 12, 1902, Ward Earll and his family---his wife and three children---were shot to death in their home near Lake Charles (Calcasieu Parish), La. The bodies were not discovered for twelve days. In the meantime, Earll's mules, horses and buggy were left at a stable in Lake Charles; evidence found in the buggy implicated Albert Edward Batson in the crime. Most of this book reports on Batson's two trials, esp. the second. Batson was found guilty and at the time of publication was under a death sentence. Dobson points out numerous discrepancies in the evidence. Fascinating. No documentation. No index.

566. Gambino, Richard. Vendetta: A True Story of the Worst Lynching in America, the Mass Murder of Italian-Americana in New Orleans in 1891, the Vicious Motivations Behind It, and the Tragic Repercussions That Linger to this Day. Garden City, New York: Doubleday, 1977. 198p. Illus.

The March 14, 1891, lynching of 11 Italian-Americans resulte ostensibly from the public's reaction to the trial of some of police chief David C. Hennessy's accused murderers. Hennessy was assasinated on October 15, 1890. Gambino contends that Hennessy's death was just the excuse needed--or manufactured---by the New Orleans economic and political elite to control the "unmanageable and intractable" Sicilian labor force. This lynching is perhaps the only one in American history to become an international incident. Highly readable, but Gambino's documentation consists only of a bibliography. No index.

567. Hair, William Ivy. Carnival of Fury: Robert Charles and the New Orleans Race Riot of 1900. Baton Rouge: Louisiana State University Press, c1976. 216p. Illus.

On Monday, July 23, 1900, an encounter between two black men and three police officers touched off one of the most violent episodes in New Orleans history. One of the blacks, Robert Charles, reacted to the meeting by wounding one of the policemen with his pistol. Charles escaped, and the manhunt began. Charles was finally located at his rooming house; he promptly killed two policemen and escaped again, this time to the nearby home of friends. Charles remained at this house while the hunt continued and twelve hours of rioting occurred on Thursday, July 26. After a day-long seige on Friday, Charles was finally killed. This book examines Charles' life prior to the New Orleans events, as well as those events. The murders committed by Charles, and the "race riot" that resulted, are good examples of how closely intwined criminal activity and racial animosity could become in the South of that era. Contains a bibliographic essay and index.

568. Hearsey, Clem G. The Six Who Were Hanged. New Orleans: n.p., 1924. 29p. Illus.

By an eyewitness to hanging of six Italians, Amite, La., May 9, 1924.

569. Hunter, Theresa M. The Saga of Jean Lafitte. San Antonio, TX: Naylor, c1940. 89p. Illus.

Simplistic version of the high spots of Lafitte's patriotic/piratical career. No documentation, bibliography or index.

570. Laffite, Jean. The Journal of Jean Laffite: The Privateer-Patriot's Own Story. New York: Vantage, c1958.

Supposedly written by Laffite in retirement between 1845 and 1850, twenty or more years after he was presumed to have died (1826). The illustrations include daguerreotypes of Laffite taken in 1839 and 1849 and a page of the manuscript, the paper of which was authenticated by the Library of Congress. Copyright held by "John A. Laffite." Probably spurious; Vantage Press is a subsidy publisher. No documentation, bibliography of index.

571. Lafitte. New York: n.p., 1828. 106p.

572. Landry, Stuart. Duelling in Old New Orleans. New Orleans: Harmanson, c1950. 48p. Illus.

Covers various duels and challenges, 1805-1908. Notes that final duel in the city took place in the City Park Oaks on June 22, 1889; H.S. Salvant and E.J. LeBreton were the parties. No documentation, bibliography or index.

573. Louisiana. Courts: Superior criminal court. Superior Criminal Court for the Parish of Orleans. State of Louisiana vs. J. Madison Wells, Thomas C. Anderson, Gadane Casanavee, Louis M. Kenner. Full Proceedings of the Trial of Thomas C. Anderson. Reported by T. Wharton Collen, Jr. New Orleans: 1878. 183p.

Trial for perjury and forgery.

574. Reeves, Thurman W., ed. From the Scarlet Past of Fabulous New Orleans: Souvenir Edition of the World Famous Tenderloin Directory "The Bluebook," with a Brief Story of Storyville. New Orleans: n.p., 1951. 20p. Illus.

Excerpts from Lulu White's 1906 bluebook giving descriptions of herself and the jazz musicians who played at her Octaroon Club bordello.

575. Rose, Al. Storyville, New Orleans; Being an Authentic, Illustrated Account of the Notorious Red-Light District. University: University of Alabama Press, c1974. 225p. Illus.

Exhaustive study of prostitution, jazz and life in Storyville. Profusely illustrated with photographs, some by Ernest J. Bellocq. Includes list of jazz musicians who played the district, locations of houses and names of their madams, etc. Poor documentation. Bibliographical note. Index.

576. Rubio Mane, Jorge Ignacio. Los Pirates Lafitte. Mexico City: Editorial Polis, 1938. 240p.

577. Saxon, Lyle. Lafitte, the Pirate. New York: Century, c1930. 307p. Illus. French ed. 1936.

History of the smuggler, pirate and hero of the Battle of New Orleans. Saxon accepts Lafitte's death by fever in the Yucatan, 1826. No documentation or index. Bibliography.

578. Tallant, Robert. Ready to Hang: Seven Famous New Orleans Murders. New York: Harper, 1952. 241p.

By the author of the classic Voodoo in New Orleans (1946). Covers murders between 1883 and 1933. Cases include David Hennessy assasination (1890), Elise Crawford poisoning (1911), Etienne Deschamps' 1892 execution for the murder of Juliette Deitsch. No documentation or index. One-page bibliography.

579. Thompson, Ray M. The Land of Lafitte the Pirate. New Orleans: Bormon House, c1943. 128p. Illus.

Describes the activities and locale of operations of Jean and Pierre Lafitte and their associates. No documentation or index. "Acknowledgements" page lists a few sources.

580. U.S. Department of State. Correspondence in Relation to the Killing of Prisoners in New Orleans on March 14, 1891. Washington, DC: Government Printing Office, 1891. 109p.

Theses

581. Adams, Margaret. "Mafia Riots in New Orleans." M.A. thesis, Tulane University, 1924.

582. Carroll, Richard Lewis. "The Impact of David C. Hennessy on New Orleans Society and the Consequence of the Assasination of Hennessy." M.A. thesis, Notre Dame Seminary (New Orleans), 1957.

Dissertations

583. Botein, Barbara. "The Hennessy Case: An Episode in American Nativism, 1890." Ph.D. dissertation, New York University, 1975. 246p.

Covers October 1890 murder of David C. Hennessy, New Orleans Police Chief, and March 1891 lynching of 11 Italians believed responsible. Aftermath of these events, which cause a diplomatic crisis between U.S. and Italy, also described.

584. Karlin, Jules Alexander. "The Italo-American Incident of 1891." Ph.D. dissertation, 1941. 421p.

585. Vyhnanek, Louis Andrew. "The Seamier Side of Life: Criminal Activity in New Orleans During the 1920s." Ph.D. dissertation, Louisiana State University, 1979. 337p.

Includes coverage of gambling and prostitution in addition to other criminal activities.

Journal Articles

586. Anderson, John Q. "Drinking, Fighting, and Fooling---Sidelights of the Social History of Antebellum Louisiana." Louisiana History 1964 winter; 5(1): 29-40.

Some discussion of dueling, including the Vidalia Sand Bar duel of 1827 near Natchez, Miss., involving James Bowie and numerous others. Also covers the role of liquor and practical jokes. Documentation.

587. Asbury, Herbert. "Gambling Hells of New Orleans." American Mercury 1936 August; 38:407-16

Discussion of nineteenth century gamblers in New Orleans and up and down the Mississippi River, including George DeVol, Jimmy Fitzgerald and William "Canada Bill" Jones. No documentation.

588. Augustin, John. "The Oaks---The Old Duelling Grounds of New Orleans." Art and Letters 1887 August; 1(4):123-34.

Claims that New Orleans famous dueling ground was first used in 1834. Individual duels are mentioned or discussed, but details and dates are given for few of them. Illustrated. No documentation.

589. Bollaert, William. "Life of Jean Lafitte, the Pirate of the Mexican Gulf." Littell's Living Age 1852 March 6; 32:433-46.

Apparently rep. from United States Magazine. Jaundiced view of Lafitte's patriotism, character and courage. Discusses Lafitte's piratical activities and role in the war of 1812 against the British. Accepts Lafitte's death in the Yucatan, 1826. No documentation.

590. Botein, Barbara. "The Hennessy Case: An Episode of Anti-Italian Nativism." Louisiana History 1979 summer; 20: 261-79.

Overview of the murder of New Orleans police chief David Hennessy (October 1890) the trial of the accused Italians and the lynching of eleven in March 1891. Notes that the case arose out of native southerners intense dislike of Italian immigrants, who were very insular in their affairs. Documentation.

591. Bryce, James. "Legal and Constitutional Aspects of the Lynching at New Orleans." Living Age 1891 June 6; 189: 579-85.

Essay on legal and other aspects of March 1891 lynching of eleven Italians in New Orleans. "Lynching is the natural and almost the necessary outcome of a state of things in which justice cannot be secured." No documentation.

592. "Buried Treasure of Jean Lafitte." Frontier Times 1924 May; 1:24-6.

593. Cable, George Washington. "Plotters and Pirates of Louisiana." Century Magazine 1883 April; 25:852-67.

Includes material on Jean Lafitte and the pirates' haven at Barataria Bay in Louisiana. No documentation.

594. Coxe, John E. "The New Orleans Mafia Incident." Louisiana Historical Quarterly 1937 October; 20(4):1067-1110.

Rep. of Coxe's LSU master's thesis, 1928. Detailed examination of the October 1890 murder of New Orleans police chief David Hennessy, trial and lynching of eleven Italians, March 1891, suspected of the crime. Documentation. Brief bibliography.

595. Cruzat, Heloise H., trans. "Trial and Sentence of Biron, Runaway Negro Slave, Before the Superior Council of Louisiana, 1728." Louisiana Historical Quarterly 1925 January; 8(1):23-7.

Contains both original French text and translation. Biran was caught and "...whipped by the public executioner at the foot of the gallows..." on July 17, 1728.

596. Cunningham, George E. "The Italians, A Hindrance to White Solidarity in Louisiana, 1890-1898." Journal of Negro History 1965; 50:22-36.

Includes some discussion of murder of New Orleans police chief David Hennessy in October 1890 and the March 1891 lynching of eleven Italians accused of his murder. Also mentions the August 9, 1896, lynching of three Italians at Hahnville, St. Charles Parish. The trio were accused of murder of Jules Gueymard and an "old Spaniard." Documentation, primarily newspaper articles.

597. Cusachs, Gaspar. "Controversy on Lafitte's Biography." Louisiana Historical Quarterly 1920 January; 3(1):100-11.

Reprints letter by J.H. Ingraham and editorial notes by J.D.B. DeBow originally published in DeBow's Review. No documentation.

598. Cusachs, Gaspar. "Lafitte, the Louisiana Pirate and Patriot." Louisiana Historical Quarterly 1919 October; 2(4): 418-38.

Covers Lafitte's piratical and patriotic activities. No documentation.

599. Dart, Henry P., ed. "A Murder Case Tried in New Orleans in 1773." Louisiana Historical Quarterly 1939 July; 22(3): 623-41.

Summary of the trial of Juan Bautista Bombara for killing Augustin; both were slaves of Antonio Thomassin. Bombara was hanged on September 20, 1773. Taken from Spanish Judicial Records of Louisiana.

600. Dart, Henry P. "The Smuggler St. Michel Confiscated by the Superior Council of Louisiana." Louisiana Historical Quarterly 1924 July; 7(3):371-413.

Proceedings in French with English translation. Smuggler Sieur Macmahon was supposedly operating from French ship St. Michel, September 1729.

601. Dart, Henry Plauche, ed. "Trial of Mary Glass for Murder, 1780." Louisiana Historical Quarterly 1923 October; 6(4):591-654.

Documents from the Spanish judicial records of Louisiana. Covers trial of Mary Glass, a free quadroon, for the torture and eventual murder (December 1779) of Emilia, a fifteen-year-old white girl. Glass was hanged for the crime on July 26, 1781. John Glass, Mary's husband, was implicated as an accessory.

602. Din, Gilbert C. "Cimmarrones and the San Malo Band in Spanish Louisiana." Louisiana History 1980 summer; 21(3): 237-62.

Describes plantation pillaging, murders, etc., of Juan San Malo band of runaway slaves, spring 1784. San Malo and two members of his band were hanged in New Orleans on June 19, 1784. Heavily documented.

603. Dobie, J. Frank. "Mystery of Lafitte's Treasure." Yale Review 1928; 18:116-34.

Discusses career of Jean Lafitte and the search for treasure he supposedly buried. No documentation.

604. "Duelling in America." Living Age 1847; 15:467-71.

Discussion of dueling, with one southern example---an encounter in New Orleans. Poor documentation.

605. Faye, Stanley. "Privateers of Guadeloupe and their Establishment in Barataria." Louisiana Historical Quarterly 1940 April; 23(2):428-44.

Pre-1812. Examines complicated activities of various privateers---nationalized pirates. Documentation.

606. Faye, Stanley. "Privateersmen of the Gulf and their Prizes." Louisiana Historical Quarterly 1939; 22:1012-94.

Discussion of Gulf pirates, including Jean and Pierre Lafitte and Dominique You. Documentation.

607. Faye, Stanley. "Types of Privateer Vessels, Their Armament and Flags, in the Gulf of Mexico." Louisiana Historical Quarterly 1940 January; 23(1):118-30.

Ships, etc., used by pirates attached to governments---"privateers." Documentation.

608. Frazier, R.D. "If Lafitte Came Back." Tangent 1913 January; 3:9-16.

609. Gayarre, Charles. "Historical Sketch of Pierre and Jean Lafitte, The Famous Smugglers of Louisiana, 1809-1814." Magazine of American History 1883; 10:284-98, 389-96.

"I propose in this paper to relate only what is based on authentic records." Author describes the Lafittes as "merchant smuggler" "averse to shedding blood." No documentation.

610. Griffin, H.L. "The Vigilance Committees of the Attakapas Country; or Early Louisiana Justice." Mississippi Valley Historical Association. Proceedings 1914-5; 8:146-59.

Covers vigilante activity in that region during a six-month period of 1859. Poor documentation.

611. Haas, Edward F. "Guns, Goats and Italians: The Tallulah Lynching of 1899." North Louisiana Historical Association Journal 1982; 13(2-3):45-58.

Covers lynching of five Italians by a mob on July 20, 1899, in Tullulah, Madison Parish, Louisiana. Documentation.

612. Himel, A.J. "Lafitte the Pirate Hero of Barataria and Galveston." Pan American Magazine 1913 September; 16:24-31.

613. "History of Lafitte." DeBow's Review 1852; 13:101-2.

Brief biographical note on Jean Lafitte dealing mainly with his French origins and activities. No documentation.

614. Hubbard, Leonidas, Jr. "Barataria: The Ruins of a Pirate Kingdom." Atlantic Monthly 1903 June; 91:806-14.

Past and present at Barataria Bay, pirate Jean Lafitte's distribution point. No documentation.

615. Hunter, John Warren. "Vindication of Jean LaFitte." Frontier Times 1950 June; 27:257-65.

Covers LaFitte's piracy/patriotic activities, La. and Texas, 1814-21.

616. Ingraham, J.H. "Lafitte--Professor Ingraham's Letter." DeBow's Review 1852; 13:422-4.

Comments on various aspects of Lafitte's piratical/patriotic activities. Notes that a chapter of Timothy Flint's History of the Valley of the Mississippi inspired his writing of a novel based on Lafitte's career. No formal, some internal documentation.

617. Inverarity, James M. "Populism and Lynching in Louisiana, 1889-1896: A Test of Erikson's Theory of the Relationship between Boundary Crises and Repressive Justice." American Sociological Review 1976 April; 41:262-80.

Sociological examination; no details of individual cases. "The analysis illustrates how econometric techniques may be applied to historical data in the process of sociological theory construction" (p. 262). Documentation.

618. Jackson, Joy. "Crime and the Conscience of a City." Louisiana History 1968 fall; 9(3):229-44.

Covers crime in New Orleans during the last two decades of the nineteenth century. Discusses vigilantism, murder of police chief David Hennessy in October 1890, gangs, etc. Documentation.

619. Karlin, J. Alexander. "New Orleans Lynchings in 1891 and the American Press." Louisiana Historical Quarterly 1941 January; 24(1):187-204.

Reactions of the nation's press to the March 1891 lynching of eleven Italians in New Orleans. Documentation.

620. Karlin, J. Alexander. "Some Repercussions of the New Orleans Mafia Incident of 1891." Research Studies of the State College of Washington 1943 December; 11:267-82.

621. Kendall, John S. "According to the Code." Louisiana Historical Quarterly 1940 January; 23(1):141-61.

Discusses several antebellum New Orleans duels. Few dates given. No documentation.

622. Kendall, John S. "Blood on the Banquette." Louisiana Historical Quarterly 1939 July; 22(3):819-56.

Covers activities of "Mafia" and "Black Hand" in New Orleans during first two decades of the twentieth century. Includes discussion of series of ax murders in 1910, 1919 and 1920 that were never solved; the 1907 kidnapping/ murder of young Walter Lamana, etc. Like so many of Kendall's interesting articles, this one has no documentation.

623. Kendall, John S. "The Humors of the Duello." Louisiana Historical Quarterly 1940 April; 23(2):445-70.

The "grim humor" of various duels in New Orleans. As usual with Kendall, few dates and no documentation.

624. Kendall, John Smith. "Notes on the Criminal History of New Orleans." Louisiana Historical Quarterly 1951 July; 34:147-73.

Brief descriptions of many murders, hangings, jail-breaks, etc., between 1830s and 1920s. Dates not always given. No documentation.

625. Kendall, John S. "Piracy in the Gulf of Mexico, 1816-1823." Louisiana Historical Quarterly 1925 July; 8(3):341-68.

Examines activities of Jean and Pierre Lafitte and other pirates. Consists primarily of quotes from New Orleans newspapers of the period, which are identified.

626. Kendall, John Smith. "Pistols for Two, Coffee for One." Louisiana Historical Quarterly 1941 July; 24(3):756-82.

Covers primarily antebellum dueling in Louisiana. Last duel in New Orleans was probably that fought in 1888 between Andre Roman and Emile Rivore. No documentation.

627. Kendall, John Smith. "The Successors of Laffite." Louisiana Historical Quarterly 1941 April; 24(2):360-77.

Discussion of piracy in New Orleans area in the first two decades of the nineteenth century. No documentation.

628. Kendall, John S. "Who Killa De Chief?" Louisiana Historical Quarterly 1939 April; 22:492-530.

A widely-cited article concerning the murder of New Orleans police chief David Hennessy in October 1890 and the subsequent trial and lynching of eleven Italians for the crime in March 1891. Long, but no documentation.

629. Kralin, J. Alexander. "Notes and Documents: The Italo-American Incident of 1891 and the Road to Reunion." Journal of Southern History 1942 May; 8:242-6.

Discusses newspaper editorial response to the lynching of eleven Italians in New Orleans on March 14, 1891. Lynchings were result of public anger over failure to convict alleged murderers of New Orleans superintendent of police David C. Hennessy. Documentation.

630. "Lafitte." DeBow's Review 1852; 13:204-5.

Letter from W.H.K., Pontotoc, Miss., concerning Jean Lafitte's participation in the battle of New Orleans.

631. Lavalett, Victor Jean. "True Story of Jean Lafitte." Gulf Coast Magazine 1909 January; 4:7-23.

632. "Life and Times of Lafitte." DeBow's Review 1852; 11: 372-87.

Covers career of pirate Jean Lafitte. Asserts that Lafitte died ca. 1818 during a battle in the Gulf of Mexico with a British sloop-of-war. No documentation.

633. "Life and Times of Lafitte." DeBow's Review 1852; 12:111-3;222.

Two brief articles on pirate Jean Lafitte.

634. "Life of Jean LaFitte, The Pirate of the Gulf." Living Age 1852 March 6; 32:433-46.

Author, identified only as "W.B.," takes a rather jaundiced view of Lafitte. "I am not inclined to agree with the Americans generally in their view of the character of Lafitte, neither as regards his ferocity in action, nor his magnanimity after it..." (p.434). Author talked to several Lafitte associates. Puts Lafitte's death in the Yucatan in 1826. No documentation.

635. Lister, Walter B. "Portrait of a Pirate." American Mercury 1926 February; 7:214-9.

Covers Jean Lafitte. No documentation.

636. Littlejohn, E.C. "Lafitte, the Lord of the Campeachy." Elite Magazine 1907 February; 1:13-5.

637. "Lynching Affair at New Orleans." Spectator 1891 March 21; 66:400-2.

638. Lyons, Grant. "Louisiana and the Livingston Criminal Codes." Louisiana History 1974 summer; 15(3):243-72.

Discusses role of lawyer Edward Livingston in drafting of La. criminal code in 1820s. Notes that Livingston once defended Jean and Pierre Lafitte for a supposed fee of $20,000. Documentation.

639. Marr, Robert H. "The New Orleans Mafia Case." American Law Review 1891; 25:414-31.

640. Meader, Louis J. "Duelling in the Old Creole Days." Century 1907 June; 74:248-59.

Discusses antebellum encounters at New Orleans, especially its famous dueling grounds, "The Oaks." Several specific duels are discussed, but dates are not always given. Illustrated. No documentation.

641. Mora, Isidro A. Beluche. "Privateers of Cartagena." Louisiana Historical Quarterly 1956 January; 39(1):74-91.

Includes discussion of such privateers---pirates in the employ of governments---as Jean and Pierre Lafitte, Dominique You, Rene Beluche. Documentation. Translated by Jane Grummond.

642. Nelli, Humbert S. "The Hennessy Murder and the Mafia in New Orleans." Italian Quarterly 1975; 19(75-6):77-95.

Discusses several possible dynamics behind the October 1890 murder of New Orleans police chief David C. Hennessy and its aftermath. Documentation.

643. "The New Orleans Massacre." Nation 1891 March 19;52: 232.

Editorial condemning the lynching of eleven Italians in New Orleans in the wake of the October 1890 assasination of that city's police chief David Hennessy. No documentation.

644. "New Orleans' War on the Mafia." Illustrated American 1891 April 4; 6:318-23.

Covers lynching of eleven Italians in New Orleans. Numerous illustrations. No documentation.

645. Persico, Joseph E. "Vendetta in New Orleans." American Heritage 1973; 24(4):65-72. Rep. Stories of Great Crimes and Trials (New York: American Heritage Publishing Co., 1974), p. 375-82.

Persico's article describes the October 1890 murder of New Orleans police Chief David Hennessy and its aftermath.

The murder of Hennessy eventually led to the March 1891 lynching/shooting of eleven Italians. "But of the eleven ...three had been acquitted, the jury could not agree on a verdict for three others, and five had never been tried" (p. 382). No documentation.

646. Pope, Whitney and Ragin, Charles. "Mechanical Solidarity, Repressive Justice, and Lynchings in Louisiana." American Sociological Review 1977 April; 42:363-8

Critical comments on Inverarity's article. Documentation.

647. Porteus, Laura L. "The Gri-Gri Case." Louisiana Historical Quarterly 1934 January; 17(1):48-63.

Translation and condensation of a June 1773 trial record from Spanish Judicial Archives of Louisiana. Four slaves were tried for plotting to poison Francisco de Bellile and his overseer.

648. Porteous, Laura L. "Torture in Spanish Criminal Procedure in Louisiana, 1771." Louisiana Historical Quarterly 1925 January; 8(1):5-22.

Summarizes a 132-page document in Louisiana Historical Archives that covers the investigation of the murder of Juan Baptiste Cezaire LeBreton (May 31, 1771) and the trial and hanging of two of LeBreton's slaves--Francisco Mirliton and Pedro Nicolas--for the crime. Torture was used to obtain confessions.

649. Rushing, Fred J., III. The Assasination of Judge T.S. Crawford, Bitter Fruit of the Tragic Era." North Louisiana Historical Association Journal 1976; 7(4):131-4.

Crawford and A.H. Harris were murdered on the highway between Columbia and Winnsboro in Franklin Parish on September 8, 1873. The motive was probably political in nature. Based on contemporary newspaper accounts. Documentation.

650. Schafer, William J. "Further Thoughts on Jazz Historiography: That Robert Charles Song." Journal of Jazz Studies 1978; 5(1):19-27.

Discusses relationship between Jelly Roll Morton's stories about Robert Charles and the facts. In July 1900 Charles --a black man--reacted to an attempt to arrest him by killing seven whites, including four policemen, before he was gunned down. Authorities were forced to lay siege for several days to a house where Charles was hiding. Charles also managed to wound twenty people; the entire incident touched off rioting in New Orleans, where Charles lived.

651. Schoonover, Frank E. "In the Haunts of Jean Lafitte." Harper's Magazine 1911 December; 124:80-91.

Impressionistic account of past and present in the Barataria bayou once frequented by Lafitte. Color illustrations by the author. No documentation.

652. Snow, Elliot. "Visit to Lafitte." Louisiana Historical Quarterly 1928 July; 11(3):434-44.

Rep. article Knickerbocker Magazine 1847 March, p. 254-61. Author probably James M. McIntosh. Discusses pursuit of Jean Lafittee by McIntosh during 1819-20 between mouth of the Mississippi River and Galveston. No documentation.

653. Spears, John R. "The True Story of Lafitte." Munsey 1902 October; 28:120-3.

Brief history of pirate Jean Lafitte's career. No documentation.

654. Tansey, Richard. "Prostitution and Politics in Antebelluem New Orleans." Southern Studies 1979; 18 (4):449-79.

Primarily a discussion of the 1854-6 anti-prostitution campaign of the Know-Nothing Party. Some discussion of the conditions of prostitution and individual cases. Heavily documented, primarily from newspaper articles.

655. Thompson, Kay C. "The First Lady of Storyville: The Fabulous Countess Willie Piazza." Record Changer 1951 February; 10(2):5,14.

Interview with former proprietress of a New Orleans bordello on employment of jazz pianists in red-light district, 1910-27.

656. Vyhnanek, Louis. "'Muggles,' 'Inchy,' and 'Mud': Illegal Drugs in New Orleans During the 1920s." Louisiana History; 1981 summer; 22(3):253-79.

Discusses illicit trade in cocaine, marijuana and heroin. Documentation, primarily newspaper articles.

657. Waddill, Frank H. "The Scene of the LeBreton Murder." Louisiana Historical Quarterly 1925 April; 8(2):266-7.

Brief note concerning the exact location of the May 31, 1771, murder of Juan Baptiste Cezaire LeBreton. According to Waddill, the murder took place on a plantation in what is now the city of Carrollton, La. No documentation.

658. White, Lula. "Blue Book. Tenderloin 400." Record Changer 1951 March; 10(3):6-7.

Facsimilie reproduction of four pages of an undated brochure (ca 1910?) by White advertising merits of her New Orleans bordello.

Miscellaneous

659. Albini, Joseph L. The American Mafia: Genesis of a Legend. New York: Appleton-Century-Crofts, c1971. 354p.

Development and analysis of U.S. syndicated crime. The assasination of New Orleans police chief David C. Hennessy is covered on pages 159-67. Some discussion of previous writers about the event. Documentation. Bibliography. Author and brief subject indexes.

660. Armstrong, Louis. Satchmo: My Life in New Orleans. New York: Prentice-Hall, 1954. 240p. Illus.

Jazz great's story of his life up to his departure from New Orleans for Chicago (1900-24). Much anecdotal material on Storyville residents, the renowned madam Lulu White, etc. No documentation, bibliography or index.

661. Castellanos, Henry C. New Orleans As It Was: Episodes of Louisiana Life. Baton Rouge: Louisiana State University Press, c1978. 367p. Illus. Rep. New Orleans: L. Graham, 1895. Intro. George F. Reinecke.

Written by a nineteenth century New Orleans criminal lawyer and newspaperman. Chapter 1, "The Labranche-Hueston Duel" (p. 1-13) describes the August 1843 encounter between Alcee LaBranche, a recently-elected U.S. representative from Louisiana and a Mr. Hueston, Baton Rouge newspaper editor. Chapter 7, "The Old Parish Prison" (p. 102-33) discusses numerous crimes and criminals including murderer Antoine Cambre and thief Paul Bertin. Chapter 9, "The Execution of Pauline" (p. 167-76) covers the March 28, 1846 hanging of a slave woman for mistreatment of her mistress. Material on pirate Jean Lafitte also included. This reprint edition includes a bibliography of articles written by Castellanos between 1892 and 1895 for the New Orleans Times-Democrat; many cover crimes such as dueling, swindling and murder. No documentation or bibliography. Index revised for reprint edition.

662. Chamberlin, Joseph Edgar. Ifs of History. Philadelphia: Henry Altemus, c1907. 203p.

Chapter 15 is entitled "If the Pirate Jean Lafitte Had Joined the British at New Orleans" (p. 129-37). No documentation, bibliography or index.

663. Cook, Fred J. The Pinkertons. Garden City, New York: Doubleday, c1974. 183p.

Intended for juvenile audience. Chapter 10, "The Pinkertons and the Mafia" (p. 119-43) covers work by the agency in the October 1890 assasination of New Orleans police chief David Hennessy. No documentation. Index.

664. Davilla, Joseph. "The Mysterious Axeman's Jazz." New Orleans, 1919.

This song, subtitled "Don't Scare Me, Papa," was written during the series of ax murders in New Orleans in 1918-1919. See Lyle Saxon, et al, Gumbo Ya-Ya, p. 87.

665. Doty, Sile. The Life of Sile Doty; the Most Noted Thief and Daring Burglar of His Time; the Leader of a Gang of Counterfeiters, Horse Thieves and Burglars of the New England, Middle and Western States; the Terror of Mexico During 1849. Toledo, OH: Blade Printing, 1880. Illus. Compiled by J.G.W. Colburn.

666. Doty, Sile. The Life of Sile Doty, 1800-1876; A forgotten Autobiography; The Most Daring Thief and Burglar of His Time. Detroit: Alved, 1948. Rep. 1880 ed. Foreward by Randolph G. Adams. Illus. 288p.

Doty was a criminal who between 1816 and his death in 1876, operated in New England, the Midwest and (so he claimed) London. On his way back from Mexico in 1847, Doty and two friends attempted to rob a house in New Orleans on the night of September 26. The thieves were met with gunfire; although Doty managed to escape, one of his cohorts was killed and the other arrested (pp. 267-8). Wellman claims that this book concerns "a thief and murderer, who had connections with several criminal rings, including the great one established by Murrell" (p. 339). Doty's only "connection" with Murrell's band was his meeting in Ohio with a man who claimed to have been an associate of Murrell's (p. 238).

667. Duff, Charles A. A New Handbook on Hanging; Being A Short Introduction to the Fine Art of Execution...Chicago: Regnery, 1955(?). 179p. Update of A Handbook on Hanging. London: Cayme Press Ltd., 1928. Also Boston, Mass.: Hale, Cushman and Flint, 1929. 129p.

Includes material on hanging of six Italians at Amite, La., May 9, 1924.

668. Ives, Burl. Burl Ives' Tales of America. Cleveland: World, c1954. 305p.

One of the tales is "The Privateer Turned Patriot" (p. 135-54) concerning Jean Lafitte.

669. Jackson, Joy J. New Orleans in the Gilded Age: Politics and Urban Progress 1880-1896. Baton Rouge: Louisiana State University Press, 1969. 355p.

Chapter 9 (p. 232-57) is devoted to "Crime and the Conscience of a City." Many types of criminal activity are discussed: prostitution; gambling; gangs of thieves such as the Shot Tower, Yellow Harry and Spiders; and organized crime. The July 1881 capture by New Orleans police officer David C. Hennessy of Giuseppi Esposito is described. Esposito, an Italian bandit, had fled to New Orleans and "formed a local underworld group which he called the Mafia." On October 15, 1890, Hennessy---by then chief of police---was assassinated; he had been investigating organized crime in the city. On March 14, 1891, a crowd of angry men entered the New Orleans prison and lynched and shot to death the eleven men they felt were responsible for Hennessy's death. The chapter is well-documented; the book contains an extensive bibliography and an index.

670. Johnston, Charles Haven Ladd. Famous Privateersmen and Adventurers of the Sea; their Rovings, Cruises, Escapades, and Fierce Battling Upon the Ocean for Patriotism and Treasure. Boston: L.C. Page, 1911. 398p. Rep. 1920.

Chapter entitled "Lafitte, Privateer, Pirate and Terror of the Gulf of Mexico (1780-1826)."

671. Lomax, John A. and Alan. Our Singing Country. New York: Macmillan, 1941.

Pages 335-41 cover "Batson" folksong, based on the murder of Ward Earll, his wife and three children near Lake Charles, La., in 1902. Albert Edward Batson was tried twice for the crimes and sentenced to death. Includes music and thirty-eight verses.

672. "The Mafia in New Orleans." Pamphlet collection. Howard-Tilton Memorial Library, Tulane University.

Cited in Asbury, The French Quarter (#559).

673. Miller, Olive Beaupre. Heroes, Outlaws and Funny Fellows of American Popular Tales. New York: Doubleday, Doran and Co., 1939, 332p. Illus.

"The Pirate LaFitte and His Ghost" (p. 116-31) concerns Jean Lafitte, his piratical activities and treasure buried by him. No documentation.

674. Mills, Elizabeth Shown and Gary B. Tales of Old Natchitoches. Natchitoches, La.: Association for the Preservation of Historic Natchitoches, 1978. 142p. Illus. Foreward by Sue Eakin. (Cane River Creole Series, vol. 3).

This title includes several chapters covering criminal activity in Natchitoches during the nineteenth century and earlier. "Murder and Justice---Colonial Style" (pp. 23-6) and "The Huntsman" (pp. 27-30) describe murders that occurred during the 1760s. "Sidelights on a Duel" (pp. covers the circumstances which led to the 1839 duel between General Francois Gaiennie and Pierre Bossier in which the general was killed. "An Affront to Honor" (pp. 71-3) describes the 1842 murder by John Cortes of a lawyer named Giles; "Nomite" (pp. 78-80) includes a description of another murder. "Showdown on Second Street" (pp. 115-8) covers the 1876 terrorization of the town by Texas' Horton gang. Each chapter is followed by a list of "Major Sources." The book includes a bibliography and index.

675. Pinkerton, William A. Train Robberies, Train Robbers and the "Hold Up" Men. Chicago: n.p., 1907. 84p. Illus. Rep. as Train Robberies and Train Robbers. Ft. Davis, TX: Frontier Book Co., 1968.

A speech given at the annual convention of the International Association Chiefs of Police. Contains material on train robber Eugene Bunch.

676. Powell, Edward Alexander. Gentlemen Rovers. New York: Scribner's, 1913. 245p. Illus.

Contains chapter on Jean Lafitte entitled "Pirate Who Turned Patriot."

677. Reader's Digest. Scoundrels and Scalawags; 51 Stories of the Most Fascinating Characters of Hoax and Fraud. Pleasantville, NY: Reader's Digest Association, c1968. 638p. Illus.

Contains a chapter by Donald Culross Peattie, "Jean Lafitte--Pirate Patriot" (p. 255-60). No documentation, bibliography or index.

678. Rhodes, Jewell Parker. "Lost Women: Marie Laveau, Voodoo Queen.: MS. 1983 January; 11(7):28-31.

Includes discussion of Laveau's career as a madam in nineteenth-century New Orleans. Brief "Reading List." Laveau died on June 16, 1881.

679. Rosen, Ruth. The Lost Sisterhood: Prostitution in America, 1900-1918. Baltimore: Johns Hopkins University Press, c1982. 245p. Illus.

Concentrates on the Progressive Era campaign to eradicate prostitution. In her introduction, Rosen writes, "The subject of prostitution on the Western frontier and in the relatively unindustrialized South has not been considered here" (p. xvi) and then proceeds to frequent use of New Orleans' famed Storyville red-light district to make her points. Despite its limitations, a fascinating portrait of prostitution at the turn of the century. Well-documented. Bibliography. Index.

680. Saxon, Lyle. Father Mississippi. New York(?): Century, 1927. 427p. Illus.

Chapter 15, "Molly Glass, The Murderess" (p. 142-58) describes the crime and execution of a free quadroon. Molly was married to John Glass, a white man. Glass was tried in New Orleans for the murder of Emilia Davis, a fifteen year-old white girl who was living in the Glass household. Molly was found guilty and hanged on July 26, 1781, in the city's public square. Saxon claims to have read the "thirty-five legal documents which constitute the court records in this case." but gives no source for these documents. The book contains an index and short bibliography.

681. Saxon, Lyle. Old Louisiana. New York: Century, c1929. 388p. Illus.

Chapter 8, "Temba Murders His Master" (p. 85-94) covers the trial and hanging of slaves for the May 31, 1771, murder of Juan Baptiste Cezaire LeBreton. Summary of trial record. Bibliography. Index.

682. Saxon, Lyle; Dreyer, Edward and Tallant, Robert, comps. Gumbo Ya-Ya: A Collection of Louisiana Folk Tales. Boston: Houghton Mifflin, c1945. 581p. Illus.

Chapter four, "Axeman's Jazz" (p. 75-92) covers the 1918-1919 series of ax murders in New Orleans. Chapter 24, "Who Killa Da Chief: (p. 505-522) covers the October 1890 murder of New Orleans police chief David C. Hennessy. No documentation. Index.

683. Tallant, Robert. Voodoo in New Orleans. New York: Macmillan, c1946. Rep. New York: Collier, 1962. 253p.

Contains material on Marie Leveau, voodoo queen of New Orleans during the nineteenth century who also ran a bordello. Brief bibliography. No documentation or index.

684. Tansey, Richard Randall. "Economic Expansion and Urban Disorder in Antebellum New Orleans." Ph.D. dissertation, University of Texas, Austin, 1981. 217p.

Includes material on prostitution and slave trading.

685. Wilson, Colin and Pitman, Patricia. Encyclopedia of Murder. New York: G.P. Putnam's 1962. 576p.

Covers primarily European and American cases. Contains at least four pre-1930 Louisiana cases: Dr. Etienne Deschamps (New Orleans, hanged for murder, May 12, 1892), Elise Crawford (New Orleans, murdered September 18, 1911), "Axe Man" murders (New Orleans, 1918) and Tom Dreher and his mistress, Ada LeBoeuf (Mason City, hanged for the murder of Ada's husband Jim, February 1, 1929). May contain other southern cases. Very "Select Bibliography." No documentation. Indexes by type of murder and name.

Newspaper Articles

686. "Criminal Court." New Orleans Bee 4 February 1830.

Reports that Jose Maria Sanchez, indicted for the New Orleans murder of Juan Callao, was found guilty of manslaughter and sentenced to twenty years in prison.

687. (Untitled) New Orleans Bee 17 February 1830, p.3.

Article noting an arsonist at work in New Orleans the previous night. "Incendiaries still infest our city, notwithstanding the utmost vigilance of the police..."

688. "Continuation of the Confession of Edward Cullen." New Orleans Bee 26 March 1830.

Cullen was hanged February 15, 1830, at Tibodauxville for the murder of Hugh Gullihor. That crime is described in this long final installment of Cullen's confession.

689. "Atrocious Murder." Charleston (S.C.) Courier 7 April 1840.

This article describes the murder in New Orleans of a tailor by his former partner.

690. "Murder." Charleston (SC) Courier 7 April 1840.

This article quotes the Lafayette (La.) Gazette as reporting the murder of William Jenkins, "Keeper of a coffee house and ten pin alley." In addition, several thousand dollars was believed to have been stolen.

691. "The City." New Orleans Daily Picayune, 19 April 1856.

Included in this column is an article about the pursuit

of Jim Chapman, "a well known thief." He was arrested aboard the steamship Michigan by New Orleans city police and managed to escape. After an "exciting chase," Chapman was finally caught for good. The thief was found carrying two pistols.

692. "The City." New Orleans Daily Picayune, 22 April 1856.

A brief article in this column describes the theft from a store in New Orleans of $5000 worth of jewelry. "The burglars operated in a very skillful manner..."

693. "The Fatal Duel at New Orleans." Charleston (SC) Daily Courier 29 August 1860.

F.W. Yates was wounded in a duel with a man named Chandler.

694. "Murder in Vienna, Louisiana." Savannah (GA) Morning News 25 March 1872.

Reports the murder on March 12 of J.N. Jackson and John Huey.

695. (Untitled) Columbus (GA) Daily Enquirer-Sun 17 July 1877; p.2,c.1.

"In St. Martin, La., a duel was the result of a difficulty at a ball which occurred between two young men, Babin and Ducrest. The arms were pistols and the distance twenty-five yards. At the first shot Ducrest was shot to the heart.

696. "The Decline of the Duello." Charleston (LA) News and Courier 24 July 1878. Rep. New Orleans Times.

Discussion of the decline of dueling. Mentions recent New Orleans duel between men named Roxborough and Saunders.

697. "Lynch Law in Louisiana." Charleston (SC) News and Courier 31 July 1878.

Notes the lynching at Monroe by four to five hundred masked men of four blacks charged with murder. Three of the victims were involved in the May 1878 murder of W.C. Fitzgerald, white constable at Trenton.

698. "Condemned to Die." New Orleans Times-Picayune 5 June 1885. Related article 6 June.

This long article reports on two blacks condemned to hang in New Orleans June 6. The background and crimes of the two murderers---Robert Williams and Foster Chase---are described. Drawings of the men are included. The second article reports on the hangings. The first article also has information on a convicted rapist, also condemned to die, who was pardoned.

699. "Homicide in St. Charles." New Orleans Times-Picayune 8 June 1885.

This article describes the shooting death of John William Kuhlman, white, at the hands of Peter Mitchell. The article also notes that in the previous year Mitchell's brother Adam had killed Joachim Williams. Both murders occurred in St. Charles Parish.

700. "Shreveport: A Murder Trial..." New Orleans Times Picayune 15 August 1885. Related article August 16.

Brief note on the opening at Belleville, Bossier Parish, of the trial of Dennis Boyd, black, for the shooting death of David Haas, December 25, 1884.

701. "Shreveport: A Negro Murder..." New Orleans Times Picayune 18 August 1885.

Notes the murder of Mingo Johnson near Keithville, fourteen miles from Shreveport.

702. "Bayou Sara: A Shooting Affray Between Two Planters." New Orleans Times Picayune 23 August 1885.

At St. Francisville, Bayou Sara, Cheston Folks fired five shots at Marcus Bankston. Three bullets hit Bankston and wounded him seriously.

703. "Carving a Wife to Pieces; The Bloody Revenge of a Roustabout; A Fresh Crime in the Slums." New Orleans Times Picayune 26 August 1885.

This long article notes the attempt by mulatto Fillmore Wyatt to murder his wife Lizzie, who had been seeing a man named Jim Taylor. Lizzie was stabbed more than twenty times and was not expected to live.

704. "A Wounded Burglar." New Orleans Times Picayune 26 August 1885.

This long article notes the search for Robert Simpson, "whose photograph adorns the rogues' gallery among the general thieves.'"

705. "Arrest of Paul Price, Murderer." New Orleans Times Picayune 27 August 1885.

Price was wanted in Plaquemines Parrish as "one of the murderers of Mrs. Cole, at Plaquemine, for which crime there have already been three persons hung..."

706. "The Plaquemines Murder." New Orleans <u>Times Picayune</u> 27 August 1885.

Notes the arrival in New Orleans of the sheriff of Plaquemines Parish to pick up fugitive and alleged murderer Bernard Provinsano, captured earlier by New Orleans police.

707. "Shreveport: Criminal Court in Bossier." New Orleans <u>Times Picayune</u> 27 August 1885.

In Bossier Parish court Beauregard Hardon, black, was sentenced to twenty years imprisonment for the murder of another black, Walker Thomas. Dennis Boyd was sentenced to hang for the December 25, 1884, murder of David Haas.

708. "Shreveport: On the Way to the Penitentiary..." New Orleans <u>Times-Picayune</u> 27 August 1885.

Notes that R.L. Jones left the city under guard to begin serving his five year sentence in the U.S. Penitentiary, Chester, Ill. Jones had been "convicted at Monroe several months ago for robbing the United States mail at Lake Providence."

709. "Attempted Robbery." New Orleans <u>Times Picayune</u> 31 August 1885.

Describes August 25 attempt by four white men and three black men to rob a train on the Louisiana Western Railroad at Shoates' Prairie near Sulphur City. Nothing was taken.

710. "Baton Rouge: Reward Offered for a Brace of Madison Parish Murderers." New Orleans <u>Times Picayune</u> 1 September 1885.

Frank and Malinda Russell were wanted for the murder of Sammy Mitchell, a nine year-old orphan living with them. Reward of $300 was being offered.

711. "Shreveport: Negro Homicides..." New Orleans <u>Times Picayune</u> 4 September 1885.

Notes on three different murders in Bossier Parish and near Shreveport.

712. "Old Rube's Ghost." Birmingham (AL) <u>Daily News</u> 15 April 1892.

Reports robbery of Illinois Central passenger train seventy-seven miles from New Orleans. "Every valuable express package" was taken. Take estimated at $3000. Three men involved, including infamous train robber Eugene Bunch.

713. "An Iberville Incident." New Orleans Daily Picayune 2 October 1896.

Porter Martin, black, was arrested for robbery in Iberville Parish.

714. "The Tucker-Fairchild Murder Case on Trial." New Orleans Daily Picayune 2 October 1896.

Notes the opening in Baton Rouge of the trial of Ed Tucker for the January 1896 murder of Sam Fairchild.

715. "Whitecapism." New Orleans Daily Picayune 2 October 1896.

This long article describes an incident of vigilantism at Camp Parapet.

716. "A Double Murderer Hanged for His Crime." New Orleans Daily Picayune 3 October 1896.

Mose Wilson, black, was executed at Farmerville for the April 1896 murder of an old black couple, Tom and Caroline Franklin.

717. "White Caps." New Orleans Daily Picayune 4 October 1896.

Attempted vigilante activity at Camp Parapet.

718. "Armand's Sensational Story of the Shooting Affray at Camp Cypress Yesterday." New Orleans Daily Picayune 24 June 1897.

Edmond Armand, owner of a restaurant/saloon at the station some thirty miles from New Orleans, claimed to have been shot by Samuel Simmons, "a bad man and mankiller, who is but a short time out of trouble for the murder of a negro at a ball..."

719. "Mrs. Ramon's Murder, Nelson Page Held After the Preliminary Examination." New Orleans Daily Picayune 24 June 1897.

Page, a black, was ordered to stand trial in New Orleans for the May 9 murder.

720. "Stole Three Parrots." New Orleans Daily Picayune 24 June 1897.

"Well known hoodlum" David Reagon boarded a steamer, stole the three birds and escaped.

721. "Bagged with His Booty." New Orleans Daily Picayune 26 June 1897.

Robert Smith,one of two black thieves wanted for a New Orleans house burglary, was arrested. Henry Jones, the second burglar, was still at large.

722. "Southern States Items of Interest..." New Orleans Daily Picayune 26 June 1897.

Notes the shooting death near Port Hickey of Charles B. Kneedler, a fisherman. He was killed by Mrs. Fannie Williams, who claimed Kneedler had made improper advances. The article also notes the shooting of William Stockwell, prominent farmer at Stony Point, by one of his black tenants, Nathan Williams.

723. "Louis Gallot Found Guilty." New Orleans Daily Picayune 30 June 1897.

Gallot had been on trial for his involvement in the embezzlement of $400,000 from the Union National Bank in New Orleans.

724. "Maud Out of Sight." New Orleans Daily Picayune 30 June 1897.

Maud McDowell, black, was wanted to testify against her lover, William Wilson, "the notorious burglar." Wilson, along with John Smythe, was in jail in New Orleans awaiting trial for the murder of Charles Daniel Gleber.

725. "Indemnity Paid for Mobbing Italians." Raleigh (NC) Gazette 14 August 1897.

About a year previously three Italians---Lorenzo Salardino, Salvatore Areno and Guiseppe Venturelia---were taken from the jail at Hanville, La., and lynched. The State Department paid $6000 indemnity to the Italian government for the incident.

726. "Italian Swindlers." New Orleans Daily-Picayune 9 January 1898.

This short article notes the arrest in St. Louis of several Italians, some of whom were believed to have been involved in two large swindling schemes in New Orleans during the past two years.

727. "Shooting in a Negro Crap Den." New Orleans Daily Picayune 10 January 1898.

At Frank Hickman's gambling parlor in Napoleonville, a shooting occurred in which one man died and two were wounded.

728. "Three Hanged in Louisiana." Raleigh (NC) Gazette 15 January 1898.

Louis Richards, George Washington and Foxli Morris were hanged at Hahnville (St. Charles Parish) for the June 1897 murder of Louis Zeigler. Richards, also known as "Creole," confessed to ten other murders since 1884; an investigation substantiated his confession.

729. "Will Austin in Jail for the Murder of Bantyeff." New Orleans Daily-Picayune 23 December 1899.

Will Austin, white, was arrested and jailed in Alexandria for the murder of Charley Bantyeff.

730. "Several Murders Disgrace the Day." New Orleans Daily-Picayune 26 December 1899.

This long article describes several Christmas Day murders that took place in New Orleans.

731. "Slidell's Tragedy." New Orleans Daily-Picayune 26 December 1899.

In Slidell "Dobb Davis and his two sons, Sam and Boy, were arrested...for the shooting of B.F. Scarbrough and the murder of his 3-year-old child..." Scarbrough had accused Davis of stealing some of his hogs.

732. "Trial of the Bossier Case Ended." New Orleans Daily-Picayune 27 December 1899.

This article describes testimony in the Covington, La., trial of Meyer Willie and Charles Fairburn for the ambush murder of Charles Bossier.

733. "Altano the Man Who Was Murdered Close to the Alhambra Plantation." New Orleans Daily-Picayune 31 December 1899. Related article December 30.

This article describes the activities in New Orleans of gambler Tony Altano and his death, probably at the hands of fellow Sicilians. In an editorial on Dec. 30, the newspaper asked, "Is it a Mafia case?"

734. "W.E. Benedict Arrested on a Charge of Murder." New Orleans Daily Picayune 31 December 1899.

This article notes the arrest of William E. Benedict (or Bennett; both spellings given), wanted for murder in Livingston Parish. Benedict "was chief of a band of whitecappers or regulators...and...is wanted with others for outrages perpetrated by the band."

735. "Bandit Kills Policeman." New York Times 25 December 1924. (p. 9)

On December 24 the Frenchman Street Branch of the Marine Bank of New Orleans was robbed of $13,000. As the robber was escaping, he shot and killed traffic policeman Jacob Uhle.

7

Mississippi

Monographs

736. Buse, William H. The Life, Confessions and Adventures of William H. Buse, Who was Executed November 19, 1858, at Jacinto, Miss., for the Murder of Thomas M'Keever, Written by Himself, Memphis, TN: Hutton and Clark, 1859. 14p.

Accused by M'Keever of stealing a jug of whiskey, Buse shot and killed him.

737. Gentry, Claude. The Guns of Kinnie Wagner. Baldwyn, Miss.: Magnolia Publishers, 1969.

738. Griffith, Frances Williams. True Life Story of Will Purvis. Purvis, MS: Booster Publishing Co., c1935. 58p. Illus.

Purvis was arrested, tried and convicted for the June 1893 shooting of Will Buckley near Columbia, Miss. On February 7, 1894, Purvis was hung at Columbia, but somehow managed to survive the attempted execution. A second execution date was set, but Purvis escaped from jail beforehand. He was captured and spent twenty-two months in jail. On December 20, 1898, Purvis was pardoned and released. Purvis was exonerated of the murder charge when Joe Beard confessed to the murder of Buckley twenty-two years later. Most of this pamphlet is made up of Purvis' own story and the testimony of witnesses at his trial.

739. Griffith, Frances William. True Life Story of Will Purvis. Lamar County (Miss.) Historical Society, 1979. 40p. Rep. 1935 ed.

740. Hammons, Ann. Wild Bill Sullivan, King of the Hollow. Jackson: University Press of Mississippi, c1980. 144p.

Investigates the facts and folklore surrounding Wild Bill Sullivan, his ancestors and descendents. In Smith Co., Miss., Sullivan and his family were and are synonymous with criminal activity and/or tall tales. Bill did kill his brother in a fight on January 31, 1903. Other murders are discussed. Includes family tree, bibliography, index. Well documented.

741. Shackleford, Thomas, comp. Proceedings of the Citizens of Madison County, Mississippi, at Livingston, in July 1835, in Relation to the Trial and Punishment of Several Individuals Implicated in a Contemplated Insurrection in this State. Jackson, MS: Mayson and Smoot, 1836.

Covers the lynching of several men believed to have been involved in the Murrell slave uprising plot. Rep. in Howard, The History of Virgil A. Stewart...Not listed in NUC Pre-1956 Imprints.

742. Sullivan, Chester. Sullivan's Hollow. Jackson: University Press of Mississippi, c1978. 93p.

More on the Sullivans, including Wild Bill, of Smith Co., Miss. See Hammons. Includes bibliography. No index.

Thesis

743. Mounger, Dwyn M. "Lynching in Mississippi, 1830-1930." M.A. thesis, Mississippi State University, 1961.

Dissertation

744. Sweterlisch, Richard Carl. "Kinnie Wagner: A Popular Legendary Hero and His 'Constituency.'" Ph.D. dissertation, Indiana University, 1976 439p.

Traces development of folklore surrounding Kinnie Wagner (1903-1958), notorious southern outlaw from Mississippi. Includes biography, a study of ballads about Wagner and a discography of commercial recordings of songs about the outlaw.

Journal Articles

745. "Bad Day for Bad Kennie." Newsweek 1956 February 13; 47(7):30-1.

Brief account of career of Kinnie Wagner, in prison for the 1924 murder of a Mississippi deputy sheriff. Describes his latest escape from Parchman prison and his capture in Scooba, Mississippi. No documentation.

746. Bishop, Edward Allen. "Missing Outlaw Loot in Mississippi." True Treasure 1973 Feb; 7:32-41.

Loot supposedly buried by outlaw James Copeland and his gang.

747. Blain, William T. "Challenge to the Lawless: The Mississippi Secret Service, 1870-71." Journal of Mississippi History 1978 May; 40(2):119-31.

Also published Mississippi Quarterly 1978 spring; 31(2): 229-40. Describes the Service's work in murder cases both related and unrelated to Ku Klux Klan activity in Mississippi. Documentation.

748. Brady, Cyrus Townsend. "Famous American Duels." Munsey's 1905 August; 33:608-16.

Includes discussion of the August 1829 duel between a Dr. Maddox and Samuel Wells. The encounter took place on an island in the Mississippi River opposite Natchez; James Bowie was involved in the brawl that developed among spectators after the duel. No documentation.

749. Bronner, Simon J. "Bad Man Monroe Legends from the Delta Region of Mississippi." Mid-South Folklore 1977 summer; 5(2):53-7.

Folktales about a murderer known as Bad Man Monroe and moonshiner Henry Brown. Collected in 1976. Greenville, Miss., from blues singer Eugene Powell. Documentation.

750. Brown, Maud Morrow. "William C. Falkner, Man of Legends." Georgia Review 1956 winter; 10:421-38.

Discusses writer William Faulkner's great-grandfather's killing of Robert Holt Hindman (1849) and Erasmus V. Morris (1851) in Ripley, Miss. Falkner was tried and acquitted on both counts of murder. Also discusses Falkner's booklet containing the confession of antebellum ax murderer A.J. McCannon. McCannon, who supposedly killed a family of four and two slaves, was hung in Ripley, the first public execution in Tippah Co. The execution supposedly took place before the Mexican War. No documentation.

751. Darkis, Fred, Jr. "Alexander Keith McClung (1811-1855)." Journal of Mississippi History 1978; 40(4):289-296.

Traces career of McClung, who was a U.S. Marshall, diplomat, colonel in the Mexican War and duelist who supposedly had killed ten men in the fourteen duels he fought. In March 1855 he committed suicide.

752. Hatfield, Joseph T. "Governor William Charles Cole Claiborne, Indians, and Outlaws in Frontier Mississippi." Journal of Mississippi History 1965; 27(4):323-50.

Most of the article concerns Claiborne's efforts to negotiate peace between white settlers and Indians in the Mississippi Territory. Some discussion of outlaws Samuel Mason, his son John, Wiley Harpe, etc. For more information the article recommends Coates (#6), a highly questionable source.

753. Haynes, Robert V. "Law Enforcement in Frontier Mississippi." Journal of Mississippi History 1960; 22:27-42.

Primarily concerns development of legal institutions. Some material on Samuel Mason and Wiley Harpe (identified as James Mason and John Sutton), horse thieves, Natchez-under-the-Hill lawless area, the George Poindexter-Abijah Hunt duel in Natchez, the Kempers (a gang that raided Spanish territory from their base in Pinckneyville), etc. Documentation.

754. Herbert, Hiram J. "The Kinnie Wagner Saga: Booze, Babes and Breakouts." For Men Only 1959 December; p. 16, 52-8.

755. Holmes, Jack D.L. "Law and Order in Spanish Natchez, 1781-98." Journal of Mississippi History 1963; 25(3): 186-201.

Administrative efforts to maintain law and order. Some material on individual cattle and horse thieves and murderers. Heavily documented.

756. Holmes, William F. "Whitecapping: Agrarian Violence in Mississippi, 1902-1906." Journal of Southern History 1969;35:165-85.

Holmes discusses the violent dirt-farmer movement that "manifested the forces of both agricultural distress and anti-Negro sentiment." (p. 166). Three southern Mississippi counties---Amite, Franklin and Lincoln---were the scene of whitecap activity in 1892-3 and again between 1902 and 1906. The men who participated in whitecap activities felt financially squeezed by the relationship between merchants and black tenant farmers; whitecapping resulted from a mixture of economic and racial forces. Holmes discusses in detail the violence against both black and white, including the role of Pinkerton detective A.J. Hoyt who was hired by Governor Vardaman to investigate the violence in Lincoln Co. Heavily documented.

757. Holmes, William F. "Whitecapping: Anti-Semitism in the Populist Era." American Jewish Historical Quarterly 1974; 63(3):244-61.

Details anti-Jewish aspects of a paramilitary movement among farmers in seven southwest Mississippi counties during the 1890s. Will Purvis was active in this movement; see Frances Griffith's biography of his strange life. Holmes has become a prolific---and excellent---chronicler of southern whitecapping.

758. Holmes, William F. "Whitecapping in Mississippi: Agrarian Violence in the Populist Era." Mid-America 1973; 55(2):134-48.

Holmes' article discusses the social context and specific events of whitecapping activity in Mississippi in the early 1890s. Members of whitecap groups, which were highly organized, saw themselves living "in a state brought to the verge of ruin by European and Wall street goldbugs..." (p. 137). Absentee landlords, Jewish merchants and unsupervised black tenant farmers were primary targets of whitecap anger and violence. This well-documented article is one of a series by Holmes on southern whitecapping.

759. Levell, William H. "On Lynching in the South." Outlook 1901 November 16; 69:731-3.

Discusses a lynching in Carrollton, Miss., during the summer of 1901. Also contains generalized discussion of causes of lynching. No documentation.

760. McKibben, Davidson B. "Negro Slave Insurrections in Mississippi, 1800-1865." Journal of Negro History 1949 January; 34:73-94.

Includes section on the July 1835 slave revolt scare--an "insurrection" supposedly formulated by John Murrell and uncovered by Virgil Stewart. McKibben rightly recognizes this entire episode as---in the words of John A. Quitman---" one of the most extraordinary and lamentable hallucinations" (p. 79). Also reprints three newspaper articles relating to this "revolt." Documentation.

761. Martin, Steve. "Missing Loot of the Mississippi Highwayman." Treasure 1977 March; 8:20-1.

Loot supposedly buried by outlaw James Copeland and his gang.

762. Matthias, Virginia Park. "Natchez-Under-the-Hill as It Developed Under the Influence of the Mississippi River and the Natchez Trace." Journal of Mississippi History 1945; 7(4):201-17.

An overview of Natchez's nineteenth century slum and crime district, comparable to Memphis' Pinch Gut and New Orleans's Swamp. Some material on Wiley and Micajah Harpe, Samuel Mason, Joseph Hare and John Murrell---the usual crowd. Sources include the usual dubious ones as well--Hall, Coates, Rothert, Walton (#s 115, 6, 154, 26).

763. Miles, Edwin A. "The Mississippi Slave Insurrection of 1835." Journal of Negro History 1957 January; 42(1): 48-60.

Covers lynchings and other events in Madison and Hinds Cos., July 1835. Primary sources are Walton and Howard. Miles states, "...it is not possible at this date to assert with authority whether such a fantastic plot existed." Miles refers to the slave revolt supposedly being led by John Murrell. See Penick for recent scholarship on the subject. The existence of a vast outlaw gang and slave conspiracy led by Murrell was easy for whites already fearful because of previous insurrections and increasing abolitionist activity to accept. Rumor and forced confessions were enough to touch off the lynchings.

764. Newell, Mrs. Samuel H., Jr. "Dr. Jeremiah Chamberlain and Oakland College." Journal of Mississippi History 1964; 26(4):322-4.

Brief article includes description of 1851 murder of Jeremiah Chamberlain, president of Oakland College now Alcorn A & M. Documentation.

765. Pittman, Walter E., Jr. "The Mel Cheatham Affair: Interracial Murder in Mississippi in 1889." Journal of Mississippi History 1981 May; 43(2):127-33.

On March 19, 1890, Mel Cheatham, a storekeeper, was hanged at Grenada, Miss. Cheatham, the first post-Civil War white to be hanged in Miss. for killing a black, had been convicted in the 1889 murder of James Tillman. Documentation.

766. Rush, Johann. "Mississippi's Copeland Clan Treasure." Treasure 1974 Oct.; 5:72-8.

Loot supposedly buried by outlaw James Copeland and his gang.

767. Rutledge, Wilmuth S. "Dueling in Antebellum Mississippi." Journal of Mississippi History 1964; 26:181-91.

Describes several pre-1862 duels. Documentation.

768. "Shame to Mississippi." Nation 1929 January 16; 128: 62.

Discusses the December 26, 1928, lynching of Emanuel McCallum (black) at Hattiesburg, Miss., and the December 31, 1928, burning alive of Charley Shepherd (black)---a convict---at Parchman, Miss. No documentation.

769. Stone, J.M. "The Supression of Lawlessness in the South." North American Review 1894 April; 158:500-6.

Generalized. Author was governor of Mississippi. Some statistics given for that state on murder, etc. No documentation.

770. Sweterlitsch, Richard. "Ballads and a Mississippi Badman." Mississippi Folklore Register 1978 spring; 12(1): 47-57.

This article examines the development of ballads based on the career of Mississippi murderer Kinnie Wagner. The article includes a brief summation of Wagner's life and the lyrics of several songs about Wagner. The composition and recording histories of those songs are also given. The tunes belong more properly to popular music than folk balladry; one was recorded (under the pseudonym Vernon Dalhart) by Tin Pan Alley singer Marion Try Slaughter. However, the songs were ballad-like and soon passed into the repertoire of rural folk singers. The author's dissertation covers similar ground. Well documented.

771. Thompson, Ray M. "Blood Spattered Gold." Down South 1960 Sept.-Oct; 3:22-4.

The "gold" is supposedly that buried in Mississippi by antebellum outlaw leader James Copeland.

Miscellaneous

772. Carroll, Thomas Battle. Historical Sketches of Oktibbeha County. Gulfport, MS: Dixie Press, 1931. 263p.

Contains material on murders, gunfights and hired killers in the Mississippi county between 1870 and 1910. See p. 139, 140, 141, 163, 173, 174, 176, 178, 182. No documentation or bibliography. Index.

773. Carver, Al. "The Fate of Kinnie Wagner." Columbia 15109. 1926.

Sound recording.

774. Claiborne, J.F.H. Mississippi As a Province, Territory State, with Biographical Notices of Eminent Citizens. Jackson, MS: Power and Barksdale, 1880. Rep. ed. Baton Rouge:Louisiana State University Press, 1964. 545p.

Pages 225-8 contain material on Natchez Trace outlaws Samuel Mason, his son John and Micajah and Wiley Harpe. Only Mississippi activities are covered and those only sketchily. Much of the material involves Governor C.C. Claiborne's proclamation of a $2000 reward for the capture of Mason's gang.

775. Dalhart, Vernon. "Kinnie Wagner." Okeh 40565. 1926.

Sound recording.

776. Dalhart, Vernon. "Kinnie Wagner's Surrender." Okeh 40685. 1926.

Sound recording.

777. Evans, David. Big Road Blues; Tradition and Creativity in the Folk Blues. Berkeley: University of California Press, c1982. 379p. Illus.

Pages 190-2 include discussion of murder of four white men and wounding of eight others by Joe Pullen in Drew, Mississippi, December 14, 1923. Documentation. Lengthy bibliography. Index.

778. Foote, Henry S. Bench and Bar of the South and Southwest. St. Louis: Soule, Thomas and Wentworth, 1876. 264p.

Foote was a lawyer as well as senator from and governor of Mississippi. This book describes lawyers and judges with whom Foote came in contact during his long career. Some scattered information of various criminal activity, including dueling. Foote describes his participation for the defense in the 1830s Vicksburg trial of robber-murderer Alonzo Phelps (p. 35-8). Includes name index, but no documentation.

779. Foote, Henry S. Casket of Reminiscenses. New York: Negro Universities Press, 1968. 498p. Rep. 1874 ed.

Foote's memoirs of his long legal and political career. Pages 250-61 describe the formation in 1835 of vigilance committees in Mississippi as a result of Virgil Stewart's discovery of John Murrell's planned "slave revolt". Also described is the July 1835 lynching of gamblers in Vicksburg. No documentation. No index. See #26.

780. Hudson, Arthur Palmer. Folksongs of Mississippi and their Background. Chapel Hill: University of North Carolina Press, 1936. 321p.

Chapter 9, "Ballads and Songs of Outlaws, Criminals and Vagrants" (p. 231-52) contains songs about real Mississippi criminals, such as murderers Kenny (sic) Wagner and Marion Drew. Hudson clearly identifies his sources. The book includes a bibliography and indices of titles and first lines.

781. James, D. Clayton. Antebellum Natchez. Baton Rouge: Louisiana State University Press, 1968. 344p.

Chapter 10, "Amusements, Vices and Disasters" (p. 254-73), includes some material on such criminal activities as gambling, murder and dueling. The book includes footnotes, index, bibliography.

782. James, Dorris Clayton. "Ante-Bellum Natchez." Ph.D. dissertation, University of Texas, 1964. 433p.

History of cultural, political, etc., aspects of pre-1861 Natchez. Some material on Natchez-Under-the-Hill area, an infamous haven for criminals.

783. Kane, Harnett T. Natchez on the Mississippi. New York: William Morrow, 1947. 373p. Illus.

Chapter 3, "Blood on the Natchez Trace" (p. 60-78) includes material on Samuel Mason, Micajah and Wiley Harpe and John Murrell. Sources include Rothert, Coates (#s 154,6 The book includes an index and bibliography.

784. "Killer Kinnie Wagner." Top Secrets 1948 February.

Comic book version of the criminal career of Mississippi's Kinnie Wagner.

785. McBee, May Wilson, comp. The Natchez Court Records, 1767-1805; Abstracts of Early Records. Baltimore: Genealogical Publishing, 1979. Rep. 1953 ed. 635p.

This book contains abstracts of civil suits, land claims, etc. Three land claims appear to involve the early nineteenth century southern outlaw Samuel Mason. In one claim (p. 418), Mason assigns rights to 400 acres in Claiborne Co., Mississippi Territory, to a William Miller. Mason, who settled the property in 1798, sold it in June 1800. The transaction was witnessed by Mason's son John, a member of his father's gang. The book includes a name index.

786. Mayer, P.L. "Wanted." National Broadcasting Company, Program 98942, 11 August 1950.

Radio dramatization of the life of Mississippi criminal Kinnie Wagner.

787. Mencken, August. By the Neck: A Book of Hangings. New York: Hastings House, c1942. 264p.

Contemporary accounts; sources given. Chapter 7, "The Hand of Providence" (p. 49-57) concerns the February 1894 case of Will Purvis. Purvis was found guilty of the murder of Will Buckley and sentenced to hang. The knot in the rope slipped, and Purvis did not die. After a legal battle he was finally released. Source is the New Orleans Item, June 6, 1920. No index.

788. Moore, Edith Wyatt. Natchez-under-the-Hill. Natchez, MS: Southern Historical Publications, 1958. 131p. Illus.

Concerns the notorious section of Natchez that served as a gathering place for thieves and other criminals during the antebellum period.

789. Reynolds, James. Ghosts in American Houses. New York: Paperback Library, 1971. 223p. Orig. ed. New York: Farrar, Straus and Giroux, c1955.

"Brickbat Charlie and Razzmatazz" (p. 109-19) describes life in the Natchez-Under-the-Hill district of Natchez, Miss., ca.1870. Details murder of Charlie Dorsey by his lover and partner in crime, Rose Mataz. No documentation, bibliography or index.

790. Rowland, Dunbar, comp. and ed. Official Letter Books of W.C.C. Claiborne, 1801-1816. Jackson, MS: State Department of Archives and History, 1917. 6 vols.

This title and Rowland's The Mississippi Territorial Archives, 1798-1803... (Nashville, TN: Brandon, 1905) contain some material on Mississippi territorial governor Claiborne's efforts to capture Samuel Mason, Wiley Harpe and other members of Mason's gang of robbers and murderers.

791. Shields, Joseph Dunbar. Natchez, Its Early History. "Edited by his Granddaughter Elizabeth Dunbar Murray." Louisville, KY: John P. Morton and Co., 1930. 274p.

Chapter 11 (p. 46-8) contains material on Samuel Mason and Micajah and Wiley Harpe. The death of Mason at the hands of Wiley "Little" Harpe is described, as well as "Little" Harpe's trial and hanging at Greenville (Jefferson Co.), Miss. Territory. These events occurred shortly after territorial governor Claiborne's offer of a reward for Mason's capture. Considering the amount of criminal activity in early Natchez, this book is very weak. No documentation.

792. Street, James Howell. Look Away: A Dixie Notebook. New York: Viking Press, 1936. 241p. Illus. Rep. Westport, CN: Greenwood Press, 1977.

Street was a newspaper reporter. Chapter 10 (p. 61-6) is called "The Story of Kinnie Waggoner." The chapter describes some incidents in the life of Mississippi criminal Kinnie Wagner. Two other chapters discuss lynchings witnessed by Street. No documentation. No index.

793. Swearingen, Mack. Early Life of George Poindexter: A Story of the First Southwest. New Orleans: published by the author, 1934. 194p.

Poindexter was an important figure in the development of the Mississippi Territory and state and eventually governor of the latter. Pages 114-6 describe the duel in Natchez, June 1811, between Poindexter and Abijah Hunt. Hunt was killed. Documentation. Annotated bibliography. Index.

Newspaper Articles

794. "The Outrage at Vicksburg." Jacksonville (FL) Courier 20 August 1835.

Describes vigilante activities against gamblers in Vicksburg. Describes lynching of four men, Dutch Bill (a saloon keeper), Samuel Smith, a Mr. North and a Mr. M'Call.

795. "A Horrible Tragedy." Jacksonville (FL) Courier 10 December 1835.

This long article describes the crimes of William H. Short. Short went to work as a wood chopper for an old man and his wife and son at Cowpens, a few miles above Natchez. After attempting to murder all three with an ax, Short fled down river about 150 miles and then robbed and murdered a new employer. Short was finally captured at Point Cowpee and hanged, probably October 30, 1835. "In his confession, which we understand will be published, he stated he would have killed any man for five dollars." Same article in Charleston (SC) Courier, 25 November 1835.

796. "Bloody Affair at Port Gibson." Semi-Weekly Mississippian (Jackson) 21 July 1854. Rep. Natchez Free Trader.

Describes two different gunfights between G.V. Moody and a Mr. Bland.

797. "Murder." Semi-Weekly Mississippian (Jackson) 21 July 1854. Rep. Vicksburg Sentinel.

Describes the Vicksburg murder of a Mr. Seddler by a Mr. Boyle. The wives of both men were witnesses.

798. "Another Murder." Semi-Weekly Mississippian (Jackson) 28 July 1854. Rep. Vicksburg Sentinel.

Notes the murder in Vicksburg of his wife by Jacob Vogh. Vogh had yet to be caught.

799. (Untitled), p. 2. Semi-Weekly Mississippian (Jackson). 18 August 1854.

Brief article noting murder of a man named Gillespie by one named May near Benela, Calhoun Co.

800. "Duel." Semi-Weekly Mississippian (Jackson) 29 August 1854. Rep. Natchez Free Trader.

Reports the August 14 duel at Bayou Bara, near Natchez, between Beechnor and Witchen. Neither man was injured.

801. "The Case of George N. Green." Semi-Weekly Mississippian (Jackson) 8 September 1854. Related articles October 24 and December 8.

Green was convicted in Marshall Co. for the murder of William L. Marmon and sentenced to hang. The governor granted a respite, and Green was finally pardoned.

802. "Horrid Murder By a Negro." Semi-Weekly Mississippian (Jackson) 8 September 1854. Rep. Natchez Free Trader.

A slave in Adams Co. killed J.E. Holmes, overseer of the plantation of Henry Metcalf. Free Trader notes this slave is the second one in jail for murdering his master.

803. "Negro Shot." Semi-Weekly Mississippian (Jackson) 12 September 1854. Related article September 15.

Reports the shooting by John Hardy of a Negro slave belonging to J.J. Morris. Took place "in this county." Hardy surrendered to authorities.

804. (Untitled), p. 2. Semi-Weekly Mississippian (Jackson) 3 November 1854.

Notes the October 28 escape from Yazoo Co. jail of three blacks under sentence of death for murder. One escapee was recaptured.

805. "The City; Alleged Accessories to Murder." New Orleans (LA) Daily Picayune, 25 April 1856.

This article notes the arrest of Bridget Boyle and Kate Saddler in New Orleans. Both women were arrested for complicity in the July 1854 murder of Kate's husband in Vicksburg, Mississippi. Bridget's husband, the alleged murderer (who was a member of the New Orleans Second District police force), had been arrested three weeks earlier "and sent to Vicksburg on a requisition from the Governor of Mississippi."

806. "Escape from Jail." New Orleans (LA) Daily Picayune. 29 April 1856 (afternoon edition).

This article notes the escape of three suspected or convicted murderers from the Raymond (Hinds County), Mississippi, Jail. The two escapees named were Jacob Vogh and Joe Irish.

807. "Duel Items." Charleston (SC) Daily Courier 20 August 1860. Rep. New Orleans Crescent 15 August.

Notes on two duels, one fought in Pascagoula by two New Orleans residents.

808. "Fire at Jackson." West Florida Commercial (Pensacola) 4 March 1869.

Reports the March 1 work of an arsonist at the office of the Clarion newspaper.

809. "Negro Lynching." West Florida Commercial (Pensacola) 4 May 1869.

"On Saturday last a young negro man named Horace in the employ of W.C. Corpwood, of Chicksaw county shot his mother through the head killing her instantly. A party of negroes, some 15 or 20 in number, took Horace to the woods and literally riddled his hide with bullets and left him to the buzzards. ---West Point Herald." Should be Chickasaw Co.

810. "A Duel in Mississippi." Charleston (SC) News and Courier 14 August 1878. Rep. New Orleans Democrat 4 August.

Describes a recent duel in Chattawa, Miss., between two New Orleans residents, John C. Golding and Benjamin Orey. Golding was slightly injured.

811. "4 Negroes Lynched." Nashville (TN) Banner 25 September 1884.

This article describes the lynching of four blacks in Brookhaven, Miss. The four men were taken by forty men from the Franklin Co. jail and hung from trees in the courthouse yard. One of the victims was charged with raping a white girl, two with the murder of blacks and the fourth with arson and robbery. "Four other prisoners were in jail at the time, one charged with rape and the others with arson, but they were unmolested. The mob left word with the jailer that if the circuit judge did not clean out the jail at the present term, they would return and make a clean sweep." The paper also noted that two other men had been lynched in the county in the past eighteen months.

812. "A Horrible Crime." New Orleans (LA) Times-Picayune. 8 June 1885. Rep. Alexandria (LA) Town Talk.

This article notes the arrest in Catahoula Parish of a man and a woman wanted in Miss. for the Washington Co. murder of her husband about two years previously. A Detective Brown, of Amite City, Miss., had been trailing the couple during that time.

813. "Shuqualak: A Town Destroyed by Incendiaries." New Orleans Times Picayune 22 August 1885.

The town's entire business section burned to the ground.

814. "Arrested on Charge of Poisoning." New Orleans Times Picayune 30 August 1885. Related article September 1.

In Holly Springs Box Doxey was arrested for poisoning his wife.

815. "Two Celebrated Murder Trials on Hand." New Orleans Times Picayune 30 August 1885.

In Holmes Co. one murder was committed a decade earlier, the other four years previously.

816. "An Unusual Case." Walthall Warden 26 February 1890. Rep. from Winona Times.

A white man named John Sheffield was found guilty of disturbing "religious worship at a negro meeting house." Sheffield was sentenced to thirty days in jail and fined ten dollars.

817. (Untitled) Walthall Warden 12 March 1890 (p. 3, c. 2).

On March 7 at Maben a man named Lynch was shot between fifteen and twenty times by John and William Cummings. Lynch died; "the origin of the difficulty" was unknown.

818. (Untitled) Walthall Warden 26 March 1890 (p. 2, c. 1).

"M.J. Cheatham was hanged in Grenada on the 19th inst., for the murder of a negro who had reported him to the grand jury...This is the first instance in the history of the State of the hanging of a white man for killing a negro."

819. "Railroader Killed." Walthall Warden 7 May 1890. Rep. from West Point Dispatch.

The article describes the circumstances surrounding the murder of a man named Hare by John Humphries, of Columbus. Hare had been abusive to his wife and step-daughter, Minnie Henderson, whom Humphries was soon to marry.

820. (Untitled) Walthall Warden 7 May 1890 (p. 2, c. 2).

"Thomas, the negro who murdered Miss Leila Lofton in Smith county has been convicted and sentenced to hang on the 28th inst."

821. "Mississippi Outrage." Birmingham (AL) Daily News 15 May 1890.

This article notes the arrest of R.W. Mullens near Meridian, Miss. Mullens was wanted for the murder of a negro in Sumter Co. (Ala.?). Mullens and the sheriff were later attacked by a group of eight or ten armed blacks; Mullens was wounded.

822. "Horrible! Horrible!" Birmingham (AL) Age-Herald 7 January 1892. Related article January 8.

A report of the lynching of Neal Sims and his nieces Beatrice and Laura are contained in this article. The lynching was supposedly done by the posse pursuing them. The report was denied in the January 8 article. The false lynching report demonstrates the heated feelings against the Sims "gang."

823. "The Dissolved Tale." Birmingham (AL) Age-Herald 9 January 1892.

This article explains that the Sims' were not lynched after all. The posse remained on the trail of Neal Sims. Beatrice and Laura Sims and their mother are described as being at Womack Hill, Choctaw Co., Ala., where they were supposed to remain and "not join the community of Simites in Mississippi."

824. "Arrested in the Pulpit." Greensboro Patriot 21 March 1894.

Reports the arrest in Birmingham, Ala., of Rev. W.M. Thompson, in charge of the Methodist church in East Birmingham. Thompson was actually William Hunt, sentenced to life imprisonment at Jackson, Miss., five years previously for the murder of his brother.

825. "Surrender of Will Purvis." Mobile (AL) Daily Register 8 March 1896.

Reports the surrender in Purvis, Miss., of Will Purvis, "the notorious White Cap." Purvis had been sentenced to hang in December 1895 but escaped with the help of friends. For more on Purvis' bizarre story, see #738.

826. "Murder Mystery Still Unsolved." New Orleans (LA) Daily Picayune 1 October 1896.

Will Pabor was tried in justice court and released for the murder near Hickory of his wife.

827. "A Negro Murder..." New Orleans (LA) Daily Picayune 7 October 1896.

John Adams, black, knifed to death Matthew Robinson, also black, in Meridian.

828. "May Be a Lynching." New Orleans (LA) Daily Picayune 25 June 1897.

Notes that sheriff of Copiah Co. had sent for troops to protect William Moseley, a black arrested for the murder of farmer John H. Strong.

829. Captain Miller Placed on Trial." New Orleans (LA) Daily Picayune 30 June 1897.

This long article describes the opening in Mississippi City of the trial of John H. Miller for the December 1896 murder in Biloxi of Jules Soule.

830. "Told in a Paragraph." Raleigh (NC) Gazette 16 October 1897.

T.E. Matthews was killed by John Fore in Copiah Co. The murder was the result of a political feud. Another item in this column notes the lynching of Henry Crowder (black) at Hernando for seducing a prominent planter's daughter.

831. "T.G. Short Murdered by Drunken Negroes." New Orleans (LA) Daily-Picayune 31 December 1899.

This crime occurred near Enterprise.

832. (Untitled). Aberdeen Examiner 29 September 1905. (p. 7, c. 4).

Notes the arrest of Alvis Gilmore, "A one eyed negro," for the murder of his wife near Athens, Miss., in June 1904. Gilmore "has been committing highway robberies in Memphis.

833. "Negroes Flee From Newton; Posse Pursues Shep Jones." Memphis (TN) Commercial Appeal, October 11, 1908.

Datelined October 10, Newton, Miss., this article describes the search by a posse and bloodhounds for Shep Jones, a black accused of murdering A.J. Wall.

834. "Lynching at Lula, Miss." Memphis (TN) Commercial Appeal, October 12, 1908. Related articles October 13, 1908.

This long article describes the assault by two blacks on train conductor J.C. Kendall. Kendall was shot twice by the two men who were "filled with whiskey and cocaine." A crowd of sixty men gathered at the depot, took the assailants from the custody of a deputy sheriff and hung them both.

835. "Lee Henderson Is Dying Game." Memphis Commercial Appeal, October 20, 1908.

Datelined Meridian, Miss., October 19, this article describes the circumstances surrounding a street pistol battle involving three men.

836. "E.R. Locke Shot at Greenwood." Memphis (TN) Commercial Appeal, October 29, 1908.

Datelined Greenwood, Mississippi, October 28, this article gives details of the shooting of Locke by either Ben or Stuart Ware, his brothers-in-law. No motive was immediately known. Although shot five times, Locke was not seriously injured.

837. "Shot Master, Hid the Body." Memphis Commercial Appeal 14 November 1908. Related article 15 November.

This article is datelined Nov. 13 from Senatobia, Miss. Boss Veazey, a prominent planter living ten miles west of Senatobia, was allegedly shot to death by Steve Veazey, from whom the planter was trying to collect a debt. Veazey's body was then thrown into the Arkabutla Creek. Steve Veazey and nine other blacks were arrested after

Argo Holloway, a witness to the killing, confessed under questioning. On November 14 a mob of one hundred men lynched Nick Veazey (Steve's cousin), who was also under arrest.

838. "Farmer Killed at Greenwood; Trouble Arose Over Crop." Memphis Commercial Appeal 16 November 1908.

Datelined Greenville, Miss., Nov. 15, this article details the murder of prominent Carroll County farmer George W. Wright by a drunken J.S. Giffen. Giffen fired two shots at the back of Wright, who was not armed; the second shot killed the farmer. The murder apparently arose from a disagreement over Giffen's starting a crop on Wright's property the previous spring. The murder occurred on a street in Greenville.

839. "Hoskins Kills Turner." Memphis (TN) Commercial Appeal 21 November 1908.

Datelined Charleston, Miss., Nov. 20, this article describes the result of an argument between W.P. Turner, a prominent hardware merchant and J.S. Hoskins, a patent specialty agent. Hoskins shot Turner, who died within minutes. Hoskins immediately surrendered to the sheriff.

840. "German Farmer Shot Four Times." Memphis (TN) Commercial Appeal 29 November 1908.

Datelined November 28 at West Point, Miss., this article describes the murder of wealthy and respected farmer F. Hiller. Hiller's horse and wagon were found first; later his body was located at Tibbee Lake, three miles south of West Point. Hiller had been shot in the back and side four times. Called perhaps the most brutal crime ever committed in Clay County, the murder was believed to have been committed by black tenants on Hiller's plantation; he had apparently had trouble with some of them. "Two of them are under arrest and officers are after suspects."

841. "Shot Down By Unknown Man." Memphis (TN) Commercial Appeal December 25, 1908. Related article December 26.

Datelined Sturgis, Miss., December 24, this article describes the murder of Dr. T.S. Richardson, prominent physician and member of the Mississippi State Board of Health. Richardson was shot twice in front of his drug store on the night of December 24. Two days earlier Richardson's store "was dynamited...and the entire front blown away." Dr. Richardson had apparently had previous problems with the man who claimed, the day after the incident, to have blown up the store. That man, currently missing, is believed to have murdered the doctor.

842. "Man Who Killed Four Given Death Penalty." Spartanburg (SC) Journal 12 July 1920.

Reports that the state supreme court had upheld the death penalty for Charles Marshall, convicted of killing Bob Miller and three members of his family at Amory. Marshall's execution date was set for August 20.

843. "Posse, Dog Trail Negro in Stabbing." New Orleans (LA) Times-Picayune 1 February 1928.

This article notes that a posse of 200 men was searching a swamp near Centreville for Henry Shaw. Shaw had stabbed---perhaps fatally---John H. Day during an argument in Rosetta.

8

North Carolina

Monographs

844. Avery, Clifton K. Official Court Record of the Trial, Conviction and Execution of Francis Silvers First Woman Hanged in N.C. Morgantown, N.C. (?): n.p., 1952 (?).

"Mr. Avery studied the Silver case and wrote several accounts for the Morgantown New-Herald. He includes all court records extant, with penetrating observations upon them." (Wellman, Dead and Gone, p. 190). Not listed in NUC Pre-1956 Imprints.

845. Bonitz, Julius A. The Murder of the Worley Family in Wayne County, North Carolina, and the Arrest, Trial and Execution of Noah Cherry, Robert Thompson, and Harris Atkinson. Containing the Shocking Details of the Atrocious Crime, and Giving a Continuity to the Events which Transpired, from the Discovery of the Bodies to the Final Sentence and Execution of the Murderers, including their Trial, Testimony and the Speeches of Counsel. Goldsboro, N.C.: Messenger Power Press, 1878.

Bonitz was editor of the Goldsboro (NC) Messenger. The three blacks were executed June 14, 1873, for the ax murders earlier that year of James and Appie Jane Worley.

846. Craven, Braxton, Naomi Wise, or the Wrongs of a Beautiful Girl, Enacted in Randolph County About One Hundred Years Ago. Greensboro, N.C.: Greensboro Patriot, 1874. Rep. Pinnacle, N.C.: n.p., 1884 (?). 21p.

Jonathan Lewis murdered his lover Naomi Wise in 1808. This title orig. published under pseudonym Charlie Vernon. Rep. in Jerome Dowd, Life of Braxton Craven (1896).

847. Evans, W. McKee. To Die Game: The Story of the Lowry Band, Indian Guerrillas of Reconstruction. Baton Rouge: Louisiana State University Press, 1971. 282 pp. Illus.

This title details the career of Henry Berry Lowry and his guerrilla force of North Carolina Lumbee Indians. As Evans notes, "In the midst of the racial strife of Reconstruction, the Lowry band started a movement which for a brief time drew support from all three races." The group's origins can be traced to anti-Confederate activity during the closing months of the Civil War. After the war the Lowry group used harrassing and foraging raids against the Reconstruction government. Rewards totaling almost fifty thousand dollars were offered for various members of the group. By 1873 many of the guerrillas had been executed or killed, and Henry Lowry had disappeared. The group's final raid on February 16, 1872, netted around twenty-two thousand dollars. This well-written and researched account includes footnotes, bibliographic essay and index.

848. Evidence of the Beasley-Harrison Kidnapping Case. Elizabeth City, N.C.: n.p., 1907 (?).

"Apparently made up of local newspaper accounts, complete with headlines, but fully covering testimony as given in court." (Wellman, Dead and Gone, p. 189). Not in NUC Pre-1956 Imprints.

849. Fitch, William Edwards. Some Neglected History of North Carolina, Being an Account of the Revolution of the Regulators and of the Battle of Alamance, the First Battle of the American Revolution. New York and Washington: Neale, 1905. 307p. Illus. Rep. New York: 1914.

850. Haigh, William H. The Trial of Mrs. Ann K. Simpson, Charged With the Murder of Her Husband, Alexander C. Simpson, by Poisoning With Arsenic...New York: A.S. Barnes and Fayetteville, NC: E.J. Hale and Son, 1851. 200p.

"A painstaking and totally dispassionate account of the indictment, trial, attorneys' pleas, and verdict of the jury." (Wellman, Dead and Gone, p. 189).

851. Husband, Hermon. An Impartial Relation of the First Rise and Cause of the Recent Differences in Public Affairs in the Province of North Carolina. Printed for the compiler, 1770. 104p.

Written by a supporter of the anti-tax vigilante activity in North Carolina, 1765-71. Included in John H. Wheeler, Historical Sketches of North Carolina (Philadelphia: 1851, 2 vols. rep. Baltimore: Regional Publishing, 1964. 480p.). See also Archibald Henderson's "Herman Husband's Continuation of the Impartial Relation."

852. Jackson, John. A Faithful Account of the Massacre of the Family of Gerald Watson, of Fayetteville County, N.C. by John Jackson, the Father-in-Law of said Watson, which Horrid Catastrophe Took Place July Last. Jackson Had For a Time Been Subject to Fits of Mental Derangement, which, it is supposed, was the Cause of His Perpretrating the Dreadful Deed. Boston: Printed for N. Coverly, 1819. 12p.

"This sounds like fiction, and Coverly, the publisher, produced a quantity of this kind of work. There is a general vagueness in details in the story. Reputedly, Jackson killed his daughter and four of her children while her husband was away." Thomas McDade, Annals of Murder, p. 149.

853. The Muddy Creek Murder Mystery. 1915(?). Illus.

"Probably printed from newspaper accounts in Winston-Salem shortly after the trial in 1915. It includes portraits of the principals and ends on a highly moralistic note." (Wellman, Dead and Gone, p. 189). Not in NUC Pre-1956 Imprints.

854. Norment, Mary C. The Lowrie History, as Acted in Part by Henry Berry Lowrie, the Great North Carolina Bandit, with Biographical Sketches of His Associates, Being a Complete History of the Modern Robber Band in the County of Robeson and the State of North Carolina. Wilmington, NC: Daily Journal Printer, 1875. 159p.

855. Norment, Mary C. The Lowrie History....Weldon, NC: Harrell's Printing House, 1895. Rep. of 1875 ed. Also serialized in Charlotte (NC) Daily Observer, March 19-June 11, 1905. 140p.

856. Norment, Mary C. The Lowrie History as Acted in Part by Henry Berry Lowrie, the Great North Carolina Bandit, with Biographical Sketches of His Associates. Lumberton, N.C.: Lumbee Publishing Co., c1909. 192p. Illus.

This volume, claims a publisher's note, is the fourth edition of the Norment history of North Carolina's guerilla band. This expanded edition includes biographical material on Henry Lowry, his brothers Steve and Tom, and other family and gang members. Although undocumented, Norment's work is a detailed examination of the robberies, murders and other "depredations" in which the Lowrys were involved in Robeson Co. between 1864 and 1874. Names, dates and places related to the crimes are given. Norment was a contemporary of the Lowrys, and her account seems fairly trustworthy. This edition contains an appendix by A.F. Olds on the condition of the Croatan Indians at the turn of the century. The book contains no index.

857. Powell, William S.; Huhta, James K.; Farnham, Thomas J., eds. *The Regulators in North Carolina: A Documentary History, 1759-1776* Raleigh, NC: State Department of Archives and History, 1971. 626p. Illus.

Includes numerous documents, dated 1759-1826, pertaining to this pre-Revolutionary vigilante movement. Also includes biographical material on many individuals. Index.

858. Powell, William S. *The War of the Regulation and the Battle of Alamance, May 16, 1771*. Raleigh, NC: State Department of Archives and History, 1949. 31p. Illus.

Brief overview of pre-Revolutionary vigilante movement in North Carolina. No documentation or index. Annotated bibliography.

859. Rankin, Hugh F. *The Pirates of Colonial North Carolina*. Raleigh: State Department of Archives and History, 1960. 72p. Illus.

1685-1720. "Includes chapters on Stede Bonnet and Blackbeard and 'A who's who of North Carolina's colonial pirates.'" (*Writings on American History*, 1959, p. 601). One-page bibliography.

860. Stedman, Andrew J. *Murder and Mystery: History of the Life and Death of John W. Stephens, State Senator of North Carolina from Caswell County*. Greensboro, N.C.: printed at the Patriot office, 1870. 40p.

861. Townsend, George Alfred, comp. *Swamp Outlaws of North Carolina. A Full Authentic and Thrilling History of the Adventures, Exploits, Battles and Ferocious Deeds of the Lowery Gang of Bandits*. Philadelphia: Old Franklin Publishing House, c1872. 62p.

862. Townsend, George Alfred, comp. *The Swamp Outlaws: Or, the North Carolina Bandits, Being a Complete History of the Modern Rob Roys and Robin Hoods*. New York: M. DeWitt, 1872. 84p.

The Lowry band conflict in North Carolina as covered by Townsend, E. Cuthbert and esp. A Boyd Henderson for the New York *Herald*. Sensationalistic.

863. *Trial of Edward Tinker, Mariner, for the Wilful Murder of a Youth, called Edward, at Carteret Superior court, September Term, 1811*. Newbern, N.C.: Hall, Bryan and Watson, 1811. 95p.

Tinker, a ship's captain, scuttled his vessel in an attempt to defraud the insurance company and then killed sailor Edward Jones, who had refused to join the fraud. Tinker was executed in September 1811.

864. Trial of the Rev. George W. Carawan, Baptist Preacher, For the Murder of Clement Lassiter, Schoolmaster, Before the Superior Court of Law of Beaufort County, North Carolina, Fall Term, 1853.

"Comprehensive and fiercely anti-Carawan, including not only a report of the trial but lurid denunciatory material on Carawan's life and character. No author is given, but it is supposed to have been written by a member of the Washington, N.C., bar." (Wellman, Dead and Gone, p. 189). Not in NUC Pre-1956 Imprints.

865. Turpin, James A. The Serpent Slips into a Modern Eden: or, Nancy Kerlee and her Crime. Raliegh, N.C.: Edwards and Broughton Printing Co., 1923. 80p. Illus.

Case of Frances Silver also covered, p. 45-67.

866. Wellman, Manly Wade. Dead and Gone: Classic Crimes of North Carolina. Chapel Hill: University of North Carolina, 1954. 190p.

Wellman's book devotes a chapter each to ten murders that occurred in North Carolina between 1808 and 1914. The crimes include the murder-for-hire of General Bryan Grimes by William Parker (Aug. 1880, Pitt Co.): Parker, who was paid by Howell Paramore, was lynched in Nov. 1888. In Nov. 1849 Ann Simpson, in love with another man, poisoned her husband Alexander with arsenic in Fayetteville. A year later she was tried, found innocent and in 1852 married Charles Young, who also died mysteriously. The third chapter describes the murder of schoolteacher Clement Lassiter by Rev. George Washington Carawan (Hyde Co., Nov. 1852). Chapter four outlines the conspiracy by Ida Warren, Sam Christy and Clifton Stonestreet that resulted in the murder of Ida's husband G.J. Warren near Winston-Salem (Aug. 1914, Forsyth Co.). The fifth crime is the kidnapping and apparent murder of eight year-old Kenneth Beasley (Feb. 1905, Currituck Co.). The sixth murder is that of Naomi Wise by Jonathan Lewis (1808, Randolph Co.). In 1872 Nimrod Jarret was shot by Balis Henderson (Macon Co.). The eighth chapter concerns the murder of John Stephens by four members of the KKK (Caswell Co., May 1870). The final chapter covers two crimes---the murder of Charlie Silver by his wife Frances (Burke Co., 1831) and the murder of Laura Foster by Thomas C. Dula (Wilkes Co., May 1866). Wellman's chapters are written like short stories, complete with extensive dialog. The only documentation is a brief listing of "Acknowledgements and Sources." The book, which has no index, is very readable but unfortunately does not give the scholarly treatment these crimes deserve.

867. West, John Foster. Ballad of Tom Dula. Durham, NC: Moore Publishing, 1971. 212p.

Study of the true story behind the "Tom Dooley" ballad. Dula murdered Laura Foster and was hanged at Statesville, N.C., May 1, 1868. Based on newspaper articles and court records.

Thesis

868. Johnson, Elmer D. "The War of the Regulation: Its Place in History." M.A. thesis, University of North Carolina, 1942. 182p.

Dissertation

869. Jones, Mark Haddon. "Herman Husband: Millenarian, Carolina Regulator, and Whiskey Rebel." Ph.D. dissertation, Northern Illinois University, 1983. 401p.

Covers Husband's role in the North Carolina vigilante movement ("Regulators"), 1767-1771, as well as other aspects of Husband's public career. See Dissertation Abstracts International 1983; 44:1180-A.

Journal Articles

870. Adams, Elijah. "The Murder of Lottie Yates." North Carolina Folklore 1958 December; 6(2):26-8.

Edited by Virgil L. Sturgill. Consists of lyrics and music of a ballad about the murder of Lottie Yates Porter by her estranged husband in Willard, Carter Co., N.C., in 1895. Oscar Porter was hanged for the crime.

871. Adams, George R. "The Carolina Regulators: A Note on Changing Interpretations." North Carolina Historical Review 1972 October; 49(4):345-52.

Describes scholarly approaches to pre-Revolution vigilante activity in the Carolinas. Earlier interpretations saw the Regulators as precursors of the Revolution. More recent scholars have treated the episodes as divorced from the Revolution and vigilante in character. Documentation.

872. Bassett, John S. "The Regulators of North Carolina (1765-1771)." American Historical Association Annual Report 1894; P. 141-212.

Covers pre-Revolutionary vigilantism. "The grievances of the Regulators were excessive taxes, dishonest sheriffs, and extortionate fees" (p. 150). Notes that Herman "Husband's part in the Regulation has been overestimated" (p. 156). Also observes, "This investigation leads to the view that the Regulation could have no direct connection with the Revolution" (p. 211). Documentation.

873. Bradley, F.W. "Old Joe Clarke." Southern Folklore Quarterly 1959 September; 23:172-4.

Reprints lyrics of a ballad concerning murderer Clarke. Ballad sung in West Virginia and North Carolina and sent to author by Dr. John Bennett of Charleston. No documentation.

874. Campbell, James M. "The Lynching of William Parker: The Criminal Justice System at Work in Nineteenth Century North Carolina." Southern Journal of Criminal Justice 1982 fall and 1983 spring; 7(2):99-109.

Covers August 14, 1880, murder near Washington, NC, of Civil War veteran Major General Bryan Grimes, the two trials of William Parker for the crime (which ended in mistrial and acquital) and the March 11, 1888, lynching of Parker at Washington. Also mentions the February 1888 lynching at Washington of three blacks being held on murder charges. Documentation, primarily newspaper articles.

875. Cooke, Arthur L. "British Newspaper Accounts of Blackbeard's Death." Virginia Magazine of History and Biography 1953 July; 61:304-7.

Includes reprints of three London newspaper articles on the killing of Edward Teach and other pirates in Ocracoke Inlet, N.C., by Virginia forces on November 22, 1718. Documentation.

876. Edward, Brother C. "The Regulators: North Carolina taxpayers take arms against the governing elite." American History Illustrated 1983 April; 18(2):42-8.

Describes anti-tax vigilante activity in North Carolina, primarily during 1760s and 1770s. Illustrated. No documentation.

877. Finger, John R. "The Saga of Tsali: Legend Versus Reality." North Carolina Historical Review 1979; 56(1):1-18.

Describes Indian hero of the removal who supposedly murdered a federal soldier and was tortured and executed. Author notes he did not play a major role in the murder and was captured and executed by Indians. Documentation.

878. Gaines, William H., Jr. "Pursuit of a Pirate." Virginia Cavalcade 1952 autumn; 2(2):12-6.

Covers the role of Virginians in the defeat of Edward Teach, "Blackbeard," and his crew in North Carolina in 1718. Illustrated. No documentation.

879. Gass, W. Conrad. "'The Misfortune of a High Minded and Honorable Gentleman': W.W. Avery and the Southern Code of Honor." North Carolina Historical Review 1979 July; 56(3): 278-97.

Discusses the November 11, 1851, courtroom murder of businessman Samuel Flemming by William Waightstill Avery, a lawyer. Murder took place in Morganton, Burke Co. Illustrated. Documentation.

880. Gordon, R.W. "Among the Hills Our Folk Songs Thrive." New York Times Magazine 1927 January 9; p. 7 and 17.

Part two of a four-part series on American folk music. Contains lyrics to "Omi Wise," based on the murder in North Carolina of Naomi Wise.

881. Henderson, Archibald, ed. "Hermon Husband's Continuation of the Impartial Relation." North Carolina Historical Review 1941 January; 18(1):48-81.

Rep. of Continuation, a 1770 pamphlet written in support of the anti-tax vigilantes active in North Carolina, 1765-71. See also Husband (#851). Documentation.

882. Hicklin, J.B. "The Carson-Vance Duel." The State, a Weekly Survey of North Carolina. 1938 Dec.; 6:9.

Covers the November 6, 1827, duel in Saluda, N.C., between Sam Carson and Robert Vance. David Crockett may have been present at this duel. See Shackford (#893).

883. Horne, Virginia. "The War of the Regulation: The First American Revolution." D.A.R. Magazine 1952 March; 86:279-82, 310.

North Carolina vigilante activity, 1764-1771. This anti-tax activity can be seen either as a harbinger of the Revolution or as the acts of criminals. No documentation.

884. Johnson, Elmer H. "Selective Factors in Capital Punishment." Social Forces 1957 December; 36:165-9.

Covers North Carolina, 1909-1954.

885. "Legends of Teach." North Carolina Folklore 1958 July; 6(1):21-2.

Reprints two articles on pirate Edward Teach, "Blackbeard," from the University of North Carolina Magazine: "Teach at Bath," by Mrs. B.F. Mayhew (Feb. 1893) and "Burying Money," by Stephen B. Weeks (1889).

886. Lewis, Henry W. "The Dugger-Dromgoole Duel." North Carolina Historical Review 1957 July; 34(3):327-45.

On November 6, 1837, Daniel Dugger and George C. Dromgoole met in a duel in Northampton Co., N.C. Dugger was killed. Dromgoole was a prominent Virginia politician. The duel arose from insults during a political argument. Heavily documented.

887. "North Carolina Slips." Outlook 1930 September 3; 156:14.

Discusses lynching of Oliver Moore, black, in Edgecombe Co., N.C. No documentation.

888. "The Origin of the Regulation in North Carolina." American Historical Review 1916 January; 21(2):320-32.

Contains several documents concerned with pre-Revolutionary vigilantism. Introduction by Archibald Henderson. Documentation.

889. "The Pirates and the Palatines: a Legend of North Carolina." North Carolina Folklore 1958 July; 6(1):23-6.

Reprinted from The Magnolia; or, Southern Appalachian (Charleston, SC), July 1842. May have been written by its editor, William Gilmore Simms. Concerns story of murder and robbery of a group of German immigrants by captain and crew of their ship off North Carolina coast in 1710. Ship supposedly reappears annually--on fire--on the anniversary of the event.

890. Pittman, Thomas M. "History of Crime and Punishment in North Carolina." North Carolina Historical Commission Bulletin 1917; 22:78-85.

Mostly generalized discussion. Some mention of individual criminals. No documentation.

891. Rights, Douglas LeTell. "The Horse Society." North Carolina Historical Review 1940 October; 17(4):347-55.

Covers a vigilante society that operated in the Winston-Salem area between 1798 and 1875. Its members were pledged to come to the aid of other members victimized by thieves. No documentation.

892. Scott, Kenneth. "Counterfeiting in Colonial North Carolina." North Carolina Historical Review 1957 October; 34(4):467-82.

Covers evolution of laws against counterfeiting, 1714-76. Includes material on specific counterfeiters, their hangings, etc. Documentation. Author has also written a monograph on counterfeiting in colonial America.

893. Shackford, James Atkins. "David Crockett and North Carolina." North Carolina Historical Review 1951 July; 28:298-315.

Includes discussion of whether or not Crockett was present at the duel between Sam Carson and Robert Vance near Saluda, N.C., on November 6, 1827. Author concludes Crockett was indeed there. Documentation.

894. Spindel, Donna J. "The Administration of Criminal Justice in North Carolina, 1720-1740." American Journal of Legal History 1981 April; 25:141-62.

Primarily concerns administrative aspects; some discussion of individual crimes and criminals. Well documented.

895. Swain, David L. "The War of the Regulation." North-Carolina University Magazine 1859-60; 9:121-61, 327-45, 456-69; and 1861; 10:17-35, 129-38.

Reprints Impartial Relation (1771) by Herman Husband, a pamphlet backing the North Carolina anti-tax vigilantes who operated 1765-1771. That pamphlet also reprinted in W.K. Boyd, ed., Some Eighteenth Century Tracts Concern-North Carolina (1927).

896. Thomas, Heath. "Alex Whitley: The Man and the Ballad." North Carolina Folklore 1960 December; 8(2):16-21.

"On a 'man of dark and evil reputation' in Stanly Co., N.C., thief, barn-burner, murderer of Bert Tucker, apprehended in Stanly Co. by a posse after the murder and lynched at Albemarle in 1892; and a ballad inspired by these events." (Writings on American History, 1960, p. 603).

897. Weeks, Stephen B. "The Code in North Carolina: Contributions to the History of the Duello." Magazine of American History 1891 December; 26:443-56.

Covers both eighteenth and nineteenth century duels. First duel in the state was fought between Alexander Simpson and Thomas Whitehurst at Brunswick, March 18, 1765. In the last duel Joseph Flanner killed William Crawford Wilkins on May 3, 1856. No documentation.

898. Wellman, Manly Wade. "Legend of Terror from Madison County." North Carolina Folklore 1972 May; 20(2): 67-72.

Examines the facts behind the legend that Alfred B. Chunn and his wife robbed and murdered guests at their tavern in antebellum Madison Co. Wellman gives two versions widely-told about these eastern Benders, including a second one involving the tavern of a William Barnett. No evidence supports the legends; the real Chunn and Barnett cannot be linked to criminal careers. Documentation.

Miscellaneous

899. Caruso, John Anthony. The Appalachian Frontier: America's First Surge Westward. Indianapolis: Bobbs-Merrill, c1959.

Chapter 5, "The Regulators of North Carolina" (p. 83-102) covers the anti-tax vigilante activity in that state during the 1760s and 1770s. Footnotes. Selected bibliography. Index.

900. Craver, Al. "Naomi Wise." Columbia 15053-D.

Sound recording of a ballad based on the ca. 1808 North Carolina murder by drowning of Naomi Wise by Jonathan Lewis.

901. Crowell, Suzanne. Appalachian People's History Book. Louisville, KY: Southern Conference Educational Fund, c1971. 129p. Illus.

Has some material (p. 5-8) on pre-Revolutionary North Carolina regulator movement. No documentation. Bibliography.

902. Emrich, Duncan. Folklore on the American Land. Boston: Little, Brown, c1972. 707p. Illus.

Pages 589-91 contain lyrics, music and some commentary on the "Frankie Silvers" ballad. Silvers was hanged in Morganton on July 12, 1833, for the murder of her husband. No documentation. Bibliography, index.

903. Harden, John. The Devil's Tramping Ground and Other North Carolina Mystery Stories. Chapel Hill: University of North Carolina Press, c1949. 178p. Illus.

"The Mysterious Death of Beautiful Nell Cropsey" describes the death of the young woman near Elizabeth City in November 1901. James Wilcox, her suitor for three years, was tried and convicted of second-degree murder. Wilcox was pardoned and released on December 20, 1920. He later committed suicide. No documentation. No index.

904. Harris, Arthur Merton. Pirate Tales from the Law. Boston: Little, Brown, 1923. Illus.

Chapter entitled "Sea Horror: Blackbeard" (p. 110-57) covers career of Edward Teach.

905. Henry, Mellinger E. "Still More Ballads and Folk-Songs from the Southern Highlands." Journal of American Folklore 1932; 45:1-176.

Pages 60-5 contain folksongs based on two North Carolina murderess, Tom Dula and Frances Silvers. Silvers was not hung at Morganton in 1908 for the murder of her husband, as noted here; the date was 1833. The Silvers ballad was supposedly composed and sung by Silvers before her execution. Pages 135-41 contain several versions of a ballad about North Carolina murder victim Naomi Wise.

906. Kay, Marvin L. Michael. "The North Carolina Regulation, 1766-1776: A Class Conflict." In Alfred F. Young, ed., The American Revolution. DeKalb: Northern Illinois University Press, 1976, p. 73-123.

907. King, Henry T. Sketches of Pitt County: A Brief History of the County, 1704-1910. Raleigh, NC: Edwards and Broughton Printing Co., 1911. 263p. Illus.

Some material on the Regulator movement; the H.F. Harris-E.C. Yellowly duel--October 1, 1847--in which Harris was killed (p. 110-2); and the murder of Willis Briley--December 23, 1867--for which two blacks, Richard Jackson and Needham Evans, were hanged on February 14, 1868. No documentation, bibliography or index.

908. Lawrence, Robert C. The State of Robeson. Lumberton, N.C.: n.p., 1939. 279p.

History of Robeson Co. Some material on Henry Berry Lowrie (sic) and his outlaw gang (p. 115-20). No documentation, bibliography or index.

909. Leach, MacEdward, ed. The Ballad Book. New York: A.S. Barnes, c1955. 842p.

Text of two versions of "Naomi (Omie) Wise," p. 793-5. Based on 1808 murder in North Carolina of Wise by Jonathan Lewis. Glossary. Bibliography. Selected list of recordings. Index of titles.

910. Neal, Lois Smathers, comp. Abstracts of Vital Records from Raleigh, North Carolina, Newspapers, 1799-1829. Spartanburg, SC: Reprint Co., c1979, c1980. 2 vols.

These two volumes abstract marriage, death and other notices from three Raleigh newspapers during the period covered. All three newspapers have been microfilmed. To find references to criminal activity, see the Subject and Title Index heading, "Death, Cause of." Such subheadings as "gunshot wound," "duelling wound" and "murder" will lead the user to appropriate entries. These volumes are part of a projected series that will abstract the newspapers through 1915.

911. Reeves, Paschal. "The 'Deaf Mute' Confidence-Man: Melville's Imposter in Action." Modern Language Notes 1960 January; 75:18-20.

Discusses an imposter who claimed to be a deaf and dumb Herman Melville in Fayetteville, N.C., in April 1850. Author believes real Melville used this incident as the basis of his novel. Documentation.

912. Phifer, Edward William Jr., Burke: The History of a North Carolina County, 1777-1920 with a Glimpse Beyond. Morganton, N.C.: privately printed, c1977. 510p.

Chapter 15, "Wars and Acts of Violence, 1777-1920" (p. 307-47) includes material on several duels, murderers and lynchings---Frankie Silver; Robert B. Vance and Samuel P. Carson (duel, 1827) and Frank Stack and Dave Boone (two blacks lynched on Sept. 11, 1889). No documentation. Bibliography.

913. Robinson, Blackwell P. A History of Moore County North Carolina 1747-1847. Southern Pines, NC: Moore County Historical Association, 1956. 270p.

Appendix C, "War of the Regulation" (p. 200-1) gives a list of Moore Co. (then a part of Cumberland Co.) men who participated in the Regulator movement. Documentation. Bibliography. Index.

914. Ross, Malcolm. The Cape Fear. New York: Holt, Rinehart and Winston, c1965. 340p.

Chapter 8, "The Regulators" (p. 79-97) discusses the pre-Revolution vigilante Movement. Apparently based on (#872). Also contains material (p. 281-4) on the murder of Naomi Wise by Jonathan Lewis (1808). No documentation. Bibliography. Index.

915. Sheppard, Muriel Early. Cabins in the Laurel. Chapel Hill: University of North Carolina Press, c1935. 313p. Illus.

Pages 25-39 cover the North Carolina case in which Frankie Silvers murdered her husband Charles on December 22, 1831. She was hanged at Morganton on July 12, 1833. Prints thirteen stanzas of a ballad Frankie supposedly wrote just prior to her execution. Also includes "The Quiltin'" a poem based on the case. No documentation, bibliography or index.

916. Short, Lillian. "Naomi Wise." American Archive of Folk Song L12.

Ballad recorded by Vance Randolph at Galena, Mo., in 1941. Wise was murdered by her lover Jonathan Lewis in 1808 in North Carolina.

917. Sprunt, James. Chronicles of the Cape Fear River, 1660-1916. 2nd ed. Raleigh, NC: Edwards and Broughton Printing Co., 1916. 732p.

"The Wilkings-Flanner Duel" (p. 231-7) describes the May 3, 1856, encounter between Dr. William C. Wilkings and Joseph H. Flanner in which the former was killed. The duel took place near Fair Bluff, New Hanover Co. Based primarily on newspaper accounts. Index.

918. Steiner, Jesse F. and Brown, Roy M. The North Carolina Chain Gang: A Study of County Convict Road Work. Monclair, NJ: Patterson Smith, 1969. 194p. Illus. Rep. 1927 ed.

Covers primarily developmental, organizational, economic and administrative aspects. Chapter 9, "Case Histories of Typical Negro Convicts," (p. 143-72) gives details on the lives and criminal careers of three black convicts. Crimes include murder, robbery, gambling and forgery. Unfortunately, assumed names are given for these men to protect their families. The book has a bibliography but no index.

919. Weems, Mason Locke. God's Revenge Against Adultry, Awfully Exemplified in the Following Cases of American Crime. 2nd ed. Philadelphia: Privately printed, 1816. 48p. Rep. 1818. and Philadelphia: Joseph Allen, 1828. 71p.

One of Weems' cases is the murder of James O'Neale by George L'Estrange of Wilmington, N.C. O'Neale had seduced L'Estrange's sister Matilda.

920. Weir, Sally Royce. Hot Springs, Past and Present. Knoxville, TN: S.B. Newman, 1906. 25p. Illus.

Covers Hot Springs, N.C. Pages 14-8 relate the legend of William Barnett, who supposedly robbed and murdered guests at his tavern in antebellum Madison Co.

Newspaper Articles

921. "A Desperate Battle." Nashville (TN) Banner 28 August 1885.

A large group of whites and blacks who had gathered at a church in the Cane Creek settlement, Rutherford Co., were attached by a gang of "white outlaws" led by Carl Michael. The door receipts were taken, and the congregation robbed. Many people were wounded in the attack.

922. "The Train Wrecker Escapes" and "The Jail Breakers Caught." Leesburg (FL) Commercial 8 April 1892.

Reports the April 2 escape from jail in Charlotte of six men, including John Boyd "who is charged with wrecking the Western North Carolina train when twenty-two persons were killed." Three escapees were later caught; Boyd was not among them.

923. "Pithy News Items." Raleigh Gazette 9 December 1893.

"Sam Neely, a colored boy burglar, was hanged at Dallas, N.C., Friday" (Dec. 8).

924. "Jim Day's Canine Scouts." Raleigh Gazette 16 December 1893.

This long article notes the arrest of Jim Day, "The most noted moonshiner in W. Va. and perhaps in Kentucky and North Carolina..." Day had been sought by government officials for more than fifteen years.

925. "The Jailer Choked to Death." Greensboro Patriot 24 January 1894.

This article describes the January 22 escape of two prisoners, Logan Meadows and Jasper Robertson, from the jail at Roxboro. In the process the men killed jailer Willis Royster. The escapees were quickly caught.

926. "A Fatal Fight at Campbellton." Greensboro Patriot 31 January 1894.

Notes the death of John Burkett during a fight with two blacks, William Campbell and William Smith.

927. "He Circulated Lead Quarters." Greensboro Patriot 7 February 1894. Rep. Davidson Dispatch.

Notes the arrest in Davidson of Lewis Workman, an old white man, for passing counterfeit quarters.

928. "Murder in the First Degree." Greensboro Patriot 7 February 1894.

Notes that Edward J. Fuller had been found guilty in Raleigh of the August 1893 murder of Ben Parker.

929. "Lynching in Alleghany." Greensboro Patriot 28 February 1894. Related article May 2.

Describes the lynching at Sparta of Daniel Slaughter, "who murdered Bare and Long in Alleghany county a few weeks ago..."

930. "Burglars Arrested." Greensboro Patriot 7 March 1894. Rep. Charlotte Observer.

Describes the arrest in Salisbury of William Littleton and Joseph B. Moore. The two men were wanted for the February 13 robbery of $200 worth of jewelry from a store in Taylorsville, Alexander Co.

931. "Escape of Three Prisoners." Greensboro Patriot 21 March 1894.

Notes the escape of three white prisoners, including Burwell Perry, from the jail at Raleigh. The other two men had been arrested for burglary.

932. "A Colored School Teacher Commits Forgery." Greensboro Patriot 18 April 1894. Rep. Fayetteville Observer.

Notes the arrest at Fayetteville for forgery of C.S. Murphy.

933. "Jail Delivery." Raleigh Gazette 19 May 1894.

Notes the escape of ten prisoners from the Raleigh jail. Among them was Orange Page, who was sentenced to hang for murder June 1.

934. "Another Burglary." Greensboro Patriot 20 June 1894. Related article June 27.

Notes the second burglary of the year of W.J. Clary's store in Greensboro. This time the thieves made off with about $100 worth of goods.

935. "Page Recaptured." Greensboro Patriot 20 June 1894.

Notes the re-capture in Jamesville, Martin Co., of Orange Page, "the notorious negro murderer." Page, under sentence of death, had escaped from the Raleigh jail May 16 with nine other prisoners.

936. "Joe Jackson Captured." Greensboro Patriot 11 July 1894.

Notes that Deputy Sheriff E.B. Miller, Wautauga Co., had captured Joe Jackson, "the High Point tough."

937. "Sentenced to Hang." Greensboro Patriot 11 July 1894. Related article Aug. 15.

Reports the end of the trial of Bob Madkins for assaulting a Miss Phillips. Madkins was found guilty and sentenced to hang at Burlington on August 10.

938. "White Caps at Reidsville." Greensboro Patriot 25 July 1894. Rep. Charlotte Observer.

Reports a visit to a house of prostitution at Reidsville by ten masked whitecappers. The madame, her daughter and husband were taken to the woods, severely whipped and told to leave the neighborhood.

939. "Bob Matkins Hanged." Greensboro Patriot 15 August 1894.

Reports that 8000 people attended the hanging of Matkins (or Madkins; see July 11 article, Greensboro Patriot). Matkins confessed before his death.

940. "A Terrible Fight." Greensboro Patriot 15 August 1894. Rep. Danbury Reporter.

This long article describes the gunfight surrounding a raid by revenue officers on moonshiners at Smith, near Danbury.

941. "Moonshine Establishment Raided." Greensboro Patriot 22 August 1894.

Reports the raid on the still of Frank Cagle in Moore Co., N,C.

942. "Murdered in Bed." Greensboro Patriot 17 October 1894.

Describes the mysterious murder in Greensboro of Samuel Tatum.

943. "Brown's Murderers Caught." Greensboro Patriot 24 October 1894.

On September 27 James Brown was found murdered in his store near Statesville. Elm M. Josey was arrested and confessed that he and Thomas Covington killed Brown.

944. "Person Jail Delivery." Greensboro Patriot 31 October 1894.

Reports the escape of seven prisoners from the Roxboro jail, among them Logan Meadows, Jasper Robertson and Robert Brooks. Those three had been arrested for murder. Meadows gave himself up the same day.

945. "Shot the Informer." Greensboro Patriot 31 October 1894.

At Mt. Airy Joe Hanes "shot and mortally wounded" Emmett Atkins. Hanes had accused Atkins of reporting his still to revenue officers. Hanes was tried and acquited on another murder charge in 1893.

946. "A Homicide in Raleigh." Greensboro Patriot 7 November 1894.

James Davis, black, insulted the wife of Charles Walton, also black; Walton shot and killed Davis. The murder occurred in a bar in Raleigh.

947. "A Moonshine Still." Greensboro Patriot 28 November 1894. Rep. Asheville Citizen.

Reports a raid on a still in the Hogback Mountain area.

948. "North Carolinians Lynch a Negro in South Carolina." Greensboro Patriot 28 November 1894.

A black who had been accused of raping a white girl in Polk Co., N.C., and released by authorities was taken to South Carolina by a mob and lynched.

949. "Records of Crime." Raleigh Gazette 19 December 1896.

Reports on crimes in the state during two years ending June 30. Notes two lynchings during that period---James F. Bergerson (white) in Beaufort Co., charged with murder; and Robert Chambers (black) in Mitchell Co., charged with attempted rape of a white woman.

950. "North State Cullings." Raleigh Gazette 2 January 1897.

Notes the offer by the governor of $100 reward for the capture of John Dixon, Buncombe Co., wanted for the murder of John Deck.

951. "Mountain Murders." Raleigh Gazette 13 February 1897.

Reports the murder in Polk Co. of two suspected moonshiners, Will and Joe Gunnell. The men were knifed and shot to death by a man named Jenkins.

952. "Dead in His Tracks---Excitement---Almost a Lynching." Raleigh Gazette 27 February 1897.

This long article reports a murder and near lynching in front of 500 spectators at a Newbern race track. Charles Bobo shot Jim Washington three times; Washington died immediately. Both men were black.

953. "North State News Notes." Raleigh Gazette 20 March 1897.

One item reports the shooting-to-death of Sam Fortner by Milt Daniel near Montezuma in Mitchell Co.

954. "North State News Notes." Raleigh Gazette 20 March 1897.

One item notes a raid on moonshiners at Glassy Mountain and "the famous 'Dark Corner.'"

955. "North State Happenings." Raleigh Gazette 24 April 1897.

One item reports the arrest of Miss Viola Brown for robbing the mails in Randolph Co. "It is thought by many that Miss Brown is a kleptomaniac. She is only 19 years old and quite pretty."

956. "North State and Liberty." Raleigh Gazette 8 May 1897.

Notes the arrest in McDowell Co. of Will Ray. After the arrest Ray was murdered during an argument with a Mr. Gregg, who had helped the deputy sheriff with the arrest.

957. "Butler Petitions for Pardon." Raleigh Gazette 5 June 1897.

Six years previously Avery Butler, then 14, had killed his father. His death sentence was commuted to life imprisonment.

958. "New Items." Raleigh Gazette 17 July 1897.

One item notes the gunshot death of Abram Davis, black, at the hands of an unknown white man. The argument resulting in the murder occurred at Charlotte.

959. "Taken to Raleigh for Safety." Raleigh Gazette 7 August 1897. Related articles Aug. 21 (p. 2), 28, Sept. 11.

At Kittrell, N.C., in Vance Co., a black named George Brodie (or Bodie) raped a white woman and was arrested and taken to Raleigh for safety. The other articles note that Brodie was sentenced to hang; the Sept. 11 article reports that hanging.

960. "A Post Office Robbed." Raleigh Gazette 4 September 1897.

Reports that the safe in the post office at Mt. Olive was blown open and $300 stolen.

961. "Under Death Sentence." Raleigh Gazette 9 October 1897. Related article October 16.

Notes the arrest in Montana of brothers George and William Cody, sentenced to hang October 4, 1894, at Marshall, N.C. The men, convicted of burglary after midnight (at the time a capital crime in N.C.), had escaped.

962. "Bankers Arrested." Raleigh Gazette 16 October 1897.

William E. Breese, W.H. Penland and J.C. Dickinson---officers and employees of the defunt First National Bank at Ashville---were arrested on indictments of embezzlement and conspiracy.

963. "North Carolina Industries." Raleigh Gazette 16 October 1897.

One item in this column discusses two murders in the state; another discusses moonshining.

964. "Told in a Paragraph." Raleigh Gazette 23 October 1897.

One item notes that George Jackson had been sentenced to death at Wilmington for rape.

965. "Convicted of Murder in Four Minutes." Raleigh Gazette 30 October 1897.

Sam Wright was found guilty of murdering W.A. Carr on October 2 at Goldsboro. Wright was sentenced to hang on November 10; his hanging was reported in the November 20 issue.

966. "Killed in a Pool Room." Raleigh Gazette 30 October 1897.

In Salisbury, N.C., Gilmore Hammond shot and killed Frank Averitt.

967. "Told in a Paragraph." Raleigh Gazette 20 November 1897.

The post office safe at Mocksville was blown open; the thieves got $300 in cash and stamps.

968. "Evans Reprieved." Raleigh Gazette 4 December 1897.

Contains the text of the governor's sixty-day reprieve for John Evans, sentenced to hang at Rockingham for rape.

969. "Negro Burned to Death." Raleigh Gazette 4 December 1897.

Nathan Willis (black), accused of murdering a white man, was taken from the sheriff by a mob and burned to death in Brunswick Co.

970. "Reward of $1000 For the Bank Robber." Spartanburg (SC) Journal 7 August 1920.

On the night of August 5 the Bank of Black Creek, N.C., was robbed of $100,000 in notes and $30,000 in "Liberty bonds and thrift stamps."

9

South Carolina

Monographs

971. Boling, Katharine. A Piece of the Fox's Hide. New York: Ballantine, 1974. 305p.

On January 15, 1921, Dora, Smiley and Marjorie Bigham and Mack and Leo McCracken were murdered on a farm near Pamplico, S.C. The five victims were members of a family that had dominated the area for decades. Edmund Bigham was tried and sentenced to death for the crimes; tried again and sentenced to prison. In 1960 Bigham was paroled; he died in June 1962. Much of the book is devoted to background on the Bighams and reports on the trials. Although well-written, the book has no documentation, no bibliography and no index.

972. Bonnet, Stede, d. 1718, defendant. The Tryals of Major Stede Bonnet and Other Pirates....London: printed by B. Crowse, 1719.

Trial was held at Charleston, S.C., in October and November 1718. Bonnet and other pirates were hanged in late 1718.

973. Brown, Richard Maxwell. The South Carolina Regulators. Cambridge, MA: Belknap Press of Harvard University Press, 1963. 230p.

Brown's work examines a colonial vigilante movement that flourished in South Carolina between 1767 and 1769. The activities of gangs of horse thieves and robbers led to the formation of the Regulators; the establishment of a circuit court system and thus the rule of law helped to moderate the need for vigilantes. Brown charts the history of the Regulators and the composition of the movement. This book is a detailed look at a type of criminal activity repeated frequently during the following 150 years as the frontier moved west. Contains a bibliography, detailed footnotes and an index.

974. Carpenter, Stephen Cullen. Report of the Trial of Richard Dennis the Younger for the Murder of James Shaw on the 10th of August 1804. Charleston: G.M. Bounethen, 1805.

Shaw had insulted Dennis' father; the young Dennis then ambushed Shaw near Charleston after the latter had refused his challenge.

975. Cash, Ellerbe Bogan Crawford. The Cash-Shannon Duel. With Appendix Containing Articles Relating to Colonel E.B.C. Cash, Capt. Wm. Boggan Cash and Capt. Robert G. Ellerbe. Comp. by Bessie Cash Irby. Boykin, S.C.: n.p., 1930. 48p. Illus. Rep. 1881 ed.

On July 5, 1880, Cash met William M. Shannon on a bridge in Darlington Co., S.C., to settle a "personal difficulty." Shannon died as a result of the duel. This pamphlet was Cash's attempt at justification, since he became "an object of the grossest misrepresentation and the most relentless persecution" after the duel. Contains extracts from letters and newspaper articles. No index.

976. Cumming, William. Conduct of George McDuffie, Esq., in Relation to an Intended Meeting between Himself and Col. William Cumming. With Some Illustrative References to a Former Affair Between the Same Parties. August, GA: Chronicle and Advertiser, 1822. 38p.

977. Mullen, Harris H. The Cash-Shannon Duel; also: Duels Around Camden, The Code of Honor. Tampa, FL: Trend House, 1963. 42p. Illus.

Covers the duel between Ellerbe B.C. Cash and William McCreight Shannon, as well as other duels. Reprints John Lyde Wilson's rulebook on dueling, The Code of Honor.

978. Nash, Roy. The Lynching of Anthony Crawford. New York: NAACP, 1916.

Rep. of Nash's article in the Independent.

979. Ravenel, Beatrice St. J., ed. Charleston Murders. New York: Duell, Sloan and Pearce, c1947. 216pp. (Regional Murder Series, vol. 7).

This book contains essays by various authors on seven Charleston, S.C., murders that occurred between 1788 and 1936. Crimes included are the murder of Nicholas Wightman by a gang of men and women (1788); the murders and robberies by John and Lavinia Fisher and their Six Mile House gang (ca. 1819); the murder of Capt. Francis Dawson by Dr. T.B. McDow (1889); and Leon A. Dunlap's killing of his moonshine competitor Frank Hogan (1927). Chapter two contains a little material on Martin Toohey. The chapters of this book are written in a conversational style with no documentation. The book lacks an index, and will be of value to scholars only as a starting place.

980. A Report in Part of the Trial of Thomas Gaynor for the Alleged Murder of His Wife. Charleston: W.P. Young, 1810.

Not listed in National Union Catalog Pre-1956 Imprints.

981. Report of the Trial of Martin Posey for the Murder of his Wife. 1850.

Not in NUC Pre-1956 Imprints.

982. Strobel, Martin. A Report of the Trial of Michael and Martin Toohey, on an Indictment for the Murder of James W. Gadsden, Esq. Charleston, S.C.: A.E. Miller, 1819.

Toohey was the leader of a gang of murderers and robbers. Gadsden was a member of a leading South Carolina family. Toohey escaped from jail, was recaptured and hung in Charleston, S.C., May 28, 1819.

983. Williams, Jack Kenny. Vogues in Villainy; Crime and Retribution in Ante-Bellum South Carolina. Columbia: University of South Carolina Press, 1959. 191p. Illus.

"The purpose of this book is to trace the patterns of lawlessness and the mechanics of law enforcement within South Carolina during the ante-bellum decades, 1790-1860" (p. vii). Chapters include "The Types of Crime," "Catching the Criminal," "The Criminal and the Courts" and "Punishment." Crimes covered range from gambling, dueling and murder to robbery and adultry. A number of specific crimes are discussed. Much of the book is devoted to the machinery of apprehension, trial and punishment. The book has an index, footnotes and an excellent bibliographic essay.

984. Zeigler, J.A. The Last of the Bighams, Being a True Story, with Ill. from the Album of a Strange Family Who by Their Own Misdeeds Have Become Extinct. Florence, SC: n.p., c1925. 230p. Illus.

Theses

985. Bowen, T.C. "Crime and Its Punishment in South Carolina Prior to 1860." M.A. thesis, University of South Carolina, 1929.

986. Folk, Edward H. "The Code Duello in South Carolina." M.A. thesis, University of South Carolina, 1924.

987. Hart, A.G. Crime in South Carolina." M.A. thesis, University of South Carolina, 1914.

988. Hindus, Michael S. "Prison and Plantation: Criminal Justice in Nineteenth-Century Massachusetts and South Carolina." Ph.D. dissertation, University of California, Berkeley, 1975. 409p.

Compares criminal justice in an urban, industrial state and a rural, slave state. Based on public documents, court and prison records, archival and other sources. Documentation.

989. Mullins, Jack S. "Lynching in South Carolina, 1900-1914." M.A. thesis, University of South Carolina, 1961.

Dissertation

990. Williams, Jack Kenny. "Crime and Punishment in South Carolina, 1790-1860." Ph.D. Dissertation, Emory University, 1953. 353p.

Journal Articles

991. Brearley, Harrinton C. "Homicide in South Carolina: A Regional Study." Social Forces 1929 December; 8:218-21.

Statistical study based on death certificates and newspaper articles. Some documentation.

992. Coleman, Alan. "The Charleston Bootlegging Controversy 1915-1918." South Carolina Historical Magazine 1974 April; 75(2):77-94.

Primarily covers political aspects. Extensive documentation.

993. Cumming, Joseph B. "The Cumming-McDuffie Duels." Georgia Historical Quarterly 1960; 44(1):18-40.

During a six-month period in 1822 William Cumming and George McDuffie met seven times and exchanged shots on two of those occasions. McDuffie was a U,S. representative from South Carolina; Cumming was an infantry colonel. Their efforts at dueling attracted the attention of John C. Calhoun, John Quincy Adams and the nation's press. Neither man was seriously wounded; the cause of the dueling centered around affronts to each man's honor by the other party.

994. "The Gentleman Criminal in South Carolina." Nation 1889 July 18; 49:44.

Discuss of treatment of white criminals in the state. Based on governor's reports on pardons. Several specific crimes and criminals are mentioned. No documentation.

995. Hindus, Michael S. "Black Justice Under White Law: Criminal Prosecutions of Blacks in Antebellum South Carolina." Journal of American History 1976 December; 63(3):575-99.

Describes various crimes and punishments, including murder and hanging. Statistics and citations to specific court cases. Heavily documented.

996. Hindus, Michael S. "The Contours of Crime and Justice in Massachusetts and South Carolina, 1767-1878." American Journal of Legal History 1977; 21(3):212-37.

Generalized discussion based on the author's monograph and dissertation. No specific crimes are discussed. Documentation.

997. Klein, Rachel N. "Ordering the Backcountry: The South Carolina Regulation." William and Mary Quarterly 1981 October; 38:661-80.

"...Regulators acted from 1767 through 1769 as the primary enforcers of order in the backcountry" (p. 661). This vigilante group primarily punished thieves. Several specific crimes and criminals are discussed. Heavily documented. Good companion to Brown (#973).

998. Lord, C.W. "Young Louis Wigfall: South Carolina Politician and Duelist." South Carolina Historical Magazine 1958; 59:96-112.

Contains biographical material on lawyer Wigfall (b.1816) of Edgefield Co. Chronicles journalistic war of words between Wigfall and Whitfield and Preston Brooks. During this activity Wigfall killed Thomas Bird (Oct. 30, 1840), a Brooks' nephew. James P. Carroll, brother-in-law of Whitfield Brooks, promptly challenged Wigfall; their duel was fought on November 4, 1840. Neither man was injured.

999. McCrady, Edward. "Lynch Law and South Carolina." Nation 1903 January 15; 76:52-3.

Disputes Matthew's claim concerning the origin of term "lynch law". McCrady notes that the practice of "regulation" began in North Carolina in 1766, not in South Carolina in 1768. Documentation.

1000. McCully, Robert S. "Letter from a Reconstruction Renegade." South Carolina Historical Magazine 1976; 77(1): 34-40.

Primarily a letter from Manson Sherrill Jolly, implicated in numerous Reconstruction murders in South Carolina.

1001. Matthews, Nancy Torrance. "The Duel in Nineteenth Century South Carolina: Custom over Written Law." Proceedings of the South Carolina Historical Association 1979; p. 78-94.

Describes various duels and work of anti-duellists. Documentation.

1002. Mullen, Harris H. "'Make Arrangements for a Hostile Meeting.'" South Carolina History Illustrated 1970 May; 1(2):26-31, 62-3.

Covers July 1880 duel in Darlington, S.C., between William M. Shannon and Ellerbe B.C. Cash; Shannon was killed. Illustrated with numerous photographs. No documentation.

1003. Nash, Roy. "The Lynching of Anthony Crawford." Independent 1916 December 11; 88:456, 458, 460-2.

Describes the October 21, 1916, lynching in Abbeville, S.C., of wealthy black farmer Crawford. Lynching was the escalated result of a dispute over seed prices. Article's photographs include ones of Crawford and Abbeville public square. No documentation.

1004. "The Simons-Snipes Duel." South Carolina Historical and Genealogical Magazine 1911 July; 12:160-2.

Discusses November 12, 1785, duel between Maurice Simons and William Clay Snipes in which Simons was killed. No documentation.

1005. "South Carolina's Shame." Nation 1926 November 17; 123: 497.

Covers the trial for murder and subsequent lynching of a black family, the Lowmans, in Aiken, S.C. Walter White of the NAACP claimed that the KKK was responsible. No documentation.

1006. Ulmer, S. Sidney. "Some Eighteenth Century South Carolinians and the Duel." South Carolina Historical Magazine 1959; 60:1-9.

Covers several individual duels in the state between 1761 and 1800. Documentation.

1007. Walker, William E. "The South Carolina College Duel of 1833." South Carolina Historical and General Magazine 1951 July; 52:140-2.

Covers October 1833 duel between John G. Adams and Govan Roach which took place at Lightwood Knot Springs. Documentation.

1008. Williams, Jack Kenny. "Catching the Criminal in Nineteenth-Century South Carolina." Journal of Criminal Law, Criminology and Police Science 1955; 46:264-71.

Concerns methods of catching lawbreakers in antebellum South Carolina. Some discussion of specific murders and vigilante activities. No documentation.

1009. Williams, Jack Kenny. "The Code of Honor in Ante-Bellum South Carolina." South Carolina Historical Magazine 1954; 54:113-28.

Covers rationale of dueling ("to provide a remedy for slander, insinuation, and personal slight," p. 115) and numerous individual duels in the state up to the Civil War. Also discusses legal aspects and professional duelists. Documentation.

1010. Williams, Jack Kenny. "White Lawbreakers in Ante-Bellum South Carolina." Journal of Southern History 1955; 21:360-73.

Includes material on duels, murder, infanticide, horse theft, robbery, etc. Several specific criminals are discussed, including David T. Hines, a forger and swindler who "remained active until he died in a Louisiana jail in 1854." Documentation, primarily newspaper articles and court cases.

Miscellaneous

1011. Green, Edwin L. George McDuffie. Columbia, SC: The State Co., 1936. 262p.

Pages 33-6 cover McDuffie's two 1822 duels with William Cumming. Documentation. Bibliography. Index.

1012. Green, Edwin L. A History of the University of South Carolina. Columbia, SC: State Co., 1916. 475p. Illus.

Pages 244-6 cover October 1833 duel between South Carolina College students John G. Adams and Govan Roach. Both men were seriously wounded; Adams died. Duel was the result of an argument over a dish of trout at dinner. November 1807 duel in which John Mayrant, James Goodwin and Powell McKra participated also discussed. No documentation or bibliography. Index.

1013. Gregorie, Anne King. History of Sumter County, South Carolina. Sumter, SC: Library Board of Sumter Co., 1954. 553p. Illus.

Chapter 12, "Nullification, Fist-fights, and a Duel" (p. 146-53) includes description of the August 1833 duel near Camden between John Hemphill and Nordecai M. Levy. Documentation. Selected bibliography. Index.

1014. Hindus, Michael Stephen. Prison and Plantation; Crime, Justice, and Authority in Massachusetts and South Carolina, 1767-1878. Chapel Hill: University of North Carolina Press, c1980. 285p.

Hindus' book examines the complex interactions among the legal, judicial and penal systems of the two states during the eighteenth and nineteenth centuries. Various chapters include material on such criminal activity as vigilantism, dueling, sexual offenses, murder, etc. This book is well-written, meticulously documented and contains a bibliography, index and numerous statistical tables.

1015. Howell, T.B. A Complete Collection of State Trials and Proceedings for High Treason and Other Crimes and Misdemeanors from the Earliest Period to the Year 1783. London: T.C. Hansard, 1816-1828. 33 vols.

Vol. 15, p. 1231-1302 covers the 1718 Charleston trial of pirate Stede Bonnet and members of his crew. Trial began October 28. Bonnet was convicted and executed Wed., December 10, 1718. Documentation. General index to set.

1016. Joyner, Charles W. Folk Song in South Carolina. Columbia, SC" University of South Carolina Press, c1971. 112p.

Contains a Murrells Inlet version of "Naomi Wise" (p. 57-8) and "Columbus Stockade Blues" as recorded by Jimmie Tarleton on November 10, 1927 (Columbia 15212) in Atlanta, Ga.

1017. King, William L. The Newspaper Press of Charleston, S.C., Charleston: Edward Perry, 1872.

On pages 164-6 King gives a list of sixty-three duels fought by Charleston citizens between 1806 and 1839.

1018. Klein, Rachel. "The Rise of the Planters in the South Carolina Backcountry, 1767-1808." Ph.D. dissertation, Yale University, 1979, 342p.

Contains material on pre-Revolution vigilante Regulator movement.

1019. Sims, J. Marion. The Story of My Life. New York: D. Appleton, 1886. 471p.

Chapter 5 (p. 88-99) covers October 1833 duel between South Carolina College students John G. Adams and Goran Roach in which Adams was killed. Other duels are also discussed. No documentation.

1020. Taylor, Amos. "The Charleston Tragedy: A New Song." 1805.

Based on the October 24, 1804, murder of John Cannon by his wife Elizabeth and her lover, Joshua Nettles. Teeters says a copy of this ballad is in the Huntington Library, San Marino, Calif.

1021. Wallace, David Duncan. History of South Carolina. New York: American Historical Society, 1934. 4 vols. Illus.

"Dueling and Its Social Background" (p. 87-97) includes discussion of specific duels and opposition to the practice. Documentation.

Newspaper Articles

1022. (Untitled). Charleston Courier 7 January 1840 (p. 2, c. 2).

This brief article describes an inquest at Givham's Ferry. A warrant was issued for and the arrest made of John Wood for the fatal stabbing of Hugh F. Buflin on December 31, 1839. Wood was jailed at Walterborough.

1023. "Schuylkill Bank." Charleston Courier 10 January 1840.

Four men (Peter Wager, Daniel Saint, J. Crosby and Ishi Craven) were indicted for "alleged participation in the fraudulent election of Directors of the Schuylkill Bank." The men posted bond; the amounts are given.

1024. "Bicknell's Counterfeit Detector." Charleston Courier 14 January 1840.

This article gives a list of counterfeit bank notes from South Carolina and Georgia. The list is taken from the Bicknell publication.

1025. "Sentence Day." Charleston Courier 21 January 1840.

This article notes the sentencing of five men for such crimes as robbery and horse theft. Fines and punishments are listed.

1026. "Robbery and an attempt to set Fire." Charleston Courier 15 February 1840.

This article describes the theft of $500 from a store in Charleston.

1027. "Robbery." Charleston Courier 25 February 1840.

This article describes the robbery of $250 from a boarder in a Charleston hotel. The thief, George Jones, was later caught.

1028. "Recovery of lost property and detection of the robber." Charleston Courier 29 February 1840.

This article notes the theft of a considerable sum of money from a passenger on the Georgetown stage. A black man was arrested and "is confined in the Georgetown jail."

1029. "Robbery of the Georgetown Post Office." Charleston Courier 3 April 1840.

This article notes the arrest of James Sanderlin for the theft of almost $300 from a letter in the post office.

1030. (Untitled). Charleston Daily Courier 4 March 1854 (p. 1).

Describes the confession of "the boy Tony," condemned for the murder of Alexander Craig and in jail in Lancaster. Tony implicated another "boy" named Dick. Quoted from Chester Standard.

1031. (Untitled). Charleston Daily Courier 28 March 1854 (p. 2).

Brief article notes that William Fowler was found guilty in Barnwell of the November 2, 1853, murder of Wise Holly.

1032. "A Dangerous Counterfeit." Charleston Daily Courier 18 August 1860.

Notes the discovery of a counterfeit twenty dollar bill in Charleston. Bill is described.

1033. " Murder in South Carolina." Charleston Daily Courier 31 August 1860. Rep. Augusta (GA) Dispatch.

Notes the stabbing death of Isaiah Golding by John Williams. Williams had apparently been illegally killing on the J.H. Hammond plantation. Both Williams and his son were arrested.

1034. "Arrest of Supposed Incendiaries in Greenville." Savannah (GA) Morning News 18 March 1872. Rep. Greenville Enterprise.

Reports the arrest of two men suspected of recent arsons in Greenville.

1035. "The Torch in South Carolina." Savannah (GA) Morning News 19 March 1872.

This long article reports the destruction caused by arsonist in Union.

1036. "Incendiarism in South Carolina." Savannah (GA) Morning News 3 May 1872.

Reports on various cases of arson around the state.

1037. "The Man Who Killed Ladd." Charleston News and Courier 20 July 1878. Related articles July 22; August 6, 9, 12.

Four federal revenue officers had been indicted for the murder of Amos Ladd, in whose house a moonshiner named Lewis R. Redmond---for whom the officers were looking---had hidden. Efforts were underway in Washington, D.C., to have jurisdiction of the case transferred.

1038. "Two of the Lowery Gang." Charleston News and Courier 23 July 1878.

John and Neill Locklear, members of Henry Berry Lowry's outlaw gang, were being tried at Bennettsville, S.C., for the February 1878 murder of Frank Bryce, "an Irish peddler." Long article.

1039. "A Bloody Affray." Charleston News and Courier 24 July 1878. Related articles July 25, 25 and August 1.

Allendale town marshall E.M. Williams shot E.R. Allen during an argument in a saloon. The sheriff attempted to arrest him, but Williams---armed with three guns---refused and was still at large. Allen later died. August 1 article has diagram of saloon giving location of each man present at the time of the murder.

1040. "Was It Wife Murder!" Charleston News and Courier 26 July 1878. Related article July 29.

The wife of Rev. Anderson Burns, black, was found dead at the bottom of a well near Eastover. Foul play at the hands of her husband was suspected.

1041. "A Bloodless Duel Near Augusta." Charleston News and Courier 2 August 1878. Related article August 6.

On the Carolina side of the river R.S. Saulsbury and J.S. Iverson exchanged shots. Neither man was injured.

1042. "The Revenue Troubles." Charleston News and Courier 5 August 1878.

Notes the arrest of several men in Pickens Co., charged with moonshining: Levi and David Stansel, William Walker and Ephraim Gilstrap.

1043. "A Brutal Crime." Charleston News and Courier 9 August 1878.

At Columbia, Greenville Co., Edna Black was murdered by having a hammer buried in her head.

1044. "An Affray in Edgefield." Charleston News and Courier 13 August 1878.

Long article describing gunbattle in which Brooker Toney and James and Thomas Booth were killed. The cause of the fight, a long-standing family feud, is discussed.

1045. "A Fatal Family Quarrel." Charleston News and Courier 15 August 1878.

In Timmonsville, Darlington Co., A.E. Woodham shot and killed his uncle, Emberry Woodham, over family difficulties. The nephew fled and was still at large.

1046. "A Scene at an Execution." Charleston News and Courier 16 August 1878.

On August 15 at Darlington, Alexander DeWitt, black, was executed for the July 1871 ax murder of an elderly white man, William Warren.

1047. "Two Men Shot." Nashville (TN) Banner 18 September 1884.

This article describes a gunfight in Columbia, S.C., between W.H. Poole and John W. Fowler, both of Laurens Co. The fight arose over Poole's broken promise to marry Fowler's niece, Mary Burdett.

1048. "Robbed Near Ridgeway." Charleston News and Courier 10 December 1890.

Farmer J.H, Clamp was robbed and beaten on the road near his home by three men; $400, the result of cotton sales, was taken.

1049. "Runs Away from the Gallows." Raleigh (NC) Gazette 19 May 1894.

"J.T. Jennings, colored school teacher under sentence of death for murder, escaped from jail in the night, disguised as a woman." The escape occurred at Columbia.

1050. "A Horrible Find." Birmingham (AL) Age-Herald 7 March 1895.

The body of Conway B. Oliver, white, was found in the woods two miles from Columbia. Oliver had been killed by a shotgun blast. T.C. Aughtrey, believed to have been intimate with Oliver's wife, was under arrest.

1051. "Split Their Heads Open." Raleigh (NC) Gazette 16 January 1897.

Reports from Maysville the murder with an ax of four people by Simon Cooper, black. A reward of $100 had been offered by the governor for a previous murder by Cooper. Cooper was captured, shot in the head "and then carried through the role of a lynching bee and riddled with bullets."

1052. "Thirteen Prisoners Escape." Raleigh (NC) Gazette 27 February 1897.

Notes the escape of prisoners from the Yorkville jail, including M.R. Reese and Dave F. Luckie. These two men had been convicted of the murder of Charles F. Williams.

1053. "Told in a Paragraph." Raleigh (NC) Gazette 23 October 1897.

One item notes that Sam Bird (black), wanted for murder in Union, S.C., had been arrested at Gastonia, N.C.

1054. "A Spirit of Blood in the Air." Charleston News and Courier 5 November 1897.

This article describes two recent murders in the state. Charles Bird shot Charles Smith, "a young white man," near Gaffney; Smith later died from the wounds. Farmer and merchant Albert R. Ballenger was killed with an ax at his store near Wellford.

1055. "Newbold Kills a Preacher." Raleigh (NC) Gazette 20 November 1897.

State detective W.H. Newbold killed Reverend J.M. Turner. Newbold, who was after moonshiners, had ordered Turner to halt, and the preacher did not stop his buggy promptly enough.

1056. "Reward of $250." Raleigh (NC) Gazette 20 November 1897.

The governor offered the reward for the capture of Constable Nowbold, who was wanted for the murder of a Mrs. Truner of Spartanburg.

1057. "Killed His Friend." Charleston News 25 December 1899.

This long article reports on the coroner's inquest into the December 23 murder of William M. Hogan. Alec Logan was charged with the crime.

1058. "Both Necks Were Broken." Charleston News 6 January 1900. Related articles same date.

This long article reports the hanging in Charleston of two blacks, Charles Wilson and Zacharias Singleton. Wilson had murdered a Private Godfrey more than a year earlier. Singleton had murdered Christopher Bennett November 3, 1899.

1059. "Augusta Man Here in Serious Trouble." Spartanburg Journal 1 July 1920.

Reports the arrest in Spartanburg of T.L. Hatcher, of Augusta, Ga. Hatcher was charged with auto theft and unlawful possession of a pistol.

1060. "Greenville Shootings Result in Two Deaths." Spartanburg Journal 6 July 1920.

Reports that Joseph E. Tipton and Jesse Cox had both died as a result of gunshot wounds received near Greenville a week earlier. Frank Martin was arrested for the shooting of Tipton and Blake Coggans for the shooting of Cox.

1061. "Two Men Killed in Pistol Duel." Spartanburg Journal 7 July 1920.

This long article reports on the gunfight on Commerce St. in Spartanburg in which Oscar L. Godfrey and William P. Cooper killed each other.

1062. "Arcadia Mills Store Entered by Thieves." Spartanburg Journal 8 July 1920. Related articles July 13, 14.

Notes the burglary of the store six miles from Spartanburg. Over $200 worth of merchandise was stolen.

1063. "Greenville Has Another Killing." Spartanburg Journal 8 July 1920.

This long article reports the arrest of Cliff Hawkins for the murder near Greenville of Josie Craig, a black woman. Hawkins was also charged with shooting and wounding "prominent farmer" William Morgan.

1064. "Wounds Prove Fatal to Negro Woman." Spartanburg Journal 10 July 1920. Related article July 14.

Reports that Julia Mitchell died as a result of gunshot wounds inflicted by her husband on the night of July 6 in Spartanburg. Mitchell was in jail on a murder charge; "domestic difficulties" were apparently the cause.

1065. "Locate Six Stills in the Last Month." Spartanburg Journal 30 July 1920.

Notes the arrest of Bob McIntyre, black, for operating a still in the Boiling Springs section of Spartanburg Co. Five other stills had been located in that area and the Golightly area during July.

1066. "Life Imprisonment for Dwinell Casey." Spartanburg Journal 31 July 1920.

Casey was convicted for the April 10 shooting death of Roy Whitmore at Woodruff, Spartanburg Co.

1067. "Enoree Man in Jail Charged with Murder." Spartanburg Journal 2 August 1920.

Claude Maddox, white, was charged with shooting to death Wayne Weir in Enoree.

1068. "Postoffice and Stores Robbed at Campobello." Spartanburg Journal 3 August 1920. Related article Aug. 4.

Little was taken from the post office, but a considerable amount of goods was stolen from the three stores.

1069. "No Action Yet in Mayfield's Case." Spartanburg Journal 4 August 1920. Related article August 5.

The governor of North Carolina was trying to extradite three white "prominent Bamberg county planters"---W.D. Mayfield, Jim Breedin, and Henry B. Sandifer--for kidnapping two black farmhands from Anson Co., N.C. and taking them to S.C. The governor of N.C. has as yet taken no action.

1070. "Raiding the Stills in Greenville County." Spartanburg. Journal 4 August 1920.

Describes the activities of R. Q. Merrick, federal prohibition officer.

1071. "Mammoth Still is Seized in County." Spartanburg Journal 5 August 1920.

Near Stone Station, Spartanbur Co. raid led by M.S. Turner, U.S. revenue agent. No arrests were made.

10

Tennessee

Monographs

1072. Crane, Sophie and Paul. Tennessee's Troubled Roots. Old Hickory, TN: Earle-Shields Publishers, c1979. 116p. Illus.

Entries on each of Tennessee's 95 county jails include lists of lynchings as well as hangings and other legal executions. Included are date, name, race and charge/crime. No documentation. Lengthy bibliography. Index.

1073. Crozier, Ethelred W. The White-Caps: A History of the Organization in Sevier County. Knoxville, TN: privately printed, 1899. 217p. Illus.

1074. Dresser, Amos. The Narrative of Amos Dresser.... New York: American Anti-Slavery Society, 1836. 42p. Illus.

Dresser was on a trip through Tennessee in 1835 when anti-slavery materials were discovered in his carriage. He was arrested and tried in Nashville by a vigilance committee of sixty men. His sentence was twenty lashes with a whip.

1075. Haynes, Milton A. Lives and Confessions of Zebadiah Payne, the Murderer and Robber of Wm. Coltart; Willis Green Carroll, the Murderer and Robber of Rev. Isaac Lindsey; and Archibald Kirby, the Pine Mountain Assassin and Murderer of Mrs. Polly Hunter; who were Executed at Nashville on the 10th February, 1843. Prepared for the Press under their Superintendance, after the Sentence of Death had been passed upon them by the Supreme Court of Tenn. by a Member of the Nashville Bar. Nashville: W.F. Bang, printers, Republican Banner Office, 1843. 48p. Also Cincinnati: Robinson and Jones, 1843.

McDade, Annals of Murder, says, "This work reports a busy day for the hangman in Nashville, Tennessee. Payne waylaid Coltart, cut his throat, robbed him, and escaped to Texas, from whence he was returned and convicted. Carroll set out for Nashville from Wilson County, accompanying Lindsey, who was carrying a large sum of money. They crossed the Cumberland River at Watson's Ferry, where Lindsey's body was found in the river, dead of a bullet wound. Carroll was brought back from Arkansas for trial. In a previous case Kirby had been convicted of killing Peter Elrod, the father of his wife's illegitimate child, but the conviction was reversed and Kirby freed. Four years later he was convicted of shooting Mrs. Hunter through the window of her house. He was convicted on the minimum of circumstantial evidence." (p. 220, #141)

1076. McBath, Will R. and Adkins, E.W. Life, Trial and Confession of John Nance, Who was Executed Rutledge, Tenn., December 27, 1867, for the Murder of Wm. M'Bee. Knoxville, TN: Brownlow and Haws, 1867. 12p.

Nance, a Union soldier, shot and killed M'Bee, a Confederate soldier, in 1864. Nance, who was intoxicated at the time, was convicted and hanged.

1077. Nall, James O. The Tobacco Nightriders of Kentucky and Tennessee, 1905-1909. Louisville, KY: Standard Press, 1939. 221p. Illus.

1078. Nicholson, John. The Tennessee Massacre and its Causes, or the Utah Conspiracy... Salt Lake City: Juvenile Instructor Office, 1884. 48p.

Memorial address delivered in Salt Lake City, September 22, 1884, for the Morman elders killed by a mob in Lewis Co., Tenn., August 1884. Wingfield, "Tennessee's Morman Massacre" (p. 34) describes the booklet as "extremely rare." (#1111)

1079. Pinkerton, Allan. Mississippi Outlaws and the Detectives. New York: G.W. Carleton, 1879. 377p. Illus.

Three titles are included in this volume; Mississippi Outlaws is on pages 9-123. Covers pursuit by Pinkerton and his oldest son William of Hillary and Levi Farrington. The brothers and members of their gang robbed a train at Union City, Tenn., on October 21, 1871. This $6000 robbery followed one in Moscow, Ky., in July 1871. The Farringtons and others were caught and returned to Union City; Hillary was killed during an escape attempt. On the night of December 18, 1871, Levi was shot to death by vigilantes; a fellow robber was strung up by the same mob. Use with caution. No documentation, bibliography or index.

1080. Spurlock, Donald E. The Brassell Hangings of Putnam County, Tennessee. Cookville, TN: n.p., c1981. 230p. Illus.

Describes the trial and hanging (March 27, 1878)in Putnam County of Joseph Lewis and George Andrew Brassell for the November 29, 1875, murder of Russell and John Allison. Includes trial transcript. Documentation. Index.

1081. Trial of Alice Mitchell for Killing Freda Ward. Forensic Psychiatry. Testimony of Drs. F.L. Sim, B.F. Turner, (etc.), Together with the Statement of the Prisoner. Memphis, TN: n.p., 1892. 52p.

Rep. from Memphis Medical Monthly 12:377-428. Case may have involved lesbianism.

1082. Vanderwood, Paul J. Night Riders of Reelfoot Lake. Memphis: Memphis State University Press, 1969. 159p.

1083. Yeatman, Ted P. Jesse James and Bill Ryan at Nashville. Depot Press, c1982. 20p. Illus.

Primarily a reprint of "Bill Ryan, Outlaw," from the Quarterly of the National Association and Center for Outlaw and Lawman History, vol. 5, no. 4, July 1980. Contains information on years spent in Nashville by Frank and Jesse James and members of their gang such as Ryan. Also includes map of James sites in Davidson Co., photographs and lyrics to two ballads by Steve Eng. Documentation.

Dissertation

1084. Taylor, Jerome Gregg, Jr. "Personal Violence as a Theme: Notable Incidents of Upper Class Violence in Nineteenth-Century Tennessee, A Teaching Guide." D.A., Middle Tennessee State University, 1978. 322p.

Examines patterns among several incidents of violence among upper class individuals, including Andrew Jackson and Edward Ward Carmack. Based on both primary and secondary sources. Documentation.

Journal Articles

1085. Bruce, Andrew A. and Fitzgerald, Thomas S. "A Study of Crime in the City of Memphis, Tennessee." Journal of the American Institute of Criminal Law and Criminology 1928 August; 19 (2, pt. 2):1-124.

A localized study based on the research of Frederick L. Hoffman, who gathered crime statistics for the Prudential Insurance Co. between 1890 and 1920. See Hoffman's Literary Digest articles, October 19, 1912, and January 19, 1918. I have not seen this article; it may be statistical in nature.

1086. Cunningham, O. Edward. "Captain Frank B. Gurly, Fourth Alabama Cavalry, CSA: Murderer or Victim." Alabama Review 1975; 28(2):83-103.

On August 5, 1862, Union General Robert J. McCook was shot by Confederate Captain Frank B. Gurly in a cavalry encounter near Deckerd, Tenn. Gurly was hunted by Union forces, finally caught in 1864 and tried, convicted of murder and sentenced to hang. President Lincoln stayed the execution, the case was reviewed again under Andrew Johnson, and Gurly eventually returned to civilian life and lived until 1920. Documentation.

1087. Daniels, Richard S. "Blind Tigers and Blind Justice: The Arkansas Raid on Island 37, Tennessee." Arkansas Historical Quarterly 1979 autumn; 38(3):259-70.

Concerns efforts to control the "blind tigers," or dives selling illegal whiskey, that began to appear on the Tennessee River island in 1911. Includes material on the July 1915 raid on the island and a map of the island. Documentation primarily newspaper articles.

1088. "A Dramatic Trial of Night Riders." Current Literature 1909 February; 46:123-6.

Covers the Union City trial of the Reelfoot Lake vigilantes. Seven photographs, including one of murdered Quentin Rankin. No documentation.

1089. Going, Allen J. "A Shooting Affray in Knoxville with Interstate Repercussions: The Killing of James H. Clanton by David M. Nelson, 1871." East Tennessee Historical Society Publications 1955; 27:39-48.

Murder occurred on September 27, 1871. Clanton, an Alabama lawyer, was in Tenn. representing Alabama in legal proceedings concerning the Alabama and Chattanooga Railroad. Nelson was found innocent at his trial. Author concludes the difficulty between the men was personal. Based primarily on newspaper accounts. Documentation.

1090. Grantham, Dewey W., Jr. "Black Patch War: The Story of the Kentucky and Tennessee Night Riders, 1905-1909." South Atlantic Quarterly 1960 spring; 59:215-25.

Brief history of the vigilantism among tobacco farmers in the two states. No documentation.

1091. Hahn, Nicholas Fischer. "Female State Prisoners in Tennessee: 1831-1979." Tennessee Historical Quarterly 1980 winter; 39(4):485-97.

Includes some discussion of pre-1930 individual female criminals, including murderesses, robbers, etc. Based primarily on Tennessee state publications. Documentation.

1092. Hall, Arthur Cleveland. "Reelfoot Lake Night Riders." Independent 1909 January 14; 66:78-84.

Discusses events leading up to the trial of eight vigilantes at Union City, Tenn., for the October 19, 1908, lynching of Captain Quentin Rankin. Rankin was connected with the West Tennessee Land Company, which claimed ownership of Reelfoot Lake and surrounding land. The well-organized "night riders" represented local protests against that claim. Author was professor of economics at Kenyon College. Photographs of posse, several "night riders" and others included. No documentation.

1093. Harvier, Ernest. "'I'll Be Hanged if I Do;' An Idyll of Tullahoma, Tennessee." Puck 1880 October 27; 8:121.

Tongue-in-cheek description of life and lynching in Tennessee.

1094. Hudelston, Jesse. "The Ballad of the Braswell Boys: A Putnam County Incident." Tennessee Folklore Society Bulletin 1980 March; 46(1):25-30.

Reprints lyrics of a ballad concerning the November 29, 1875, robbery/murder of Russell and John Allison and the March 27, 1878, hanging of George and Joe Brassell for the crime. See Spurlock (#1080). Little documentation.

1095. Kaser, David. "Nashville's Women of Pleasure in 1860." Tennessee Historical Quarterly 1964 December; 23 (4):379-82.

Description of prostitution based on 1860 census data for Nashville. Enumeration of prostitutes in that locale for that year probably unique. Some of the 207 professionals listed in the census are named. No documentation.

1096. Koch, Charles R. "The Night Riders." Farm Quarterly 1954 spring; 9(1):56-8, 94, 96, 98, 100.

Vigilantism in Tennessee and Kentucky, 1906-08.

1097. Lanier, Robert A. "The Carmack Murder Case." Tennessee Historical Quarterly 1981; 40(3):272-85.

This article describes the background of the murder of Edward Garmack (former Tennessee senator and prominent newspaper editor) in Nov. 1908 and the 1909 trials of and appeals by Robin and Duncan Cooper. Robin Cooper shot Carmack to death; his father Duncan, a well-known politician, was a witness to the shooting. The November 9 shooting resulted from political differences over prohibition between Carmack and the Coopers, as well as Carmack's insistence in print that the elder Cooper "was connected with the Nashville underworld." The article contains an account of the Memphis murder, the trial of the Coopers (both were found guilty) and the appeal to the state Supreme Court. Duncan Cooper was pardoned by the governor, and the charges were eventually dropped against his son. Lanier concludes that the murder was not the result of a conspiracy and that Carmack "fired the first shots." The article is well documented and relies heavily on legal documents pertinent to the case.

1098. Lowe, Maggie J. "The Murder of Munroe Bynum." Tennessee Folklore Society Bulletin 1954 March; 20(1):9-13.

Ballad and other material relating to 1887 murder of Bynum at Bradyville, Tenn. Bynum was killed by Silas T. Lands, C.B. Curlee and Jack Chapman; their motive was robbery. Includes lyrics and music. Some documentation.

1099. Marshall, Park. "John A. Murrell and Daniel Crenshaw." Tennessee Historical Magazine 1920 April; 6(1):3-9.

Early debunking of the myths surrounding Murrell as a result of the Stewart narrative. Describes Murrell's and Crenshaw's convictions for horse theft. No documentation. See #26.

1100. "Memphis; May 22, A.D., 1917." The Crisis 1917 July; 14(3):supplement (4p.).

Excerpts from Memphis "white daily papers" concerning rape/ax murder of Antoninette Rappal by Ell Persons (black). Persons was lynched by torture and burning on May 22. Related article August 1917 issue (p. 185-8).

1101. "Mob Murder." The Crisis 1916 Nov.; 13(1):24-5.

Describes the recent lynching at Hohenwald, Tenn., of blacks Wiley Tidwell and Manuel Carter for the killing of Bud Burns at the Gordonsburg mines. Law enforcement officers were searching Lewis and Maury counties for a third black. The Crisis, published by the NAACP beginning in November 1910, often contained brief notes on lynchings of blacks in the south. No documentation.

1102. O'Dell, Ruth W. "An East Tennessee Ghost Tale." Tennessee Folklore Society Bulletin 1954 June; 20(2):42-3.

Concerns the Hawkins Co. "Long Dog," a ghost dog that appeared in the area where the John A. Murrell gang supposedly robbed and murdered a family. No documentation.

1103. "Reelfoot Lake Night Riders on Trial." Independent 1908 December 31; 65:1584-5.

Brief article concerning trial at Union City, Tenn., of vigilantes for the October 19, 1908, murder of Quentin Rankin. No documentation.

1104. Robertson, James I., Jr. "Frolics, Fights and Fire-water in Frontier Tennessee." Tennessee Historical Quarterly 1958 June; 17:97-111.

Generalized discussion of such criminal activity as dueling, robbery, moonshining, etc., 1780's-1840s. Documentation.

1105. Smith, Bolton. "Memphis Lynching." New Republic 1917 August 11; 12:51.

Discusses the recent lynching of Ell Person ten miles from Memphis. No documentation.

1106. Taylor, Hillsman. "The Night Riders of West Tennessee." West Tennessee Historical Society Papers 1952; 6:77-86.

Obion Co. and vicinity, 1908-9. Covers Reelfoot Lake vigilantism in which Quentin Rankin was murdered and trial of some of the "Night Riders." Documentation.

1107. Taylor, Jerome G., Jr. "Upper Class Violence in Nine-teenth Century Tennessee." West Tennessee Historical Society Papers 1980; 34:28-52.

This article describes the involvement in violent activity of three members of Tennessee's nineteenth-century upper crust---Sam Houston, Nathan Bedford Forrest and Joseph A. Mabry. Events included are Houston's duel with General William A. White in 1826; Forrest's murder of Andrew Gould, a soldier under his command, in 1863; and Mabry's "three shooting incidents" between 1870 and 1882. Also mentioned is a duel between Mabry's father, Joseph, and Dr. William A. Leland in Tuscaloosa in April or May 1838. This well-written article includes footnotes.

1108. "Tennessee Murderers Condemned." Outlook 1909 January 16; 91:92.

Brief article concerning conviction of vigilantes at Union City, Tenn., for the October 19, 1908, murder of Quentin Rankin. No documentation.

1109. Tucker, David M. "Miss Ida B. Wells and Memphis Lynching." Phylon 1971 summer; 32:112-22.

Covers Wells' Memphis newspaper campaign against lynching that she conducted in the 1890s. Includes discussion of specific lynchings, including the March 1892 lynchings in that city of Tom Moss, Calvin McDowell and Will Stewart, leaders of the People's Grocery. Documentation is primarily newspaper articles.

1110. Vanderwood, Paul J. "Night Riders of Reelfoot Lake." Tennessee Historical Quarterly 1969 summer; 28(2):126-40.

Examines the 1908 episodes of vigilantism in west Tenn. that climaxed in the October 1908 lynching of Quentin Rankin--a representative of the West Tennessee Land Company against which much of the activity was directed----and the subsequent trial of several of the "night riders." Vanderwood has also written a dissertation and a monograph on the subject. Well-documented from newspaper articles, interviews, etc.

1111. Wingfield, Marshall. "Tennessee's Mormon Massacre." Tennessee Historical Quarterly 1958 March; 17:19-36.

Feeling against Mormon missionaries was high in Lewis Co., Tenn., in the early 1880s; in August 1884, this hatred resulted in the death of several Morman elders at the hands of a mob. This well-documented article describes the background and aftermath as well as the event itself. Based primarily on newspaper accounts.

1112. Wolfe, Margaret Ripley. "Bootleggers, Drummers, and National Defense: Sideshow to Reform in Tennessee, 1915-1920." East Tennessee Historical Society Publications 1977; 49:77-91.

Concentrates on political efforts. Some material on individual bootleggers, including description of a May 13, 1916, raid on a Nashville establishment run by Burt Bachering. Documentation.

Miscellaneous

1113. Bane, Michael. White Boy Singin' the Blues: The Black Roots of White Rock, New York: Penguin, c1982. 269p.

Primarily covers influence of Memphis blues on rock music. Includes discussion of January 25, 1892, murder of Freddie Ward by Alice Mitchell in Memphis and Memphis murderer Will "Wild Bill" Latura. No documentation or bibliography. Index.

1114. Breazeale, J.W.M. <u>Life As It Is; or, Matters and Things in General, Containing, Amongst Other Things...History of the Harps, (Two Noted Murderers)...</u> Knoxville: Printed by James Williams, at the Office of "The Post," 1842. 256p.

Primarily a history of the early days of Tennessee. Chapter 16 (p. 136-51) is the "History of the Harps," a fairly detailed account of the activities in Tenn. and Ky. of the murderous Harpe brothers, Micajah and Wiley. Breazeale claims to have obtained his information on Micajah Harpe's death "from a gentleman...who received his information from one of the persons engaged in the capture and execution of Harp." No documentation.

1115. Guild, Josephus C. <u>Old Times in Tennessee, with Historical, Personal, and Political Scraps and Sketches</u>. Nashville: Tavel, Eastman, Howel, 1878. 503p.

Guild was a Nashville judge. Chapter 5 (p. 92-106) contains the reminiscences of John L. Swaney, mail carrier from Nashville to Natchez between 1796 and 1804. This chapter has material on robber/murder Samuel Mason (called Tom in this account), including descriptions of specific robberies. The execution of Wiley "Little" Harpe is also described. The book includes material on duels fought by Sam Houston and Andrew Jackson. No documentation. No index.

1116. Humphreys, Cecil C. "The History of the Reelfoot Lake Region." Master's thesis, University of Tennessee, Knoxville, 1939. 95p.

Contains a chapter on the 1908 episode of vigilantism in the Reelfoot Lake vicinity.

1117. Isaac, Paul Edward. "Prohibition and Politics in Tennessee, 1885-1920." Ph.D. dissertation, University of Texas, 1961. 467p.

Covers primarily legal and private efforts to achieve prohibition. Includes material on the 1908 of ex-senator Edward Ward Carmack by Robin Cooper in Nashville.

1118. Lee, George W. <u>Beale Street, Where the Blues Began</u>. College Park, MD: McGrath, 1969. 296p. Rep. 1934 ed. Foreward by W.C. Handy.

Includes discussion of gambling, illegal narcotics and prostitution. Elmwood Sam, who began operation of a dope ring in Memphis in December 1924, is discussed (p. 70-4). Chapter 7 (p. 104-18) is devoted to "the brightest shining of all the beauties" (p. 106), prostitute Birdie Butler. Chapter 3 (p. 33-56) concerns River George, a black who killed white postmaster Fred Smith near Holly Rock, Miss., and fled to Memphis, where around 1900 he murdered several other people, including a police officer and Sadie Brown, one of his mistresses. George was finally killed by police during a raid on a crap game. Chapter 4 (p. 57-61) describes the early 1892 murder of Freddie Ward by another woman, Alice Mitchell. Events surrounding Will "Wild Bill" Latura's 1908 slaughter of four people in Hammitt Ashford's saloon are discussed (p. 92-4). Other murders are also mentioned. No documentation, bibliography or index.

1119. Lowe, Walter Edgar. "History of Reelfoot Lake." M.A. thesis, George Peabody College, 1930. 196p.

Chapter 3, "Reelfoot Lake Involved in Legal Actions" (p. 105-69) contains an account of the "Night Riders," a vigilante group formed in western Kentucky and Tennessee in 1907. The aim of the organization was to force tobacco farmers into an association that could control the price of that crop. The "Night Riders" were also determined to fight the West Tennessee Land Company's ownership and control of the Reelfoot Lake area in Tennessee. The lawless activity reached a peak with the 1908 lynching of Quentin Rankin, a lawyer and stockholder in that company. This murder resulted in a spectacular trial of eight men; the trial is also described in this chapter. Footnotes. Bibliography. No index.

1120. McIlwaine, Shields. Memphis Down in Dixie. New York: Dutton, c1948. 400p.

Traces origin of "Stagolee" folk figure (p. 199-200) to Memphis-based riverboat captain Stacker Lee. Describes Memphis murderer Bill Latura as a "notorious saloon-keeper" (p. 362). No documentation or bibliography. Index.

1121. Miller, William D. Memphis During the Progressive Era 1900-1917. Memphis: Memphis State University Press, 1957. 242p. Illus.

Chapter 5, "Sodom and Gomorrah" (p. 87-103) covers various types of criminal activity including prostitution, organized crime, murder and drug use. Prostitutes such as Grace Stanley and Eva Furgerson are described. The murder of William Wooten by his brother Jesse in late May 1901 is discussed. Underworld kingpins John Persica, George Honan, Jim Kinnane and Ed Ryan are mentioned. The career of murderer Will "Wild Bill" Latura is summarized.

1122. Miller, William D. "Myth and New South City Murder Rates." Mississippi Quarterly 1973 spring; 26:143-53.

Mostly statistics and causal factors. Only specific crime discussed is the April 1917 burning at the stake of a retarded black accused of decapitating a white girl. This lynching took place on the outskirts of Memphis, was attended by 5000 people and presided over by a local minister. Documentation.

1123. Moore, John Trotwood and Foster, Austin P. Tennessee, the Volunteer State, 1769-1923. Nashville: S.J. Clarke, 1923. 4 vols.

Volume 1 (p. 388-94) has material on Wiley and Micajah Harpe, Samuel (called Tom) Mason, John Murrell and his associate Daniel Crenshaw. Documentation. No bibliography. Index.

1124. Phelan, James. History of Tennessee: The Making of a State. Boston and New York: Houghton Mifflin, 1889. 478p.

Chapter 32 is devoted to John A. Murrell. Includes "List of Authorities."

1125. Williams, Samuel Cole. Beginnings of West Tennessee: In the Land of the Chickasaws, 1541-1841. Johnson City, TN: Watauga Press, 1930. 331p.

Chapter 37, "John A. Murrell, the Outlaw" (p. 246-9) is taken primarily from Stewart (See #26); nothing new. Williams does denigrate some of Stewart's more extravagant claims. Documentation. Bibliography. Index.

Newspaper Articles

1126. "A Bloody Family Fight." Savannah (GA) Morning News, 3 January 1872. Rep. from the Memphis Appeal, December 29, 1871.

This article describes the shooting in Memphis of a Mr. and Mrs. Groves by Joe Musso. Musso was married to one of the Groves' daughters, and the old couple was trying to mediate after Musso had threatened to kill his wife. Musso picked up a pistol and shot four or five times. Mr. Groves' wound was considered fatal; Mrs. Groves' was not as serious.

1127. "Hunting a Murderer; Revenue Officers Unable to Find Commissioner McDonald's Slayer." Nashville Banner, 29 August 1884.

This article describes the hunt in Overton and surrounding counties for Riley Piles, murderer of McDonald. The article also notes the death of two deputy marshalls in Macon County; one of them, Henry Seagraves, was killed several years previously. The article mentions that the area is "a good field for the manufacture of moonshine whiskey."

1128. "Killing in Bledsoe County." Nashville Banner 30 August 1884.

This brief article describes the shooting of William Fergueson at Crocker's Neck on Bee Creek. Fergueson was about to attack John Seals, and Seals shot him four times. Seals then disappeared.

1129. "Robbed by Negroes; Operations of a Band Who Fleeced a Number of Persons." Nashville Banner 1 September 1884.

The article describes the work of a group of black robbers in the Nashville area who lure unsuspecting victims to a house and rob them.

1130. "The Mormon Murder." Nashville Banner 2 September 1884 Related articles September 6, 8.

This article has some information concerning the "recent" murder of two Mormon elders in Lewis County.

1131. "Meyer Moskovitz." Nashville Banner 17 September 1884. Related articles September 14, 15, 16.

This article describes the sentencing of Moskovitz to life imprisonment for being an accessory to murder.

1132. "An East Tennessee Tragedy." Nashville Banner 24 September 1884.

"Capt. E.T. Johnson shot and killed Maj. Edison Henry at Hayesville, Greene County, yesterday, and surrendered to the authorities. Henry seduced Mrs. Johnson a year ago and the latter, after making a confession to her husband, committed suicide at Indianapolis. Johnson was formerly supervisor of pensions for Tennessee and North Carolina, and Henry had a wife and family residing in New York."

1133. "Shot Down; An Aged Tollgate-Keeper Killed Near Shelbyville." Nashville Banner 25 September 1884.

This article describes the murder of a tollgate-keeper named Wade and the wounding of his wife. The two were shot by D.P. Brown and W.F. Pigg after Mrs. Wade demanded a toll from the pair. Both men were arrested.

1134. "Chattanooga: A Murder Mystery Unravelled." New Orleans (LA) Times-Picayune 10 June 1885.

1135. "Tennessee Moonshiners." Nashville Banner 18 July 1885.

This article notes the comments of a U.S. marshal concerning eleven stills in Overton Co. and five in Putnam Co.

1136. "The Keesee Case." Nashville Banner 23 July 1885. Related article July 17.

This brief article describes the preliminary trial in Nashville of Frank P. Keesee, charged with embezzlement of almost $29,000 from the Rock City Building and Loan Association. Keesee, out on bond, failed to appear; his lawyer and bondsman were also absent.

1137. "Child Murder." Nashville Banner 11 August 1885.

This article notes the arrest of Annie Davenport, a black, for the poisoning of the child of Willie Plummer, also black. The two women had quarreled previously.

1138. "A Bold Robbery." Nashville Banner 17 August 1885.

Albert Coombs and Charles Monk, two recent arrivals from England, were being sought for the robbery of about $600 worth of jewelry from the Nashville residence of W.B. Wallwork.

1139. "Shot to Death." Nashville Banner 17 August 1885.

This article describes the fatal shooting of DeWitt Dobbins by Jordan Brown during an argument. Both men were black. Brown was arrested.

1140. "Killed in Knoxville." Nashville Banner 20 August 1885.

Horace Foster, a young lawyer, knifed Ben Wilkinson to death in a saloon. Wilkinson had accused Foster of cheating.

1141. "John A. Hide." Nashville Banner 26 August 1885.

This article describes the arrest in Sherman, Texas, of Hide, wanted in Nashville for forgery.

1142. "Murdered in Fentress." Nashville Banner 1 September 1885.

Special deputy marshal S.W. Pile was ambushed by moonshiners on August 29 in Jamestown, Tenn., and was believed to be dying.

1143. "The Luddington Murder." Nashville Banner 2 September 1885. Related articles August 17, 18, 19.

This article notes the arrest of William Cole for the murder of Ike Luddington, a L & N brakeman, in Nashville. The murder, committed by "two negroes," occurred on August 16. Cole claimed that his partner George Wilson, alias Dave Anderson, actually committed the murder.

1144. "Knoxville Lynchers." Nashville Banner 5 September 1885. Related article September 4.

Lee Sellers, charged with the murder of George E. Maines, was taken from the Knoxville jail by a mob of masked men who attempted to lynch him. The attempt was unsuccessful, and Sellers was then shot to death.

1145. "Blood for Blood." Nashville Banner 7 September 1885. Related editorial September 9.

Charles Williams, a black slate roofer who "had given the police much trouble" shot and killed street car conductor Polk Mitchell in Chattanooga on September 6. Williams was arrested and then taken from the jail and lynched by a mob of two hundred men.

1146. "Moonshiners Arrested." Nashville Banner 10 September 1885.

U.S. Marshal Hart Freeman comments on how he caught seven moonshiners in Henry County.

1147. "The Carter Murder." Nashville Banner 21 September 1885. Related articles September 10, 15.

This long article describes the jury's verdict in the Nashville trial of Edward Petty, Obie Sawyers and Thomas Cartwright for the murder of James Carter.

1148. "Dangerously Wounded." Nashville Banner 21 September 1885.

During an argument over the effects of liquor, Joseph Page shot William Hamlett. "...there is little hope of his recovery," the article notes concerning Hamlett.

1149. "The Miller Murder." Nashville Banner 23 September 1885. Related articles July 29, 30; August 6; September 14, 17.

This long article describes the opening in Nashville of the preliminary trial of John and Bates Bradley for the July 1885 murder of U.S. Deputy Marshal Lee Miller. The testimony of several witnesses is summarized.

1150. "Moonshiners; The Facts Concerning the Recent Raid in Carroll County." Nashville Banner 28 September 1885. Related articles September 23, 25.

U.S. Deputy Marshal W.I. Overton attempts to set the record straight concerning a raid on September 20 on several illicit stills. This lengthy letter gives Overton's detailed version of those events.

1151. "Tom Owens; The Alleged Murderer of Meyer Friedman Arraigned for Trial." Nashville Banner 28 September 1885. Related article August 29.

Owen, a black man, was charged with the April 12, 1884, slaying in Nashville of Friedman. This article notes the selection of a jury; the members' names are listed.

1152. (Untitled), Walthall (MS) Warden 26 February 1890 (p. 1, c.2).

"A negro, named Hardy Ballard, was sentenced to hang in Memphis on the 5th of April for the murder of a street car driver."

1153. "Negro Shoots Whitecappers." Raleigh (NC) Gazette 23 October 1897.

At Milan, Tenn., the home of Dot Price (black) was attacked. Price killed William Sires (white) and fatally wounded four others.

1154. "Told in a Paragraph." Raleigh (NC) Gazette 23 October 1897.

A.K. Ward was on trial in Memphis for embezzling $250,000.

1155. "Told in a Paragraph." Raleigh (NC) Gazette 18 December 1897.

One item notes that Mynatt Leach was hanged at Clinton in Anderson Co. for the February 17 murder of J.D. Heck.

1156. "Shot By a Woman." Raleigh (NC) Gazette 15 January 1898.

On the outskirts of Memphis, Mrs. Mary Sandbrink, a widow, fatally wounded Dr. Shep A. Rogers, prominent Memphis physician. Sandbrink then shot and killed herself. Rogers had been engaged to the woman.

1157. "Bold Hold-up on Adams Ave." Memphis Commercial Appeal, 13 October 1908.

Describes robbery and beating of J.F. Weaver and S.H. Moredock by three white thieves. The incident occurred "within a half block of one of the most prominent and busiest corners" in Memphis.

1158. "New Reward in Whitehead Case." Memphis Commercial Appeal, 13 October 1908. Related article November 14, 1908.

Describes new reward offered for the killer of Harry Whitehead, a shoe clerk murdered on September 19. Contains a long statement by the uncle of the deceased.

1159. "Carroll, Bank Robber, Caught; Broke Jail Six Years Ago." Memphis Commercial Appeal, 15 October 1908.

Describes arrest in Cincinnati, Ohio, of George Carroll, alias "Doc Davenport," Carroll and James Lonergan, alias "Whispering Jim," had robbed the bank in Whiteville, TN, on the night of December 6, 1902 and fled to Memphis with $2000. Carroll and others were arrested, tried and sentenced. While awaiting appeal, Carroll and two other men escaped.

1160. "Steals $2,000 worth of Jewels." Memphis Commercial Appeal 18 October 1908.

During the absence from home of Mrs. Robert A. Parker, Jr., a thief entered the house and took some of her jewelry. Other valuable jewelry was left behind. The missing pieces are described.

1161. "Horse Stolen on Main Street." Memphis Commercial Appeal 24 October 1908. Related articles October 25 and 28.

Describes the theft around noon October 23 of a horse and buggy belonging to deputy sheriff J.T. Mullins. The theft occurred "within a hundred feet of the courthouse." The two thieves, John Kelley and Robert Hastle, were arrested that afternoon when they attempted to sell the rig.

1162. "Painters Look for A. Kaufman." Memphis Commercial Appeal 24 October 1908.

This article describes the hunt for A. Kaufman, wanted for arson in Crawfordsville, Ark., and for embezzlement from the treasury of the Memphis local of the Painters and Decorators Union.

1163. "Desperate Fight with a Negro." Memphis Commercial Appeal 26 October 1908.

The article describes the altercation in Memphis, Oct. 24, between L.E. Royster, a printer, and Dan Ingram, a black man. Royster accused Ingram of stealing $21 from him. That night Ingram went to Royster's home and attacked the printer with a knife. Royster managed to escape death when a black woman came to his aid.

1164. "Highwaymen Cut Victim's Throat." Memphis Commercial Appeal, 26 October 1908.

Two black men robbed J.A. York of $10 dollars and also cut the victim's throat. The incident occurred on Front Street in Memphis at five A.M. on October 25.

1165. "Dynamiter is Shot to Death." Memphis Commercial Appeal, 30 October 1908.

Near Bloomington, Tenn., Willis Meadows and his son Lee were ambushed and shot to death on the night of October 27. The Meadows were believed to be members of a group of men that had recently been terrorizing the town because of a disagreement with local officials.

1166. "Says Fisher Killed Wife." Memphis Commercial Appeal, 30 October 1908.

This article describes testimony in the case of Dr. J.B. Fisher against the Pacific Mutual Life Insurance Company. The doctor had sued the company to force it to make payment on the life insurance policy on his deceased wife. The company's witnesses accused Fisher of murdering his wife. This sensational trial was featured in numerous other articles before and after the above date.

1167. "Citizens Robbed, Police Idle." Memphis Commercial Appeal, October 31, 1908.

This article describes five robberies that occurred in Memphis the night of October 30.

1168. "George Cook Killed in Jail." Memphis Commercial Appeal, October 31, 1908.

Datelined Kingston, Tenn., October 30, this article describes the killing of George Cook by thirty masked men. Cook was being held in Roane County jail for the murder at Southwest Point of John King, a ferryman. Cook was also suspected of a murder in Chattanooga.

1169. "Murdered and Thrown in Car." Memphis Commercial Appeal, November 2, 1908. Related article November 3.

Describes the discovery of the body of Lee Marshall. Marshall, a travelling salesman, was shot twice and his body concealed in a railroad coal car. The body was found in the car near Montgomery Park in Memphis.

1170. "Senator Carmack Killed in a Street Duel." Memphis Commercial Appeal, November 10, 1908. Related articles November 11, 12, 13 (w/photos), 14, 25, 26 and December 23, 24, 25, 29.

Former U.S. Senator Edward Carmack was killed by Robin Cooper, son of Colonel Duncan B. Cooper. Incident occurred as a result of editorials written by Carmack that criticized the elder Cooper for his connections with the "'Democratic machine' and its methods." The elder Cooper was present but did not fire a shot. This article contains an eyewitness account of the crime.

1171. "Kills Man Who Insulted Her." Memphis Commercial Appeal, 12 November 1908. Related articles November 13, 14.

This article describes the murder of S.P. Craig by Mrs. A.W. Bonds. Craig, who had once boarded in the Bonds' household, supposedly harassed Mrs. Bonds over a period of time and then, on the night of Nov. 11, followed her across a field to a "lonely spot." Fearing for her life, Mrs. Bonds fired three shots at Craig, reloaded her pistol and shot three more times. She surrendered to police the following morning.

1172. "Duel with 2 Negroes; C.E. Thompson Wounds One and Puts Another to Flight." Memphis Commercial Appeal 16 November 1908.

Two black men attempted to rob Thompson as he was walking along railroad tracks toward his home early Saturday evening. Thompson, who was carrying his pistol in his hand, fired at one of the blacks several times; the other retreated, firing at Thompson, who was not hit. The wounded robber managed to crawl into the weeds near the tracks. A search of the site and hospitals the next day failed to turn up the wounded man.

1173. "Desperate Negro Shot to Death; Fatally Wounds Negress." Memphis Commercial Appeal 20 November 1908.

Ralney Hill, a fish peddler known as a desperate man and under surveillance by police, shot his lover Gertrude Robinson during an argument. Attracted by the noise, a crowd of men pursued and fired at Hill, who returned the fire as he ran. A man in a buggy pursued Hill and finally shot and killed him with a rifle. The identity of the buggy driver was unknown.

1174. "Negroes Shoot Two Officers." Memphis Commercial Appeal 23 November 1908. Related articles November 25, 26, 27.

This article, datelined Nov. 22 from Tiptonville, Tenn., describes the attempt by two deputy sheriffs to arrest three blacks who were disturbing public worship services at Owl City, four miles east of Tiptonville. The blacks escaped, were followed by a posse of 150 men and by dark were surrounded in a dense thicket. A lynching was expected.

1175. "Bill Latura Kills 3 Men." Memphis Commercial Appeal, December 11, 1908. Related articles December 12 (w/photos) and 22.

Describes the murder by Latura of three blacks in Hammett Ashford's saloon at the corner of Fourth St. and Beale Ave. in Memphis. Latura entered the saloon around midnight and opened fire with a Colt's automatic pistol; in addition to the deaths, numerous people were injured, including two seriously. Latura surrendered when the police arrived and refused to give a reason for his crime. This long article includes descriptions by eyewitnesses and information about the many victims.

11
Fiction

1176. Agee, George W. Rube Burrow, King of Outlaws and His Band of Train Robbers, An Accurate and Faithful History of their Exploits and Adventures. Chicago: Henneberry Co., 1890. Rep. Old West 1968 spring; 4(3):67-96.

Described as the most accurate of the many dime novels based on the career of Burrow. Adams notes, "The author was superintendent of the Western Division of the Southern Express Company and gives a fairly accurate account of Burrows (sic) life and activities" (p. 18).

1177. Baldwin, Joseph G. The Flush Times of Alabama and Mississippi; A Series of Sketches. Gloucester, MA: Peter Smith, 1974. 244p. Rep. 1853 ed.

Baldwin's humorous sketches include "An Affair of Honor" (p. 141-3), a barbed satire of dueling. "John Stout, Esq., and Mark Sullivan" covers Washington Co., Ala., murderer Sullivan. Other sketches also include crime and criminals.

1178. Banks, Polan. Black Ivory. New York: Harper, 1926. 305p.

Based on the career of pirate Jean Lafitte.

1179. Barnum, George H. Rube Burrows, the Famous Outlaw, Murderer and Train Robber. Chicago: George Henry Barnum, 1890 64p. Illus.

Probably a dime novel.

1180. Bell, Sallie Lee. Marcel Armand, a Romance of Old Louisiana...Boston: Page, c1935. 343p.

Armand is portrayed as a lieutenant of pirate Jean Lafitte.

1181. Bethea, Jack. Bed Rock. Boston: Houghton Mifflin, 1924.

"Realistic story of coal mining in Alabama with conflict arising from bootlegging and sabotage." Gerhardstein, p. 143.

1182. Bowen, Mrs. Susan Petigru King. Lily: A Novel. New York: Harper, 1855. 330p.

According to Ravenel, Charleston Murders, p. 4, this novel is a highly fictionalized account of the early nineteenth century murder in Charleston, S.C., of Harriet Mackie, the "poisoned bride." Listed in Wright, American Fiction 1851-1875, no. 325.

1183. Brewer, Willis. The Children of Issachar. New York: Putnam's, 1884.

This novel deals with Reconstruction in Alabama; one of the subplots concerns the murder by poison of Hal Neilson, former lover of Catherine Vinnell. Neilson had threatened to expose the relationship to her new love Alfred Rowe. Vinnell is tried and acquitted.

1184. Brown, William Garrott. A Gentleman of the South. New York: Macmillan, 1903. 232p. Illus.

This novel by an Alabama author is set in the antebellum "Black Belt," probably Mississippi's. Climax of the work is a duel by moonlight between the two male principals.

1185. Carr, John Dickson. Papa La-Bas. New York: Harper, 1968. 277p.

Murder mystery set in New Orleans in 1858.

1186. Charnley, Mitchell V. Jean Lafitte, Gentleman Smuggler. New York: Viking, 1934, 240p.

Includes Lafitte's piratical and "patriotic" activities.

1187. Complete Official History of Rube Burrows and His Celebrated Gang. A Story of His Life and Exploits, Without a Parallel in Crime and Adventure. Birmingham: Lyman and Stone, n.d. 141p. Illus.

According to Adams (p. 75), "This is perhaps the rarest of the books on Rube Burrows and gives a fairly accurate account of his operations."

1188. Devereux, Mary. Lafitte of Louisiana. Boston: Little, Brown, 1902. 427p.

Based on the career of Gulf Coast pirate Jean Lafitte.

1189. Donaldson, Madelaine H. (Everett). The Thrilling and Extraordinary Adventures of Miss Madelaine H. Everett, Who Was Abducted from the Bloomington Ladies Seminary in Florida...Was Finally Rescued by Her Friends at an Auction Mart in Havana, Where She Was About to Be Sold as a Slave. Philadelphia: Barclay and Co., 1859. 40p. Illus.

The title says it all. Listed in Wright, American Fiction 1851-1875, no. 2498.

1190. Fletcher, Inglis. Lusty Wind for Carolina. Indianapolis: Bobbs-Merrill, 1944. 509p.

Covers efforts of North Carolina plantation owners to fight off pirates, 1718-1725. Pirate Anne Bonney is a character. Novel is part of the author's Albemarle Series.

1191. Fox, Richard K. Rube Burrows' Raids; Historic Highwaymen; Night Riders of the Ozark, or, The Bald Knobbers of Missouri. New York: K. Fox, c1891. 45p. Illus.

Rube Burrows' Raids is a brief (12p.) and fanciful version of the career of the Alabama train robber. Adams (p. 75) calls it "sensational fiction."

1192. Gaither, Frances. The Red Cock Crows. New York: Macmillan, 1944. 313p.

Based on the attempted slave rebellion centered at Livingston, Miss., in 1835---the rebellion supposedly led by John Murrell. Murrell is not a character, although a vigilante Committee of Safety---similar to the real one at Livingston---figures prominently. Author lived in Alabama and Mississippi.

1193. Greene, Ward. Death in the Deep South: A Novel About Murder. New York: Stackpole Sons, c1936. 283p.

Based on the Leo Frank case. Filmed as They Won't Forget (1937).

1194. Hamilton, Lillian Opal. Zeb Harkins. New York: Vantage Press, c1952. 127p. Illus.

Contains fictionalized material based on career of Mississippi criminal Kinnie Wagner.

1195. Harris, Joel Chandler. Tales of the Home Folks in Peace and War. Freeport, New York: Books for Libraries Press, 1969. 417p. Rep. 1898 ed.

The short story "The Cause of the Difficulty" (p. 345-76) concerns the murder of a young lady by the man who had been courting her "for two or three years..." Set in Georgia.

1196. Harrison, William. Pretty Baby. New York: Bantam, 1978. 184p.

Novelization of the film of the same title. Based on the career of photographer E.J. Bellocq, who recorded Storyville prostitutes ca. World War I.

1197. Hawkeye, Harry (pseud.) Rube Burrows the Outlaw. A Book of Thrilling Adventure and Desperate Deeds, Narrating Actual Facts and Obtained from Principals and Eyewitnesses. Baltimore: I. & M. Ottenheimer, 1908. 172p.

Dime novel.

1198. Hooper, George W. Down the River; or, Practical Lessons Under the Code Duello. New York: E.J. Hale and Son, 1874. 268p. Illus.

Written by an Alabama author, this novel details the July through September 1873 comical attempts at dueling in Georgia, Florida and Alabama among four principles. The book is filled with correspondence, newspaper articles, etc. Savage satire. An appendix reproduces John Lyde Wilson's The Code of Honor...(1838).

1199. Ingraham, Joseph Holt. The Pirate: or, Lafitte of the Gulph of Mexico. London: J. Cunningham, 1839. 80p. Rep. New York: Garrett Press, 1970. 216p. Forward by J.V. Ridgely.

Probably first of many novels based on career of pirate Lafitte. Also rep. Upper Saddle River, NJ: Literature House, 1970. Modern printings are under title Lafitte, The Pirate of the Gulf.

1200. Ingraham, Prentiss. Lafitte, The Pirate of the Gulf. Cleveland: Arthur Westbrook Co., 1931. 223p.

1201. Jennings, Gary. Sow the Seeds of Hemp. New York: Norton, 1976. Rep. New York: Avon, 1982. 269p.

Based on the legendary career---as opposed to the factual one---of John A. Murrell. Includes "The Ballad of John Murrell." Author also wrote bestseller Aztec.

1202. Judson, Edward Zane Carroll. The Mysteries and Miseries of New Orleans. New York: Akarman and Ormsby, c1851. 104p.

Supposedly and expose of New Orleans' underworld. Published under Judson's pseudonym, Ned Buntline.

1203. Kester, Vaughan. The Prodigal Judge. New York: Grosset and Dunlap, c1911. 448p. Illus.

Outlaw John A. Murrell is a main character in this novel set in Tennessee and North Carolina.

1204. Kroll, Harry Harrison. Rogues' Company. A Novel of John Murrell. Indianapolis: Bobbs-Merrill, 1943. 412p.

Foster, Sense of Place, (#251) says, "An excellent fictionalized account of the notorious outlaw John Murrell. Based on factual records, this book is especially good in its treatment of dialect, customs, manners, etc." (p. 92) Beware of such hype. Adams describes the novel as a "collector's item" (p. 220).

1205. LeMay, Alan. Pelican Coast. Garden City, New York: Doubleday, 1929. 329p.

Piracy and smuggling in New Orleans in the early 1800s; Jean Lafitte is a character.

1206. Lucas, Lucas, John Paul, Jr., and Groome, Bailey T. The King of Scuffletown, A Croatan Romance. Richmond, VA: Garrett and Massie, 1940. 238p.

Based on North Carolina guerrilla band the Lowrys, esp. leader Henry Berry Lowry.

1207. Lytle, Andrew Nelson. The Long Night. Indianapolis: Bobbs-Merrill, c1936. 331p.

A son tries to avenge the death of his father at the hands of Alabama criminals. Set in antebellum period.

1208. Miers, Earl Schenck. Pirate Chase. New York: Holt, Rinehart and Winston, c1965. 129p. Illus.

Edward Teach is a character in this juvenile novel.

1209. Monley, Marline. Rube Burrow, or Life, Exploits and Death of the Bold Train Robber. New York: n.p., 1898.

Dime novel. Not listed in National Union Catalog Pre-1956 Imprints.

1210. Moore, John Trotwood. *Hearts of Hickory: A Story of Andrew Jackson and the War of 1812*. Nashville: Cokesbury, 1926. 450p.

Defense of New Orleans, 1814; one of the characters is pirate Jean Lafitte.

1211. Murray, Albert. *Train Whistle Guitar*. New York: McGraw-Hill, c1974. 183p.

Set in small-town Alabama during the 1920s, this novel features the state's nineteenth-century black train robber, Morris "Railroad Bill" Slater as a major influence.

1212. Ransom, Reverand A. *A Terrible History of Fraud and Crime; the Twin Brothers of Texas. Lives, Trial, Confession and Execution at Savannah, Georgia, for the Cruel, but Mistaken Murder of their Beautiful Sister, Emily Eganus. With Full Confession of Many Other Awful Murders, Incendiaries, Highway Robberies, and Garrotting, while Connected with the Lawless Band of Land Pirates of Texas and Kansas*. Philadelphia: M.A. Milliette, 1858. 42p. Illus. German ed. same year, *Die Zwilling-Bruders von Texas*.

Adams calls this work "bloody fiction" (p. 290). The two brothers were described as members of Murrell's clan. Wright, *American Fiction 1851-1875*, no. 1996

1213. Ray, Clarence E. *The Alabama Wolf. Rube Burrows and His Desperate Gang of Highwaymen*. Chicago: Regan, n.d. 188p. Illus.

Adams (p. 293) notes that this book was "written by Ray for sensational reading and sale on trains" and has little "historical value."

1214. Ray, Clarence E. *Rube Burrows, King of Outlaws and Train Robbers. A Faithful History of Their Exploits and Adventures*. Chicago: Regan, n.d. 191p. Illus.

Probably much the same (if not exactly) as Ray's *Alabama Wolf*.

1215. Rayner, Emma. *Visiting the Sin; a Tale of Mountain Life in Kentucky and Tennessee*. Boston: Small, Maynard, 1900. 448p.

Revenge in the mountains.

1216. Robinson, Benjamin. Dolores: A Tale of Disappointment and Distress, Compiled, Arranged and Edited from the Journal, Letters and Other MSS of Roland Vernon, Esq. New York: E.J. Hale and Sons, 1868. 180p.

Wellman (#866, p. 41) says this novel is based on the life of North Carolina murderess Ann Simpson. Book is set in North Carolina. Wright, American Fiction 1851-1875, no. 2061.

1217. Sancton, Thomas. Count Roller Skates. Garden City, New York: Doubleday, 1956. 383p.

Set in red-light district of Storyville, New Orleans, pre-World War I.

1218. Savage, Lee. Silver Street Woman. Garden City, NY: Doubleday, 1954. Rep. NY: Pocket Books, 1955. 339p.

Love and prostitution in antebellum Natchez, Miss.

1219. Shepard, Odell and Willard. Holdfast Gaines. New York: Macmillan, 1946. 647p.

Covers events from conclusion of revolution to War of 1812; pirate Jean Lafitte is a character.

1220. Simms, William Gilmore. Border Beagles; A Tale of Mississippi. Philadelphia: Carey and Hart, 1840. 2 vols. Rep. New York: AMS Press, 1970. 495p.

Novel based on John Murrell's legendary outlaw clan. Listed in Wright, American Fiction 1774-1850. Twelve other editions published between 1855 and ca. 1901.

1221. Simms, William Gilmore. Confession: or, the Blind Heart. Philadelphia: Lea and Blanchard, 1841. 2 vols. Rep. New York: AMS Press, 197?. 398p.

Set in Charleston, SC, and Montgomery, Ala., this novel concerns Edward Clifford and the murder of his wife Julia. Also material on dueling. Eleven other editions published between 1856 and 1899.

1222. Simms, William Gilmore. Richard Hurdis; or, The Avenger of Blood. A Tale of Alabama. Philadelphia: Carey and Hart, 1838. 2 vols. Rep. New York: AMS Press, 1971 (?). 403p.

Based on stories of the John Murrell clan/conspiracy Simms heard during his travels through Alabama and Mississippi in the 1830s. Listed in Wright, American Fiction 1774-1850. Ten other editions published between 1855 and ca. 1901.

1223. Simms, William Gilmore, Voltmeier. Columbia: University of South Carolina Press, 1969. 446p. Rep. 1869 serialization.

Voltmeier was a Jekyll-Hyde figure---intellectual American landowner and enigmatic frontier outlaw. Set in the mountainous border region of North and South Carolina during the 1830s.

1224. Slaughter, Frank G. Sangaree. Garden City, NY: Doubleday, 1948. Rep. Popular Library, n.d. 318p.

Piracy and love along the Georgia coast, 1780s.

1225. Sperry, Armstrong. Black Falcon; A Story of Piracy and Old New Orleans. Philadelphia: John C. Winston, 1949. 218p.

Jean Lafitte is a character.

1226. Stahl, Ben. Blackbeard's Ghost. Boston: Houghton Mifflin, 1965. 184p. Illus.

Edward Teach returns to a Carolina town in the 1960s. Film version by the Disney studio in 1968.

1227. Stephens, Charles Asbury. The Ark of 1803, A Story of Louisiana Purchase Times. New York: A.S. Barnes, 1904. 340p. Illus.

Riverboat journey from Ohio to New Orleans in 1803. Wiley and Micajah Harpe and Samuel Mason appear as characters.

1228. Stewart, Catherine. Three Roads to Valhalla. New York: Scribner, 1948. 307p.

Murder, romance and tragedy in Jacksonville, Fla., during reconstruction.

1229. Stockton, Frank Richard. Kate Bonnet; The Romance of a Pirate's Daughter. New York: D. Appleton, 1902. 420p. Illus. Rep. New York: Scribner's, 1903. 357p. Rep. New York: Appleton, 1905.

Kate is the daughter of pirate Stede Bonnet. Bonnet and Edward Teach's activities off the Carolina coast are included.

1230. Stout, F.E. Rube Burrows; or, Life, Exploits and Death of the Bold Train Robber. Aberdeen, MS: n.p., c1890. 78p. Illus.

Adams (p. 339) notes this title is "Said to be the rarest of all the books about this bold outlaw..." Title page says "By detective F.E. Stout, of Aberdeen, Miss."

1231. Tallant, Robert. The Pirate Lafitte and the Battle of New Orleans. New York: Random House, 1951. 186p. Illus.

Jean and Pierre Lafitte are characters.

1232. Thompson, William Tappan. Major Jones's Scenes in Georgia. Philadelphia: T.B. Peterson, c1843. Rep. Upper Saddle River, NJ: Gregg Press, 1969. 186p.

Humorous sketches. "The Duel" (p. 136-60) lampoons dueling; "The Anti-Rail-Rode Man" (p. 179-86) does the same for lynching.

1233. Ward, William. Rube Burrow of Sunny Alabama: The True Story of the Prince of Train Robbers...Cleveland: Arthur Westbrook Col, 1906 (?). 191p.

Dime novel; "Adventure Series no. 8."

1234. Weems, Mason Locke. The Devil in Petticoats, or God's Revenge Against Husband Killing. New ed. by C.J. Ramage. Saluda, S.C.: n.p., 1935. 27p. Rep. 1878 ed. Orig. pub. 1816.

Describes the Edgefield Co., S.C., murder of John Cotton by his wife Rebecca. Highly florid style.

1235. Wellman, Manley Wade. Flag on the Levee. Ives Washburn, 1955.

Includes dueling and Jean Lafitte.

1236. Wellman, Paul I. The Iron Mistress. Garden City, New York: Doubleday, c1951. 404p.

Based on the life of James Bowie. Covers his relationship with pirate Jean Lafitte and his participation in the Vidalia Sand Bar duel outside of Natchez, Miss., in 1827. The demi-monde of Natchez (prostitutes, gamblers, etc.) is described.

1237. Wellman, Paul I. The Iron Mistress. New York: Pocket Books, 1953. 492p.

Paperback edition.

1238. Welty, Eudora. The Robber Bridegroom. New York: Harcourt, Brace, c1942. Rep. New York: Harcourt Brace Jovanovich, c1970. 185p.

Wiley and Micajah Harpe appear as characters (Little and Big Harp) in this novel of early nineteenth century life along the Mississippi River. Adapted as a musical play by Alfred Uhry, 1976.

1239. Welty, Eudora. The Wide Net and Other Stories. New York: Harcourt, Brace, 1943. 214p.

Contains the story "A Still Moment" in which circuit rider Lorenzo Dow, outlaw John Murrell (named "James") and naturalist John Audubon meet on the Natchez Trace. Audubon shoots a heron, and the trio disperse.

12

Films

1240. Blackbeard's Ghost. 1968. Color 107m. D: Robert Stevenson. Peter Ustinov, Dean Jones, Suzanne Pleshette, Elsa Lanchester.

Disney film based on Ben Stahl's 1965 novel in which eighteenth century pirate Edward Teach returns to a Carolina town in the 1960s.

1241. The Buccaneer. 1938. 90m. b&w. D:Cecil B. deMille. Frederic March, Akim Tamiroff, Walter Brennan.

Based on pirate Jean Lafitte's activities during the war of 1812. Lafitte helps Andrew Jackson defend New Orleans against the British. "Sprightly adventure romance with generally good production and acting." (Halliwell, Halliwell's Film Guide, p. 105).

1242. The Buccaneer. 1958. 121m. Technicolor. D: Anthony Quinn. Yul Brynner, Claire Bloom, Charles Boyer, Inger Stevens.

"Slow, slack and stolid remake" (Halliwell, p. 105) of 1938 film in which Anthony Quinn played a minor role. Based on activities of pirate Jean Lafitte during the War of 1812.

1243. Buccaneer's Girl. 1950. 77m. Color. D: Frederick de Cordova. Yvonne DeCarlo, Elsa Lanchaster.

DeCarlo plays a New Orleans singer involved with pirates.

1244. Gambler from Natchez. 1954. Color. 88m. D: Henry Levin. Dale Robertson, Debra Paget, Thomas Gomez.

Set in the 1840s.

1245. I Am a Fugitive from a Chain Gang. 1932, 90m. b&w. D: Mervyn LeRoy. Paul Muni, Glenda Farrell, Preston Foster.

Based on Robert Burns' autobiographical book, I Am a Fugitive from a Georgia Chain Gang. Burns co-wrote script.

1246. The Lawless Breed. 1952. 83 min. Technicolor. D: Raoul Walsh. Rock Hudson, Julie Adams, Hugh O'Brian, John McIntire, Dennis Weaver.

John Wesley Hardin's story comes to the silver screen as Hudson plays the Texas outlaw and Adams his wife Jane. Part of the film is set in south Alabama, where Hardin spent time hiding from the Texas Rangers in the town of Pollard (Polland in the film). The film's ending is totally Hollywood---Hardin is released from prison and the family returns to south Alabama. In actuality, Hardin's wife was dead by the time he left prison; Hardin himself died a gunfighter's death in El Paso in 1895.

1247. Night Rider. 1979. Color. 78m. D: Hy Averback. David Selby, Percy Rodrigues, Kim Cattrall.

Made-for-television film. New Orleans-dandy-by-day dons a sword and mask after dark to seek revenge for his family's murder.

1248. Pretty Baby. 1978. 109m. Color. D: Louis Malle. Brook Shields, Keith Carradine, Susan Sarandon.

Based on the life of E.J. Bellocq, who photographed New Orleans prostitutes ca. World War I. Despite a sleep-walking performance by Carradine, the film has a good feel for the city's demi-monde.

1249. Sangaree. 1953. 94m. Color. D: Edward Ludwig. Gernando Lamas, Arlene Dahl, Patricia Medina.

Based on Frank G. Slaughter's novel about piracy along the Georgia coast in the 1780s.

1250. They Won't Forget. 1937. 94m. B&W. D: Mervyn LeRoy. Claude Rains, Gloria Dickson, Edward Norris.

Based on Ward Greene's novel Death in the Deep South, which was based on the Leo Frank case. "Harrowing to watch" (Halliwell, p. 762).

1251. The Travelling Executioner. 1970. 95m. Color. D: Jack Smight. Stacy Keach, Mariana Hill, Bud Cort.

Muddled but fascinating story of Keach who travels the early twentieth-century south charging $100 per execution in his electric chair. Filmed in Alabama, including Kilby Prison.

13

Drama

1252. Rutland, Lucile. Lafitte, A Play in Prologue and Four Acts. - New York: printed at the Goerck Art Press, 1899. 96p.

1253. Uhry, Alfred. The Robber Bridegroom. 1976. Music by Robert Waldman.

Musical version of Eudora Welty's novel in which Wiley and Micajah Harpe are among the characters. Filmed version with Marjoe Gortner shown on Showtime cable television network in 1982 (?).

1254. White, John Blake. "Modern Honor: A Tragedy in Five Acts."

Anti-dueling play by a South Carolina resident of the nineteenth century. Manuscript in John Blake White Papers, South Carolina Historical Society.

1255. Wilkinson, Elizabeth. Monsieur Lafitte (Jean Lafitte) Pirate-Patriot, South Louisiana, 1808-1815. New Orleans: Louisiana Printing Co., 1924. 14p.

14

Sources

Adams, Ramon F. Six-Guns and Saddle Leather: A Bibliography of Books and Pamphlets on Western Outlaws and Gunmen. Norman: University of Oklahoma Press, c1954.

America: History and Life. Santa Barbara, CA: American Bibiliographical Center, Vol. 1, 1964-vol. 20 (1), 1983.

Amercian Historical Association. Writings on American History. 1092-03; 1906-1940; 1948-1981.

Beers, Henry Putney. Bibliographies in American History: Guide to Materials for Research. New York: H. W. Wilson, 1942.

Combined Retrospective Index Set to Journals in History 1838-1974. Washington, D. C.: Carrollton Press, 1977. 10 vols.

Comprehensive Dissertation Index 1861-1972 (vol. 28: History). Ann Arbor, MI: Xerox University Microfilms, 1973.

Comprehensive Dissertation Index, Five-Year Cummulation, 1973-77. (vol. 13: History). Ann Arbor, MI: Xerox University Microfilms, 1979.

Comprehensive Dissertation Index, 1978, 1979, 1980, and 1981 Supplements. (vol. 4, pt. 2: History). Ann Arbor, MI: Xerox University Microfilms, 1979, 1980, 1981, 1982.

Cushing, Helen Grant and Morris, Adah V. Nineteenth Century Readers' Guide to Periodical Literature 1890-1899. New York: H. W. Wilson, 1944. 2 vols.

Davis, Bruce L., comp. Criminological Bibliographies, Indexes, and Review Articles of the Literature of Crime Study in the United States. Westport, CT: Greenwood Press, c1987.

Sources

Davis, David Brion. Homicide in American Fiction, 1798-1860: A Study in Social Values. Ithaca, NY: Cornell University Press, 1957.

Gerhardstein, Virginia Brokaw. Dickinson's American Historical Fiction. 4th ed, Metuchen, NJ: Scarecrow, 1981. 312p.

Halliwell, Leslie. Halliwell's Film Guide; A Survey of 8000 English-Language Movies. New York: Scribner's, c1977.

Hotchkiss, Jeanette. American Historical Fiction for Children and Young People. Metuchen, NJ: Scarecrow, 1973. 318p.

Kuhlman, Augustus Frederick. A Guide to Material on Crime and Criminal Justice. New York: Wilson, 1929. Rep. Montclair, NJ: Patterson Smith, 1965.

Library of Congress. National Union Catalog of Manuscript Collections. Washington, D.C.: Library of Congress, 1959-1980.

McGarry, Daniel D. and White, Sarah Harriman. World Historical Fiction Guide. 2nd. ed. Metuchen, NJ: Scarecrow, 1973.

Marcus, Marvin. Criminal Justice Bibliography. 2nd. ed. Atlanta, GA: Georgia State University, c1976. 658p.

National Union Catalog of Pre-1956 Imprints. Mansell, 1968-1981. 754 vols.

Owen, Thomas M. "A Bibliography of Alabama" in American Historical Association Annual Report 1897. U.S. House of Representatives 55th Cong. 2nd. Sess., Document no. 577. U.S. Congressional Serial Set no. 3710.

Recently Published Articles. Vol. 1, 1976- Vol. 7, 1982. Washington, D.C.: American Historical Association.

Readers' Guide to Periodical Literature. New York: H.W. Wilson, 1900-1930. Vols. 1-8.

Pool's Index to Periodical Literature 1802-1906. New York: Peter Smith, 1938. 6 vols.

Sandoe, James. "Criminal Clef: Tales and Plays based on Real Crimes." Wilson Library Bulletin 1946; 21:299-306.

Thorton, Mary Lindsay, comp. A Bibliography of North Carloina, 1589-1956. Chapell Hill: University of North Carolina Press, 1958.

Wright, Lyle H. American Fiction 1774-1850: A Contribution Toward a Bibliography. San Marino, CA: Huntington Library Publications, 1948. Rev. ed.

Wright, Lyle H. American Fiction 1851-1875: A Contribution Toward a Bibliography. San Marino, CA: Huntington Library, 1957.

Author/Editor Index

Author/Editor Index

Author/Editor Index

Personal Name Index

Personal Name Index

Personal Name Index

Personal Name Index

T

Subject Index

A

B

Subject Index

Subject Index

About the Compiler

A. J. WRIGHT, M.L.S., is Clinical Librarian, Department of Anesthesiology, University of Alabama at Birmingham School of Medicine. His primary research interests are various aspects of the history of American anesthesia and the history of southern crime in the United States. He has published widely in both areas.

www.ingramcontent.com/pod-product-compliance
Lightning Source LLC
LaVergne TN
LVHW101500200926
848483LV00001B/178